Inspiralize
Everything

Inspiralize
Everything

An Apples-to-Zucchini
Encyclopedia of Spiralizing

Ali Maffucci

Clarkson Potter/Publishers

New York

Published in the United States by Clarkson Potter/Publishers,
an imprint of the Crown Publishing Group, a division of
Penguin Random House LLC, New York.
clarksonpotter.com

CLARKSON POTTER is a trademark and POTTER with colophon
is a registered trademark of Penguin Random House LLC.

Book and cover design by Amy Sly
Photographs by Evan Sung

Library of Congress Cataloging-in-Publication Data
Names: Maffucci, Ali, author.
Title: Inspiralize everything: an apples-to-zucchini encyclopedia of
spiralizing / Ali Maffucci.
Description: First edition. | New York: Clarkson Potter/Publishers
[2016] | Includes index.
Identifiers: LCCN 2016009208| ISBN 9781101907450
(pbk.: alk. paper) | ISBN 9781101907467 (ebook)
Subjects: LCSH: Cooking (Vegetables) | Spiralizers (Utensils) |
LCGFT: Cookbooks.
Classification: LCC TX801.M243 2016 | DDC 641.6/5—dc23
LC record available at https://lccn.loc.gov/2016009208

ISBN 978-1-101-90745-0
eBook ISBN 978-1-101-90746-7

Printed in the United States of America

10 9 8 7 6 5 4 3 2 1

First Edition

"Everything you see here I owe to spaghetti." —Sophia Loren

To my "best bud" and
love of my life:
Lu, this one's for you

Contents

Introduction

On a typical Saturday morning, my husband, Lu, and I wake up early, go for an invigorating run outside together, and end up at our local farmer's market. We check in with the farmers about what's fresh, what's coming soon, and how life is. Many of our meals begin right there with the very people who plant and harvest our food. We walk through the market, loading up on seasonal, spiralizable (not a word in Webster's dictionary, but definitely in mine) veggies, finding all colors of the rainbow—red onions and bell peppers, orange carrots and sweet potatoes, golden beets, green zucchinis and cucumbers, and purple kohlrabi, depending on the season. At that point, I'm already thinking about what we'll be eating for dinner all week—will it be Greek-Style Shrimp Scampi (page 253)? Turkey Picadillo with Green Bell Pepper Noodles (page 50)? Hot-and-Sour Soup with Daikon Noodles (page 188)? The possibilities are limitless.

I still remember the first bowl of zucchini noodles I ever ate. My mother, a type 1 diabetic, was experimenting with raw veganism to help regulate her blood sugar levels. She discovered spiralizing, and invited me over to try an Asian-style raw zucchini noodle dish. As I spun my fork in the crunchy green "noodles," I was wary. Growing up in an Italian-American family, I was accustomed to eating heaping portions of spaghetti and dipping crusty, oven-heated slices of white bread into the pool of leftover sauce in the bottom of the bowl. How could sliced zucchini hold a candle to those meals? Well, that dinner was one that changed everything for me.

If you're familiar with my story, you know that I actually went home that night with my mother's spiralizer (thanks, Mom!) and started spiralizing nonstop. After three months, I quit my corporate job, launched Inspiralized.com, and made spiralizing my new lifestyle. I was blessed to garner an audience fairly quickly, and, before the two-year mark, to write a *New York Times* bestselling cookbook, *Inspiralized*. Fast-forward, and here we are. Who would've thought zucchini noodles could be so impactful? I promise, if you haven't already tried them, once you do, you'll be just as smitten as I am. And eventually, you, too, will *Inspiralize Everything*.

I still adore pasta today, but spiralizing has since transformed family dinners—and the way I cook, eat, and live every day. In the past, I would head straight to the living room after I finished at the table so I could lie flat on the couch, belly up, and let the food coma take over. Now, after a spiralized meal, I go for a walk around the block with Lu, full of energy and feeling nourished and satisfied. We'll breathe the fresh air into our lungs, soak up the day's last minutes of sunlight, and end up down by the Hudson River, taking in the gorgeous views of downtown Manhattan from our neighborhood in Jersey City. Not only does this help us digest our food after a meal, but we're also able to enjoy some quiet time to ourselves, talking about our day and feeling gracious. Since launching Inspiralized, I haven't cooked a bowl of "regular" pasta at home. When I dine out at restaurants, of course I'll order a plate of piping-hot fresh gnocchi in an aromatic tomato-basil sauce and signal the waiter to bring over more bread—God forbid a drop of sauce goes unslurped! I would never neglect my roots or deprive my taste buds. But on the whole, my eating is more balanced than ever before. (Plus, I can classify these meals as "research"—consider it a job perk.)

Opting for a clean-eating lifestyle changes everything—your energy levels skyrocket, your mood becomes more positive, your focus improves, and your waistline shrinks. Overall, you become a better version of yourself. You'll be grateful for the food you eat, as it not only strengthens your body, but also provides you with the vigor needed to live and enjoy your optimal life. After discovering spiralizing, my whole perspective on eating healthy changed: I started to focus on eating whole, real ingredients and stopped getting caught up in the minutiae of dieting. I discovered moderation, the concept of nourishing your body from the inside out, and, most

important, committing to a lifestyle rather than a temporary diet. Spiralizing is a way to eat lighter and more nutritiously, but still have the dishes and flavors I love to eat most (like pasta!). Once I went all-in with spiralizing, I lost 30 pounds and was able to finally find the weight my body feels best at and that I can maintain without obsessing over what I'm eating. I was freed from the chains of yo-yo dieting and calorie counting and can honestly say that spiralizing has led me to the healthiest and happiest body I've ever had.

All my success and positive results have only driven me to keep spiralizing. I have new tricks, cooking methods, ingredients, and of course recipes to share with you. In writing this cookbook, no rock was left unturned, or, ahem, *unspiralized*. Want a thinner noodle? I can show you how to get that (page 15). Having difficulty spiralizing large, tough vegetables? No problem—I've got you covered (page 15). I even found a new vegetable to spiralize (page 46)! Based on all your helpful feedback, I've included new categories and classifications for the recipes, such as Dairy-Free, No Cook, and Saves Well (see page 23 for a full list of indicators). You'll find dishes from all different cuisines—Thai, Chinese, Indian, Greek, Cuban, American, and, of course, Italian. Every recipe can be easily adapted to suit your preference or dietary needs. And everything here is meant to be a fully satisfying meal. You may have a hearty salad for lunch (like Fried Green Tomatoes with Avocado Ranch Kohlrabi, page 148) and an ample bowl of soup for dinner (like Slow-Cooked Carnitas Soup with Chayote Noodles, page 114).

Spiralizing can be used not only to re-create noodle and rice dishes, but also to make everyday meals

more interesting. Whether or not vegetables were meant to be this extraordinary, they are now—and when you spiralize, you'll impress yourself and friends with what comes out of your kitchen. Simply put, after reading this book, you'll be able to masterfully spiralize everything from Apples to Zucchini.

When my grandparents call to invite us over for Sunday night dinner, we grab the keys, run out the door, and drive the hour to their house from Jersey City, picking up a bottle of Chianti, Brunello, or Montepulciano (my grandfather's favorites) on the way. We know we'll arrive to a delicious, home-cooked meal, overflowing with love. We'll toast to good health and do what we do best: eat together. I cherish these moments deeply. But as for Monday night? That dinner will be Inspiralized.

How to Inspiralize Everything

BACK TO BASICS

Regardless of whether you've been spiralizing for ages or you're a newbie, it's important to know what you're doing with this gadget before you start cooking. Here are some simple definitions to get you started:

spiralizer (noun) *[spy-ruh-lahyz-er]*
1 a kitchen tool that turns vegetables and fruits into noodles.

spiralize (verb) *[spy-ruh-lahyz]*
1 to turn vegetables and fruits into noodles with a spiralizer.

inspiralize (verb) *[in-spy-ruh-lahyz]*
1 to make meals healthier and more creative by incorporating spiralized vegetables.
2 to replace traditional pasta, noodles, and rice with spiralized vegetables.

inspiralized (adverb)
1 a meal made with spiralized vegetables that's now healthier and more inspired because of it.

What can I spiralize?

For a vegetable or fruit to qualify as spiralizable and for best results, it must be:

- Without a tough pit or an interior with large, tough seeds.
- At least 1½ inches in diameter.
- At least 2 inches in length.
- Not soft or juicy inside.

There are a few exceptions to the above, however. Some vegetables and fruits may go through the spiralizer, but not well—the noodles won't look great, and the process will most likely waste much of the vegetable or fruit. Eggplant seemingly satisfies the guidelines, but due to its spongy flesh, it shreds and produces a seedy, mushy mess instead of noodles. Cantaloupes, persimmons, and some other foods are spiralizable, but I wanted to focus on the most versatile produce—but feel free to experiment and get creative! On the opposite end of the spectrum, we have bell pepper. They are hollow, but they can be spiralized quite successfully (more on that on page 47).

For a flawless experience, stick to these rules and the vegetables and fruits covered through the book. In developing these recipes, I've tried to include the produce that's readily available at local grocery stores and farmer's markets in the continental United States.

Which spiralizer should I use?

Now that your mind is racing with the endless possibilities of vegetable- and fruit-noodle meals, let's talk about your gadget. There are many types of spiralizers out there; each will produce a slightly different result, and each has its pros and cons. But no matter what kind you have, you can make every single recipe in this cookbook. If you *don't* have a spiralizer and aren't quite ready to invest, I have a solution for that, too! Check out the Tip Box on the right.

Everything on the market is primarily plastic and easy to clean and maintain. You can find spiralizers at specialty kitchen retailers, big-box chains, grocery stores, online—pretty much anywhere these days. They essentially break down into two main categories: handheld and countertop.

Handheld: These spiralizers require you to manually spin the produce through. They are small and best used on thinner vegetables like carrots, zucchini, and cucumbers. They are a great starting point if you don't want to invest in a larger tool, or simply don't have the room for one in your kitchen. They're also a solid option if you plan to bring your spiralizer with you when you're traveling or if you primarily want to spiralize zucchini.

Countertop: These spiralizers secure to a surface, offering more leverage and, therefore, the ability to handle vegetables and fruits of all sizes and shapes. The produce moves through with a crank of the handle instead of with your hand. These tend to take up more space and take a bit more time to clean (see page 16 for instructions on that).

So which one do I use? After trying out pretty much every model on the market, I decided to take the best features of what was out there and design my own: the Inspiralizer, which can be ordered at Inspiralized.com. But it comes down to personal preferences—one spiralizer doesn't fit all, so just do your research and choose one that best meets your needs.

If you don't have a spiralizer but do want to enjoy these recipes, you have a few options. A mandoline, julienne peeler, regular vegetable peeler, knife, or even the widest holes on a box grater can help you make noodles out of all vegetables. These methods are more time-consuming than spiralizing, but they work.

How do I spiralize?

Now that you've got your gadget, let's break down the steps. Here's how it works.

PREPARE YOUR PRODUCE

First, you'll need to get your vegetable or fruit ready to be spiralized. The opening text in each specific produce section specifies what steps to take for that item. But speaking generally, you'll want to slice off the ends of your vegetable so they are flat and even. Doing so will create a surface area that the spiralizer can properly secure to. Without this step, the vegetable will misalign, wobble, fall off, and ultimately cause your noodles to come out improperly. You don't have to slice the ends off apples, beets (if they're perfectly round), bell peppers, or pears— the spiralizer will just latch right on.

Next, if the outer skin is inedible or unpleasant to eat (like with a knobby, hairy celeriac), peel it before spiralizing. If the outer skin *is* edible and you prefer to eat it, no need to peel.

If your produce exceeds 6 inches in length, halve it. Some vegetables can be very round, large, and heavy, making it tough for them to stay secured to the spiralizer. To combat this issue, using a sharp knife, trim the edges off to make a rectangular shape no more than 5 inches wide. You can use the excess in another recipe or eat it as a snack.

CHOOSE A BLADE

If you're working with a gadget that has multiple blades, you get to decide your noodle shape, depending on which blade you choose to spiralize with. All the brands and models out there produce similar shapes with blades that we'll refer to here as A, B, C, and D.

BLADE A: Yields thin, ribbonlike noodles, similar to a pappardelle.

BLADE B: Yields thicker-shaped noodles, similar to a bucatini or fettuccine.

BLADE C: Yields linguine-shaped noodles.

BLADE D: Yields spaghetti-shaped noodles or, with some models, angel hair–shaped noodles. If you cannot find a vegetable with a diameter of at least 1½ inches, always use this blade. If yours is a three-blade tool, use blade C instead.

The Inspiralizer displays these letters on a blade-changing knob. If you're using another brand, check the manual so you know which blade yields which noodle shape. Most have either comblike teeth or triangular spokes for slicing. The smaller the distance between the teeth or the smaller the spokes, the thinner the noodle it will produce. The blade without any spokes is always blade A. Every recipe in this book indicates which blade you should use to prep your produce.

Since writing *Inspiralized*, I taught myself a new trick to adjust the width of the noodles without necessarily changing the blade. It's especially helpful if you love angel hair spaghetti and don't have a spiralizer with blade D, or if you're creating a thick pasta sauce and simply want a sturdy noodle. It's easy: just apply more or less pressure as you spiralize. To achieve thinner noodles, spiralize slowly and gently using light pressure. To achieve thicker noodles, spiralize more quickly with strong pressure. This technique works with any blade.

Time to spiralize!

You've got your vegetable or fruit and you've got your blade—you're ready to go! Take a peek at the manual that came with your tool. In general, if yours is a countertop model, you'll first secure the machine to the countertop. Then load on the vegetable or fruit, first aligning its center on the central coring blade, and then securing the spokes of the handle into the other end. Start cranking and watch the magic happen!

While you're spiralizing, if you notice that spiralizing yields more half-moon-style noodles instead of full spirals, it is most likely because your vegetable has moved off the center of the coring blade and isn't slicing evenly. To combat this, simply remove and recenter the vegetable.

After the blade indication in the ingredients lists, you'll often see "noodles trimmed." Just take kitchen shears and roughly cut the noodles so you don't have any that are super long. If you're cooking for kids, this step is especially important, as they may want to play with their noodles if they are too long, and won't easily be able to chew them. You can trim the noodles after the vegetable or fruit is fully spiralized or every couple of seconds as you spiralize.

CLEANING YOUR SPIRALIZER

Once you have the proper brush (see page 21 for details), cleaning your spiralizer is easy. Place the gadget under running water and, using soap, scrub the blades in a circular motion until all the food bits are washed away. Most important is the timing—it's essential to clean your spiralizer right after you use it to avoid staining and discoloration. After washing, place it on a rack and let it air-dry, or carefully pat it dry with a kitchen or paper towel.

What can I make with spiralized vegetables?

In the recipes in this book, sometimes the spiralized produce is the hero of the dish, and other times it's the sidekick. No matter how the produce is incorporated, it always adds texture, flavor, and nutrients. You probably know by now that the most popular way to incorporate spiralized vegetables is to use them in place of regular pasta and noodles. You won't think twice about eating a big bowl of spaghetti or pad Thai when it's light in calories and carbs, but still bursting with flavor. Some other easy ways to include them are in soups and stews, salads, pasta salads, casseroles, breakfast dishes, and baked goods. But it's not *just* about the noodles . . .

RICE

Ginger-Crab Fried Daikon Rice (page 191)? Chicken and Celeriac Rice Soup (page 108)? Why not! Spiralized rice is a great replacement for rice in any traditional use. To make it, first spiralize your vegetable with blade C or D. Pack the noodles into a food processor and pulse in 3-second intervals until they become ricelike. Take care not to overpulse, or you'll end up with shredded vegetables or mush. If there are any pieces that don't break down properly, pick them out and pulse them again separately.

Some vegetable rices require their excess moisture to be squeezed out before use in recipes. If you're using daikon radish, jícama, turnip, or zucchini, place the rice in a kitchen or paper towel and wring it out over the sink before cooking with it.

The Best Veggies for Ricing

- Beets
- Butternut squash
- Carrots
- Celeriac
- Daikon radish
- Jícama
- Kohlrabi
- Parsnips
- Rutabaga
- Sweet potatoes
- Turnip
- Zucchini

NOODLE BUNS

Spiralized noodles can also be enjoyed in the form of a bun, which can be used as the base for sandwiches, as burger buns, as miniature pizzas, or simply on their own. I bet you didn't think you could spiralize avocado toast (page 170)! To make buns, spiralize your vegetable with blade C or D. You can use any spiralizable produce, but starchy vegetables are best—parsnip, rutabaga, sweet potato, and potato.

Season the noodles with salt and pepper and cook them in some heated olive oil in a nonstick skillet until tender. You can also substitute cooking spray for the olive oil and cover the pan to let the noodles steam. Once they're cooked, transfer the noodles to a bowl, add one beaten egg per medium vegetable, and toss to coat. Pack the noodles into a ramekin or a similar vessel and place aluminum foil, parchment, or wax paper directly on top, pressing down with your hands or a weighted can. Let the noodles set for at least 15 minutes in the refrigerator. Heat 1 tablespoon olive oil in a large skillet over medium-high heat. When the oil is shimmering, invert the molded noodles into the pan. Sear until the buns are firm and browned on both sides, 5 to 7 minutes total.

THE INSPIRALIZED KITCHEN

You've got your gadget all set up, but what about the rest of the kitchen? It's absolutely crucial for a healthy home cook to be well-equipped in terms of pantry items and cookware. If not, cooking can be frustrating and disappointing, and you'll probably end up ordering in pizza. As the saying goes, failure to prepare is preparing to fail. So let's prepare!

The pantry

I've included an updated list of must-have items for a healthy Inspiralized pantry. In addition to the initial setup, it's important to occasionally (every month, if you cook regularly) survey what you're running low on and what you aren't using. Perhaps the foods you aren't using as much will inspire you to make something new! If you have the essentials on hand, you won't end up halfway through a recipe saying, "Oh no! I'm out of crushed tomatoes!" I've been there and it's *non bene*. Many of the pantry items listed here are great for cooking whether or not your meal is Inspiralized. Some of these ingredients are new to this book, so definitely take a moment to assess what you have!

Extra-virgin olive oil: A heart-healthy fat, and my favorite to cook with. If you're going to have one oil in your pantry, make it extra-virgin olive. Investing in a quality olive oil is essential (and totally worth it), as it cooks well and has a gentler, less processed flavor.

Extra-virgin coconut oil: The flavor of this oil makes it ideal for stir-fries; plus, it's packed with healthy fatty acids. As a bonus, it can be used in your beauty routine for facial masks, moisturizing, and more. It is solid at cold temperatures and often melted before use, either in the microwave or directly in a skillet on the stove.

Assorted canned beans (black, kidney, white, chickpeas): If your pantry is stocked with beans, you can always easily whip up a quick protein-packed meal. Always buy "no salt added," and be sure to rinse and drain your beans to remove about 40 percent of the sodium.

Low-sodium chicken, beef, and vegetable broth: Whether you're making soup, braising meat, or cooking sauce, you'll need broth. Broths also add flavor when used for simmering legumes.

Sesame oil: This is a must for many Asian dishes. All you need is a teaspoon or two to add significant flavor—it's potent!

Nuts (pistachios, almonds, walnuts, pecans, cashews, pine nuts): Whether used as a garnish or eaten as a snack, nuts are a versatile part of any pantry, and are packed with healthy fats, protein, and antioxidants.

Seeds (hemp, chia, sunflower): These superfoods can be used as a nutritional garnish or more completely, like in pudding, salad dressing, or baked goods. I love the pleasantly nutty taste of hemp hearts, which are called for in a few of these recipes.

They are an excellent source of protein, omega-3s fatty acids, magnesium, and dietary fiber.

Low-sodium soy sauce: Not only is soy sauce an essential part of Asian dishes like stir-fries and soups, but it's also great to have on hand to add salty umami flavor to pretty much anything. Soy sauce does typically contain gluten, so if your diet is gluten-free, look for a brand that works for you, or try alternatives like tamari and coconut aminos.

Flours (tapioca, almond meal and flour, coconut flour): Whether you're gluten-free or just want to infuse more nutrients into your meals, these less-processed wheat-free flours are the ones to have. They have a low glycemic index, so they won't give you that sugar-level roller-coaster feeling.

Vinegars (red wine, rice, balsamic, apple cider): Having a variety of vinegars on hand allows you to make all different kinds of dressings in a pinch, or even to create marinades, glazes, and sauces for veggies and proteins.

Dried herbs and spices (chili powder, parsley, rosemary, thyme, basil, curry powder, coriander, oregano, paprika, cumin, garlic powder, red pepper flakes, bay leaves, onion powder): These are the seasonings I use every week and consider must-haves to add healthy, low-calorie flavor to anything.

Sea salt and peppercorns (with a grinder): When using freshly ground pepper and salt, you don't need as much because of its freshness. They're also less processed!

Dried fruits (apricots, raisins, cranberries): Dried fruit jazzes up even the most lackluster salad, but it can also be tossed with nuts for a snack that's just sweet enough.

Bottled sauces (tomato-basil, teriyaki): When there's just no time to make a sauce from scratch, having healthy canned and jarred options on hand can take a lot of pressure off dinner plans—just make sure there are no additives or other processed ingredients such as dairy, xanthan gum, or sugar in the sauce. I like Victoria Fine Foods pasta sauces when I can't make my own.

Worcestershire sauce: For making robust stews and grilled dishes in the summertime, this sauce is crucial.

Canned coconut milk: I like to cook with full-fat coconut milk, but if you're watching your calories and fat count, the lite stuff works great, too. Use it to marinate chicken, stir into curries and soups, flavor sauces, or even add into oatmeal. Coconut cream is an excellent substitute for cream in many sauces. It infuses a dish with healthy fatty acids and naturally hydrating electrolytes. To get coconut cream, as it will be called for in some ingredient lists here, refrigerate a can of full-fat coconut milk for at least 24 hours without disturbing it. When you open the can, carefully scoop out the white solids from the top—that's the coconut cream (discard the liquid left in the can or reserve it for another use). One 14-ounce can typically yields about 1 heaping cup of the coconut cream.

Tahini: This condiment, usually sold in paste form, is made from ground sesame seeds. It's my favorite finish on bowl meals—I'll roast some spiralized veggies, throw in some quinoa, and drizzle over some tahini and lemon juice for a quick, easy, flavorful meal.

Nut butter: When making nut butter–based sauces (like a Thai peanut sauce), it's important to have a healthy, smooth nut butter with no added sugars. I like almond butter best, but peanut and cashew are great, too. Stock your pantry with what you like!

Curry paste (red and green): Curry pastes are essential to, well, curries, but they also work well as a marinade for veggies and stirred into yogurt-based sauces or even meatball mixes.

Nutritional yeast flakes: This versatile vegan ingredient enables you to make dishes taste cheesy without the cheese. These flakes can be pureed into sauces like Alfredo or simply sprinkled like a grated cheese on top of salads.

Healthy grains (quinoa, lentils, farro, barley): These grains are sustainable sources of protein and nutrients, making them ideal to keep you feeling full and nourished.

Maple syrup and honey: I keep these sweeteners on hand for baked goods and dressings.

Country Dijon mustard: A quality grainy Dijon mustard can be used in many different ways; for tart dressings and vinaigrettes, for crusting fish and meat, or obviously as a spread. It's low in calories and adds a strong bite of flavor!

Canned tomatoes (whole peeled, diced, crushed) and tomato paste: A pantry is not complete without canned tomatoes, which are used in sauces, soups and stews, braises, and so many others. These are especially helpful in the wintertime, when fresh tomatoes aren't available. My grandparents almost always used Tuttorosso tomatoes, and now that's what I use, too, but find whatever brand suits your preference. Opt for "no salt added" when possible.

Olive oil cooking spray: I try to avoid using canola oil in my cooking because many are genetically modified and partially hydrogenated, so I always buy olive oil cooking spray. Certain spiralized veggies (like zucchini) just need a few spritzes of spray in a heated pan.

Water-packed tuna (chunk light): An easy-to-use lean protein, water-packed tuna is low in calories and packed with essential omega-3s. Try tossing it together with zucchini noodles, lemon juice, and red pepper flakes for a quick dish.

Other pantry items

There are some pantry items that aren't crucial, but as you grow your pantry and start cooking more, you may want to include them as well.

Ground flaxseed: Sprinkled over salads and breakfast bowls, flaxseed adds a nutty, textural topping that's high in antioxidants and omega-3s.

Gluten-free oats: Not only for breakfast and cookies, oats are also great to fold into meatball mix as a binding alternative to bread crumbs.

Other spices: Nutmeg, cinnamon, ground ginger, turmeric, herbes de Provence, garam masala, Chinese five-spice.

Tools

This probably won't shock you, but I'm kind of a gadget nut. I own everything from a 4-minute pizza maker to a strawberry huller. Those may not be essential to an Inspiralized kitchen, but there are certain kitchen tool must-haves that I use regularly and couldn't cook healthfully without.

Wok: If you're cooking more than two large spiralized vegetables, you will need to do so in batches or use a larger vessel, such as a wok. I use my wok when I'm making dinners for more than two people, since it's large enough to hold all the noodles before they wilt and cook down.

Food processor: Some of the recipes here require a food processor, a tool that allows you to make your own healthy sauces and dressings. Sometimes you can get around it by chopping ingredients super small and stirring them together, but I promise this tool is worth the investment. Most important, you can't make spiralized rice without it!

Tongs: Once you start spiralizing, you'll be doing a lot of tossing, which requires a pair of delicate but sturdy tongs. I prefer stainless steel with a rubber grip, which are strong but gentle enough to handle the daintiest of vegetable noodles.

Vegetable peeler: Many vegetables need to be peeled before they're spiralized (if their flesh is unpleasant or inedible). Certain veggies have tough, knobby exteriors that are difficult to peel. Look for a solid peeler that has a rubber grip for leverage and a stainless-steel blade.

Round palm brush: In my kitchen, I keep a separate brush for the spiralizer—one that has tough bristles and a palm grip. Don't try to use a regular sponge to clean the blades of your spiralizer—the tool will eat it right up. See page 16 for more details on how to clean the spiralizer.

Quality chef's knife: One of the first things I did when I started Inspiralized was invest in a sharp, good-quality chef's knife. My world changed— preparing food for cooking is infinitely better with a great knife, and you don't know until you know. I use both Zwilling and Wüsthof knives.

Nonstick skillets: Vegetable noodles can be fragile, so nonstick skillets are all I ever use when cooking them to avoid breakage. When purchasing a set of nonstick skillets, look for PFOA-free ones.

HOW TO USE THIS COOKBOOK

When I brought the spiralizer home for the first time, I was eager to get started. I'm sure you're feeling excited and ready to start making these recipes. But before you dig in, I have just a few more notes. My goal with this cookbook is not only to inform you of every nuance of spiralizing, but also to prepare you for it. I want you to have a seamless experience when following along, so I've designed it to be as user-friendly as possible. The recipes here are divided by vegetable or fruit, rather than by type of dish as they were in *Inspiralized*. The Apple section, for example, features recipes using spiralized apples. This way, you can cook with what's in season, what's fresh at the market, or what you already have on hand. In fact, I encourage you to cook your way down the whole produce aisle!

Each recipe also includes a section called Also Works Well With. Here, I'll list other vegetables that would spiralize well in that recipe. For example, the Broccoli Rabe and Sausage Parsnip Pasta (page 174) calls for parsnips, but it would also work well with spiralized butternut squash. This flexibility is one of the things I love most about spiralizing—it truly transforms the way you think about produce and encourages you to eat something you may never have considered before. With an easy swap, a simple tomato-basil zucchini pasta can also become a celeriac pasta or a sweet potato pasta. Although Zucchini is the last chapter in this book, it's a great place to start. Once you're acquainted with this veggie, you'll understand the full potential of spiralizing and realize that the possibilities are truly endless.

The spiralized ingredient in each recipe will be written in this format:

1 medium zucchini, spiralized with BLADE C, noodles trimmed

To translate, the vegetable should be spiralized prior to beginning the recipe, along with all the other ingredient preparation like slicing and dicing. Whichever blade is specified is the one you should use to spiralize. If we're making rice, it will say that, too. If you see the star vegetable listed, but it *doesn't* indicate which blade to use, you will find those instructions in the recipe steps, as that specific preparation needs to happen at a specific time. This will come up for making noodle buns, or for making macaroni-style noodles or chips, like with Grams's Tuna and Macaroni Salad (page 62). It will also come up when a recipe requires a longer cooking method; instead of setting up a full *mise en place*, the spiralizing can happen while another part of the recipe is cooking in order to save time. But in general, when tackling the recipes in this

book or otherwise, I strongly encourage you to read the whole recipe first, and to fully prepare the ingredients as listed. This way, you won't have to turn off the stove mid-simmer with an "Oops, I forgot to mince the garlic!" Your whole cooking experience will be more harmonious.

Indicators

Each recipe includes a bunch of indicators to give you an at-a-glance overview.

DIFFICULTY LEVEL

The number of spirals signifies how difficult the recipe is to make.

∿ **One spiral:** Very easy, no or not much cooking required, basic spiralizing

∿∿ **Two spirals:** Medium difficulty, more preparation or cooking required

∿∿∿ **Three spirals:** Most difficult, many steps required and more handling of the spiralized vegetables

But don't let a three-spiral recipe intimidate you—it mainly means that the recipe will take you more time, on account of the extra steps involved. Each recipe also indicates how long it will take to prep and cook so that you can prepare—mentally and logistically.

Diet and feature classification

If you follow a certain dietary lifestyle, I've included indicators to classify the recipes by diet:

Vegan

Vegetarian

Gluten-free

Paleo

Dairy-free: This dietary feature is new to this book, indicating that the recipe contains no dairy.

Dairy-free (opt.): This indication means the dairy listed in the ingredients is not integral to the dish and can be omitted without sacrificing much flavor.

I've also included some nondietary cooking features to give you a bit more background information on each dish.

Low-Cal: Under 300 calories per serving.

No Cook: Doesn't require any heated cooking, so it is mostly assembly-based.

Saves Well: Works well as leftovers (so you may want to make extra!).

One Pot: Cooked in one pan or pot for the easiest cleanup.

All recipes include the following nutritional information: calories, carbohydrates, protein, fat, fiber, and sugar. This information was calculated primarily using data from the USDA National Nutrient Database for Standard Reference.

A note about salt

In my opinion, salt should always be added according to your taste preferences, but sparingly—at least to start! You can always add more, but it's impossible to take out. And if you're cooking for other people, remember that everyone's taste buds are different. Aside from a couple of baked goods, you won't find many recipes in this book that necessitate a specific amount of salt. I will, however, indicate when you should salt "generously." Almost always, I instruct to "taste and adjust the seasoning to your preference." Seasoning is crucial, so don't skip it! Stick a spoon into the dressing or sauce, give it a taste, and then adjust accordingly. Just be mindful of how much salt you add, as too much can cause issues like high blood pressure, which can lead to scarier issues like heart failure and obesity.

Now you know all of my spiralized secrets! If you're a new cook, you're about to surprise yourself with how easily you can whip up nutritious and flavorsome meals. If you're a seasoned cook, you'll enliven your repertoire with this new technique. I've made a point to offer recipes that are foolproof, filling meals that you'll want to come back to all the time and will soon become a part of your weekly dinner rotation. Ready? Time to *Inspiralize Everything*!

Apple

Before Inspiralized, apples were really only for baking into pies, making fruit salads, snacking on, or to pick as a totally Instagrammable fall activity. They come in so many varieties with beautiful colors and unique flavor profiles; there's definitely an apple out there for everyone! If you like tart, opt for a Granny Smith, but if you like sweet, grab a Fuji. Try them all and see what tickles your taste buds.

Once Inspiralized, apples take on a new life—they're integral to bountiful salads, stirred into yogurt for a sweet crunch, and served up as toppings to appetizers and meats. They're even useful as an edible garnish, like in the Creamy Roasted Butternut Squash Soup with Apple Noodles on page 28. By spiralizing apples, you'll uncover their true potential.

NUTRITIONAL BENEFITS: Apples are loaded with vitamin C, which is where the old saying "An apple a day keeps the doctor away" comes from. They also contain high amounts of fiber and have been proven to reduce levels of LDL, the "bad" cholesterol.

PREPARATION AND STORAGE: Remove the stem prior to spiralizing. I don't recommend saving spiralized apples due to browning, but if you must, seal spiralized apple in an airtight container covered with water and a bit of lemon juice for up to 2 days.

BEST BLADES TO USE
- Blade C
- Blade D

BEST COOKING METHODS
- Raw
- Sauté in a skillet over medium heat for 5 minutes

Crabless Crab Cakes
with Green Apple Guacamole

～～ | Vegetarian
～～ | Gluten-Free
～～ | Dairy-Free

TIME TO PREP 30 minutes
TIME TO COOK 15 minutes
SERVES 4 to 6

NUTRITIONAL INFORMATION
(for 1 of 6 servings)
Calories: 311
Fat: 21 g
Sodium: 725 mg
Carbohydrate: 30g
Fiber: 6 g
Sugar: 8 g
Protein: 5 g

Yes, these crab cakes are crabless! It seems like an oxymoron, but once you make them, you'll get it—and smell it. Thanks to Old Bay seasoning, Dijon mustard, and hearts of palm, these cakes are fit for a steakhouse. The proverbial cherry on top is definitely the green apple guacamole. Its tart sweetness ties all the flavors together, offering a refreshing balance to the potent Old Bay. The spiralizer creates the perfect apple noodle to give each forkful a crunch!

For the cakes

Kernels from 4 medium ears of corn (about 2 cups)

¼ cup minced onion

¼ cup minced green bell pepper

¼ cup mayonnaise (I prefer homemade or vegan—see Tip)

1 (15-ounce) can whole hearts of palm or artichoke hearts, drained, diced, and lightly smashed

2 teaspoons Old Bay seasoning

2 tablespoons chopped fresh flat-leaf parsley

2 teaspoons Dijon mustard

⅓ cup gluten-free bread crumbs, plus more as needed, or ½ cup almond meal

Salt and pepper

For the guacamole

3 avocadoes, cubed

2 large garlic cloves, minced

Juice of 2 limes

Salt and pepper

2 medium jalapeños, seeded and finely minced

1 small red onion, diced

2 vine tomatoes, seeded and diced

½ cup fresh cilantro, chopped

1 *large green apple, spiralized with* BLADE C

2 tablespoons extra-virgin olive oil

1 Heat a large skillet over medium-high heat. When water flicked onto the skillet sizzles, add the corn, onion, and bell pepper and cook until tender, 3 to 5 minutes. Transfer 1 cup of the mixture to a food processor and pulse until coarse-smooth. Transfer to a medium bowl and add the mayonnaise, hearts of palm, Old Bay, parsley, mustard, and bread crumbs. Season with salt and pepper and stir well.

2 Line a baking sheet with parchment paper. Using your hands, form the mixture into twelve cakes, 2 inches in diameter, and transfer to the prepared baking sheet. Refrigerate for 10 to 15 minutes to bind.

3 Make the guacamole. Place all the guacamole ingredients in a medium bowl and stir together until combined but some chunks of avocado still remain. Taste and adjust the seasoning to your preferences, adding more salt, cilantro, lime, or jalapeño as needed. Refrigerate until ready to serve.

4 Heat 1 tablespoon of the olive oil in a large skillet over medium-high heat. When the oil is shimmering, add six cakes and cook for about 2 minutes per side or until golden brown. Transfer to a platter. Wipe down the skillet, add another 1 tablespoon of the olive oil, and cook the remaining cakes.

5 Serve two or three cakes and about ½ cup of guacamole on each plate.

I prefer to make my own mayonnaise to ensure that the ingredients are wholesome. Or I'll use a vegan brand such as Sir Kensington's. To make your own, in a food processor or by hand, blend together 1 egg yolk and 1½ teaspoons fresh lemon juice. While whisking rapidly to emulsify, slowly stream in ½ cup avocado oil, 1 teaspoon at a time. Season with salt and pepper.

Creamy Roasted Butternut Squash Soup
with Apple Noodles

Vegan
Vegetarian
Gluten-Free
Paleo
Dairy-Free

TIME TO PREP 10 minutes
TIME TO COOK 1 hour
SERVES 4 (about 6 cups)

NUTRITIONAL INFORMATION
Calories: 370
Fat: 13 g
Sodium: 396 mg
Carbohydrate: 57 g
Fiber: 12 g
Sugar: 30 g
Protein: 4 g

ALSO WORKS WELL WITH
Pear

Spiralized vegetables and fruits don't always have to be the main attraction of a dish—they work exquisitely as garnishes, too. Actually, that was their original purpose. They artistically topped dishes in restaurants, where the highlight of a meal is frequently its inventive presentation. While they're a nice finishing touch in this cozy dish, they also offer a sweet zing and cold crunch that elevates this classic autumnal soup.

1 large butternut squash (about 3 pounds), halved lengthwise and seeded

1 tablespoon coconut oil, melted

Salt and pepper

2 teaspoons extra-virgin olive oil

1 small shallot, minced

2 garlic cloves, minced

1/8 teaspoon ground nutmeg (just a pinch)

1 teaspoon chili powder

2 cups low-sodium vegetable or chicken broth

1 (15-ounce) can lite coconut milk

2 sweet red apples (I like Gala)

1 tablespoon roasted and salted shelled pepitas

If your taste buds prefer a sweeter soup, stir in a teaspoon or two of maple syrup.

1 Preheat the oven to 425 degrees. Line a baking sheet with parchment paper. Put the butternut squash cut-side up on the prepared baking sheet and drizzle the inside of the squash with the coconut oil. Rub it in with your fingertips or a brush. Season with salt and pepper. Flip over the squash and bake for 45 minutes or until the flesh is easily pierced with a fork. Let cool for 5 to 10 minutes or until cool enough to handle. Use a spoon to scoop out the flesh and transfer it to a bowl, discarding the skin.

2 While the squash cooks, heat the olive oil in a medium skillet over medium heat. When the oil is shimmering, add the shallot and cook for 3 minutes or until softened. Add the garlic and cook for 30 seconds or until fragrant.

3 Transfer the shallot and garlic to a high-speed blender. Add the squash, nutmeg, chili powder, broth, coconut milk, and salt and pepper to taste and pulse until creamy, about 1 minute. Taste and adjust the seasoning to your preferences.

4 When the soup is blended, spiralize the apples with **BLADE D**. Divide the soup among four bowls and add apple noodles, pepitas, and more pepper.

Apple-Walnut Muffins

When I was in school, my mother used to buy giant, grapefruit-size muffins from Costco and freeze them. After school, she'd take one out, toast it, and slice it—then we'd all devour it in a matter of seconds. My favorite flavors were always the ones with nuts or fruit. These muffins are my healthy version, using real, whole ingredients like mashed bananas, cinnamon, and coconut oil, which give them an extra nutrient and flavor boost. They are best served with strong coffee and a sunny disposition.

Vegetarian
Gluten-Free
Paleo
Low-Cal
Saves Well

TIME TO PREP 20 minutes
TIME TO COOK 30 minutes
MAKES 6 large or 12 mini muffins

NUTRITIONAL INFORMATION
(for 1 of 6 servings)
Calories: 226
Fat: 7 g
Sodium: 230 mg
Carbohydrate: 21 g
Fiber: 5 g
Sugar: 11 g
Protein: 6 g

ALSO WORKS WELL WITH
Pear

Cooking spray

½ cup coconut flour

¾ teaspoon baking soda

½ teaspoon salt

2 teaspoons ground cinnamon

½ teaspoon ground nutmeg

3 large eggs

3 tablespoons maple syrup

2 teaspoons vanilla extract

2 tablespoons plain unsweetened almond milk

1 tablespoon coconut oil, melted and cooled to room temperature

1 ripe banana, mashed

1 Honeycrisp apple, spiralized with BLADE B, noodles trimmed

½ cup chopped walnuts

1 Preheat the oven to 350 degrees. Coat a large muffin tin with cooking spray and line the wells with strips of parchment paper or paper liners.

2 In a medium bowl, combine the coconut flour, baking soda, salt, cinnamon, and nutmeg. In a separate medium bowl, combine the eggs, maple syrup, vanilla, almond milk, coconut oil, and banana. Add the dry ingredients to the wet. Add the apple and stir until the batter is smooth. Fold in the walnuts.

3 Pour the batter into the prepared muffin tin and bake for 30 minutes or until a toothpick inserted into the center of a muffin comes out clean.

To move these muffins from breakfast to dessert, add some dark chocolate chunks or a tablespoon of unsweetened raw cacao powder to the batter.

Curried Apple Egg Salad Wrap

Vegetarian
Gluten-Free
Low-Cal
No Cook

TIME TO PREP 20 minutes
SERVES 2 to 4

NUTRITIONAL INFORMATION
(for 1 of 2 servings)
Calories: 199
Fat: 4 g
Sodium: 135 mg
Carbohydrate: 28 g
Fiber: 4 g
Sugar: 18 g
Protein: 15 g

If you asked me what kind of photos consistently receive the most "likes" on the Inspiralized Instagram account, the answer would undoubtedly be my collard green wraps. I love creating this bulging burrito-style lunch using collards and spiralized veggies. This egg salad version is rich with flavor from the curry powder in my classic fayonnaise, made with Greek yogurt for a lighter choice that's higher in protein and lower in fat. Its creamy texture gets a surprisingly crunchy bite thanks to the celery and apple noodles. The egg salad can be prepped ahead of time and kept in the fridge for three days, making it ideal for work lunches. If you can't find collard greens, use Bibb lettuce or romaine instead.

For the curried fayonnaise

⅔ cup plus 2 tablespoons nonfat plain Greek yogurt

1 tablespoon whole-grain or Dijon mustard

½ teaspoon garlic powder

1 tablespoon fresh lemon juice

½ teaspoon curry powder

Salt and pepper

⅛ teaspoon cayenne pepper

For the apple mixture and wrap

1 *apple*

2 tablespoons raisins

½ cup diced celery

1 hard-boiled egg, peeled and chopped

2 large or 4 small collard green leaves, stems trimmed

½ cup alfalfa sprouts

1 Make the fayonnaise: Combine all the fayonnaise ingredients in a large bowl and whisk until combined. Set aside.

2 Make the apple mixture: Slice the apple halfway through lengthwise to create a slit, being careful not to pierce through its center. Spiralize using **BLADE B**. Add the apple, raisins, celery, and egg to the bowl with the fayonnaise. Toss to combine thoroughly.

3 Pack the curried egg salad into the middle of the collard leaves, dividing it evenly. Top with sprouts and roll like a burrito, tucking in the ends. Secure both ends with a toothpick and halve before serving.

Not a fan of the curry flavor? Omit it from the fayonnaise and make this a regular egg salad sandwich.

Ginger Pear and Apple Sangria

Vegetarian
Dairy-Free
No Cook

TIME TO COOK 4 hours
SERVES 6

NUTRITIONAL INFORMATION
Calories: 312
Fat: 0 g
Sodium: 10 mg
Carbohydrate: 44 g
Fiber: 1 g
Sugar: 38 g
Protein: 0 g

My college roommate Stacey used to make the best cocktails. On Friday mornings, she would prepare a batch of sangria and leave it in the refrigerator, and then we'd enjoy it later that night, once classes were done. Stacey's sangria was fun and festive and always signified the best part of the week: the start of the weekend. What I loved most was that she always used a lot of fresh fruit—and the chunks of alcohol-soaked fruit were fun to eat! This spiralized version looks even prettier than the original with its elegant and colorful spirals. While Stacey always made red sangria, I've updated my version to use white wine and a hint of ginger beer. Bring on summer!

1 (750-ml) bottle sauvignon blanc (or other dry white wine)

½ cup white rum

¼ cup brandy

1 (12-ounce) bottle ginger beer

1 tablespoon honey

1 *Gala apple, spiralized with* BLADE C

1 *Bartlett pear, spiralized with* BLADE C

1 In a large serving pitcher, combine the wine, rum, brandy, ginger beer, and honey. Stir until the honey has dissolved. Add the apple and pear noodles and stir.

2 Enjoy immediately, or for best results, refrigerate for at least 4 hours and up to 8 hours before serving.

Beet

Beets are my jam! They're sweet and earthy all at once. They are always in season, are readily available in grocery stores, and tend to be the ideal size for spiralizing. Beets come in several different varieties, although red ones tend to hog the spotlight. Some of my other favorites are the golden beet and the Chioggia beet, which resembles a candy cane with its stripes. They're common in Mediterranean cooking, but they work well in all different cuisines, as you'll see here.

While beets have a lot going for them, the red ones get messy no matter how you prepare them—whether roasted in foil or spiralized raw, they'll bleed. To avoid staining your hands, wear gloves when handling them. I have reusable kitchen gloves just for this purpose! To avoid staining your spiralizer, wash it immediately after use. If need be, scrub your hands or spiralizer with warm water and kosher salt to help remove discoloration.

NUTRITIONAL BENEFITS: Beets significantly help lower blood pressure thanks to their naturally occurring nitrates. Their concentration of betaine helps fight inflammation. In addition to immune-boosting vitamin C, beets contain powerful phytonutrients that may help ward off cancers. In fact, beet extract is a popular ingredient in natural cancer-fighting supplements.

PREPARATION AND STORAGE: Peel the beet completely, then slice off the ends to make flat, even surfaces. Store in an airtight container in the refrigerator for up to 5 days. Beet noodles can also be frozen for up to 8 months for future use.

BEST BLADES TO USE
- Blade C
- Blade D

BEST COOKING METHODS
- Raw
- Boil for 2 to 3 minutes
- Sauté over medium-high heat for 7 minutes
- Roast at 425 degrees for 5 to 10 minutes

Spiced Lamb Skewers
with Beet Noodles

≈≈ | Gluten-Free
≈≈

TIME TO PREP 20
TIME TO COOK 20
SERVES 4

NUTRITIONAL INFORMATION
Calories: 443
Fat: 34 g
Sodium: 112 mg
Carbohydrate: 10 g
Fiber: 2 g
Sugar: 2 g
Protein: 25g

ALSO WORKS WELL WITH
Sweet Potato, Butternut
Squash, Broccoli, Rutabaga

Since launching Inspiralized, I feel like I've circled the globe by way of food. I'm always looking to healthfully re-imagine my and my readers' favorite meals found while traveling. After one of my readers came back from her honeymoon in Turkey, she wondered if I could re-create the lamb skewers she'd enjoyed there. Challenge accepted. Here we have filling beet noodles that enhance the flavors in the meat and pair well with the yogurt sauce. I'm humbled to be able to bring back someone else's happy memory—and to make a new one for myself.

For the beet noodles

2 large red beets, peeled, spiralized with *BLADE C*, and noodles trimmed

Salt and pepper

For the skewers

1 pound ground lamb

1 teaspoon ground cumin

2 teaspoons ground coriander

¼ teaspoon paprika

2 garlic cloves, finely minced

1 tablespoon minced fresh mint

Salt and pepper

1 tablespoon extra-virgin olive oil

For the yogurt sauce

½ cup nonfat plain Greek yogurt

1 tablespoon minced shallot

2 teaspoons minced fresh cilantro

2 teaspoons fresh lemon juice

¼ teaspoon paprika

Salt and pepper

¼ cup chopped roasted pistachios, for garnish

1 Make the beet noodles. Preheat the oven to 425 degrees. Line a baking sheet with parchment paper and arrange the beet noodles on it, spacing them apart. Season with salt and pepper. Roast for 10 to 15 minutes or until al dente.

2 Meanwhile, make the skewers. In a large bowl, stir together all the ingredients for the skewers except the olive oil. Form the mixture into eight balls, then thread them onto four metal or soaked wooden skewers.

3 Heat the olive oil in a large grill pan or skillet over medium-high heat. When the oil is shimmering, add the skewers and cook for 5 minutes per side, flattening the meat mixture slightly with a spatula.

4 Meanwhile, make the yogurt sauce. Whisk together all the ingredients for the yogurt sauce in a small bowl.

5 Divide the beet noodles among four plates and top with one skewer each. Drizzle with the yogurt sauce and garnish with pistachios.

If lamb isn't your thing, try ground turkey. If you don't eat meat, the vegetarian meatballs on page 109 work well instead.

Tahini Beet Noodle Bowl
with Falafel

 Vegetarian
Gluten-Free
Dairy-Free
Low-Cal

TIME TO PREP 25 minutes
TIME TO COOK 1 hour
SERVES 4

NUTRITIONAL INFORMATION
Calories: 266
Fat: 15 g
Sodium: 359 mg
Carbohydrate: 30 g
Fiber: 10 g
Sugar: 7 g
Protein: 10 g

ALSO WORKS WELL WITH
Butternut Squash, Sweet
Potato

Somewhere along the way on my Inspiralized journey, I fell in love with tahini. Tahini sauces complement almost every single meat, grain, and vegetable out there. Maple-tahini, lemon-tahini, garlic-tahini, avocado-tahini—I've tried them all. Made from ground sesame seeds, this paste has a nutty flavor that just seems to go with everything. Here, the falafel, beets, and tomatoes are full of robust Mediterranean flavor—a perfect match for my beloved tahini. This homemade falafel is a lighter version, baked instead of fried. Trust me—this dish will transport you right to your favorite falafel spot, whether it's a stand in Israel or a cart on a New York City sidewalk.

3 tablespoons chopped fresh parsley

2 garlic cloves, minced

1 teaspoon lemon zest

Juice of 1 large lemon

1¼ teaspoons ground cumin

1 teaspoon ground coriander

¼ teaspoon chili powder

Salt and pepper

1 (15-ounce) can chickpeas, rinsed, drained, and patted dry

¼ cup almond flour

¼ cup diced red onion

2 large beets, peeled, spiralized with **BLADE D**, *and noodles trimmed*

1 tablespoon chopped fresh cilantro

½ cup quartered seeded cherry tomatoes

½ cup diced cucumber

1 teaspoon extra-virgin olive oil

For the tahini dressing

2 tablespoons tahini

1 tablespoon fresh lemon juice

1 teaspoon honey

⅓ teaspoon garlic powder

1 tablespoon extra-virgin olive oil

Salt and pepper

1 Preheat the oven to 375 degrees. Line a baking sheet with parchment paper.

2 Make the falafel. In a food processor, combine the parsley, garlic, lemon zest, lemon juice, cumin, coriander, chili powder, and salt and pepper to taste. Pulse to completely combine, about 30 seconds. Add the chickpeas and pulse until incorporated but still chunky.

3 Transfer the mixture to a medium bowl and add the almond flour and onion. Mix again to form a dough. Using your hands, form the mixture into eight balls and place them on the prepared baking sheet. Press down with a spatula to flatten them into patties, cupping to keep them compact. Refrigerate for 15 minutes to firm up.

4 Transfer the baking sheet to the oven and bake for 35 to 40 minutes or until the patties are firm and browned, flipping once halfway through.

5 Spread the beets on the second prepared baking sheet, spacing them apart, and roast with the falafel for 15 minutes or until al dente.

6 Meanwhile, in a small bowl, combine the cilantro, tomatoes, cucumbers, and olive oil. Season with salt and pepper and set aside.

7 Make the tahini dressing. Place all the ingredients for the dressing in a food processor and pulse until creamy. Slowly add 1 to 2 tablespoons water as needed to thin. Taste and adjust the seasoning to your preferences. Set aside.

8 Divide the beet noodles among four bowls and top each with two falafel patties and a spoonful of the tomato mixture. Drizzle with the tahini dressing to finish, and serve immediately.

For a crispier, more traditional falafel, heat 2 tablespoons olive oil in a skillet and sear the patties for 2 minutes per side before transferring to the oven.

Chicken Tagine
with Apricot Golden Beet Rice

Gluten-Free

TIME TO PREP 15 minutes
TIME TO COOK 45 minutes
SERVES 4

NUTRITIONAL INFORMATION
Calories: 403
Fat: 22 g
Sodium: 517 mg
Carbohydrate: 21 g
Fiber: 4 g
Sugar: 10 g
Protein: 28 g

ALSO WORKS WELL WITH
Turnip, Butternut Squash,
Carrot, Kohlrabi, Celeriac,
Sweet Potato

My inspiration for this chicken dish came from Daniel Boulud's Mediterranean French restaurant Boulud Sud in New York City. I saw the recipe featured in the *New York Times*, made it, and loved it. In fact, I loved it so much that I decided to Inspiralize it. Although the spiralized version is not nearly as elaborate as the original, this traditional North African stew boasts robust, deeply spiced flavors. It is typically served over a starch like couscous, but here we use golden beet rice instead, which adds beautiful color, as well as nutrients such as fiber and calcium.

1 tablespoon extra-virgin olive oil

1½ pounds chicken legs and thighs

   Salt and pepper

½ yellow onion, diced

2 carrots, diced

2 garlic cloves, minced

1 (½-inch) piece fresh ginger, peeled and minced

½ teaspoon ground coriander

½ teaspoon ground cumin

¼ teaspoon ground cinnamon

1½ cups low-sodium chicken broth

¼ cup slivered blanched almonds

¼ cup dried apricots, chopped

1 cup canned chickpeas, rinsed and drained

2 *large golden beets, peeled, spiralized with* **BLADE D**, *then riced (see page 16)*

1 tablespoon fresh cilantro, for garnish (optional)

1 Heat the olive oil in a large Dutch oven or pot with a lid over medium-high heat. Season the chicken with salt and pepper. When the oil is shimmering, add the chicken to the pan without crowding, working in batches if necessary. Sear the chicken for about 7 minutes, flipping once, until both sides are golden brown. Set aside on a plate.

2 Immediately add the onion and carrots to the pan, season with salt and pepper, and cook until softening, 5 to 7 minutes.

3 Add the garlic to the pan and cook until fragrant, about 30 seconds. Add the ginger, coriander, cumin, and cinnamon and cook, stirring, until fragrant, about 1 minute. Add ½ cup of the chicken broth and scrape up any browned bits from the bottom of the pan.

recipe continues

4 Return the chicken to the pan, fitting the pieces into a single layer as best as possible. Pour over the remaining 1 cup chicken broth. Increase the heat to high and bring the liquid to a boil. Reduce the heat to low, cover the pan, and simmer for 25 to 30 minutes or until the chicken is no longer pink in the center and its juices run clear.

5 Reserving the vegetables in the pot, transfer the chicken to a plate and cover with foil to keep warm. Add the almonds, apricots, chickpeas, and beet rice to the pot. Increase the heat to medium-high and bring to a steady simmer. Reduce the heat to low, cover, and cook for 5 minutes more or until the beet rice softens.

6 Transfer the rice mixture to a serving platter and top with the chicken. Garnish with cilantro, if desired, and serve immediately.

To minimize prep and for a different variety of sweetness, try tossing in golden raisins in place of the apricots.

Green Curry Golden Beet Noodle Bowl

Vegan
Vegetarian
Gluten-Free
Paleo

TIME TO PREP 15 minutes
TIME TO COOK 15 minutes
SERVES 4

NUTRITIONAL INFORMATION
Calories: 343
Fat: 24 g
Sodium: 316 mg
Carbohydrate: 25 g
Fiber: 9 g
Sugar: 11 g
Protein: 7 g

ALSO WORKS WELL WITH
Turnip, Radish, Zucchini,
Cabbage, Carrot, Kohlrabi,
Chayote

This basic bowl is the perfect introduction to coconut curry. In fact, once you've mastered this recipe, I bet you'll be inspired to create your own version. You may want to try a red paste instead of green, or add protein—lentils, chicken, and even a strong fish like salmon would work well on top. Maybe you want to include snap peas, broccoli, or bean sprouts in addition to or instead of the green beans that are called for here. Spiralized curry bowls are comforting, filling, easy, and clearly customizable! Have fun with it.

1 tablespoon coconut oil

2 garlic cloves, minced

2 teaspoons minced fresh ginger

½ *small yellow onion, peeled, spiralized with* **BLADE A**, *noodles trimmed*

4 scallions, diced, dark green parts kept separate

1½ to 2 tablespoons Thai green curry paste

1 (15-ounce) can coconut milk

3 cups low-sodium vegetable broth

4 *small golden beets, peeled, spiralized with* **BLADE A**, *noodles trimmed*

4 ounces green beans, ends trimmed

Salt

½ cup cashews

1 Thai red chile pepper, thinly sliced

Handful of fresh Thai basil or cilantro leaves

1 Heat the coconut oil in a large pot over medium-high heat. When the oil has melted, add the garlic, ginger, half of the onion noodles, and the white and light green parts of the scallions. Cook for 30 seconds or until fragrant, then carefully add the curry paste, watching out for splatter.

2 Add the coconut milk and broth to the skillet and cook, stirring to combine, for 30 seconds. Add the beet noodles and green beans and season with salt. Reduce the heat to medium-low, add the cashews, and simmer for 5 to 7 minutes or until the noodles are softened.

3 Divide the curry among four bowls and garnish with the dark green parts of the scallions, chile slices, and Thai basil leaves.

Oven-Fried Goat Cheese
with Figs, Bitter Greens, and Beet Noodles

Vegetarian
Gluten-Free

TIME TO PREP 10 minutes
TIME TO COOK 15 minutes
SERVES 4

NUTRITIONAL INFORMATION
Calories: 446
Fat: 31 g
Sodium: 381 mg
Carbohydrate: 18 g
Fiber: 8 g
Sugar: 9 g
Protein: 16 g

ALSO WORKS WELL WITH
Butternut Squash, Sweet Potato

The only thing better than cheese is warm cheese. Baked Brie and *queso* are a thing for a reason! This Inspiralized cheese plate offers the best of everything— savory oven-fried cheese, nutritious greens, elegant fruit, and crunchy vegetables. Take it up a notch with some sliced Genoa salami. This dish will add style to any party—try it with a light wine and good company.

½ cup slivered almonds, roughly chopped

1 (8-ounce) log goat cheese, chilled and sliced into 8 rounds

2 *medium red beets, peeled, spiralized with* **BLADE D**, *noodles trimmed*

Salt and pepper

For the dressing

3 tablespoons extra-virgin olive oil

2 tablespoons apple cider vinegar

1 teaspoon country Dijon mustard

1 teaspoon minced shallot

1 teaspoon fresh lemon juice

1 teaspoon honey

Salt and pepper

4 cups chicory

1½ cups chopped endives

4 Mission figs, quartered lengthwise

To chop the almonds, place them in a food processor and pulse until no large pieces remain. Just be sure to stop before they're ground into a powder.

1 Preheat the oven to 350 degrees. Line two baking sheets with parchment paper.

2 Spread the almonds over a small plate. Dip each goat cheese round in the almonds and turn to coat all over, pressing the nuts to adhere. Place the coated goat cheese rounds on one of the prepared baking sheets.

3 On the other baking sheet, lay out the beet noodles, spacing them apart, and season with salt and pepper.

4 Bake the goat cheese and beets together for 10 minutes or until the cheese is warmed through and the beet noodles are al dente. Remove the beet noodles and set aside to cool for 2 minutes. Turn the oven to broil and bake the goat cheese for 2 minutes more or until the almond crust is golden brown, watching carefully to ensure the nuts don't burn.

5 Meanwhile, whisk together all the ingredients for the dressing in a large bowl.

6 Add the beet noodles, chicory, and endives to the bowl with the dressing and toss to combine.

7 Divide the beet and greens mixture among four plates and top with with two baked goat cheese rounds and figs.

Bell Pepper

If you've been cooking out of *Inspiralized*, this section may be new to you. Since that book was published, I discovered that you *can* spiralize bell peppers. Actually, I was putting together a spoof video showing that certain vegetables and fruits can't be spiralized, like ripe avocado and some others. When I went to spiralize the bell pepper, it worked! I never posted the video, because I quickly got sidetracked by this game-changing discovery and realized that this veggie has its own amazing flavor, texture, and purpose. So let me formally introduce you to . . . bell pepper noodles!

Spiralizing bell peppers can simply help you make fajitas faster or quicken the prep for stir-fries, but these colorful noodles also have the power to build the base for complete, creative meals. In red, orange, yellow, and green, they brighten up pretty much any dish.

NUTRITIONAL BENEFITS: While all bell peppers are packed with antioxidants and dietary fiber, red have the most vitamin C and contain beta-carotene, which provides anti-inflammatory benefits. All bell peppers are very low in calories, making them ideal if you're on a diet.

PREPARATION AND STORAGE: Using a small paring knife, carefully slice just around the stem and remove it entirely, pulling out the seeded middle that's attached. Then flip over the pepper and gently tap it against a garbage can or bowl to release any remaining seeds. (If you just snap the stem off but don't remove the seeded interior, you'll have a mess when you spiralize, but it will still work.) Attach the handle to the widest part of the bell pepper (the top, where the stem was sliced off). Store the noodles in an airtight container in the refrigerator for up to 5 days.

BEST BLADE TO USE
- Blade A

BEST COOKING METHODS
- Raw
- Blanch
- Sauté over medium-high heat for 5 to 7 minutes
- Roast at 450 degrees for 20 minutes

Spiralized Shakshuka

Whenever I see shakshuka on a menu, I think of the first official get-together I had with my bridesmaids, at a brunch spot in the SoHo neighborhood of New York City. We toasted with mimosas, discussed bachelorette party ideas, and laughed over jokes about my long road to finding the perfect husband, all while I dug into the shakshuka. This bright, spicy meal can be served as breakfast, or just as easily as dinner. This spiralized version creates more texture and interest with its noodles and gets bonus points for being super easy to prepare.

Vegetarian
Gluten-Free
Paleo
Dairy-Free
Low-Cal
One Pot

TIME TO PREP 10 minutes
TIME TO COOK 25 minutes
SERVES 6

NUTRITIONAL INFORMATION
Calories: 157
Fat: 8 g
Sodium: 129 mg
Carbohydrate: 14 g
Fiber: 5 g
Sugar: 8 g
Protein: 10 g

ALSO WORKS WELL WITH
Sweet Potato

1 tablespoon olive oil

1 *small white onion, peeled, spiralized with* **BLADE A**, *noodles trimmed*

1 large garlic clove, minced

1 *green bell pepper, spiralized with* **BLADE A**, *noodles trimmed*

1 *red bell pepper, spiralized with* **BLADE A**, *noodles trimmed*

Salt and pepper

2 tablespoons tomato paste

1 teaspoon chili powder

1 teaspoon ground cumin

1 teaspoon paprika

1/8 teaspoon cayenne pepper

1 (28-ounce) can no-salt-added diced tomatoes

6 whole large eggs

1½ teaspoons chopped fresh parsley, for garnish

1 Heat the olive oil in a 10-inch skillet with a lid over medium-high heat. When the oil is shimmering, add the onion and garlic and cook until the onion is slightly softened, about 5 minutes. Add all the bell pepper noodles, season with salt and pepper, and cook for 5 minutes or until softened.

2 Add the tomato paste and stir to combine. Add the chili powder, cumin, paprika, and cayenne and cook for 2 minutes to allow the flavors to develop. Add the diced tomatoes and their juices and cook until the liquid begins to reduce and thicken, 5 to 7 minutes. Taste and adjust the seasoning to your preferences.

3 Create six cavities in the tomato mixture with a spoon. Crack one egg into each cavity, cover the pan, and simmer until the eggs are just set, 5 to 7 minutes.

4 Garnish with the parsley and serve.

For a kick of salty flavor, sprinkle feta over the shakshuka as soon as you pull it out of the oven.

Turkey Picadillo
with Green Bell Pepper Noodles

Gluten-Free
Paleo
Dairy-Free
Saves Well

TIME TO PREP 15 minutes
TIME TO COOK 20 minutes
SERVES 4

NUTRITIONAL INFORMATION
Calories: 384
Fat: 20 g
Sodium: 629 mg
Carbohydrate: 23 g
Fiber: 7 g
Sugar: 17 g
Protein: 36 g

ALSO WORKS WELL WITH
Zucchini, Sweet Potato,
Jícama, Rutabaga

Remember the Bikini Bolognese from *Inspiralized*? Well, imagine it traveled from Italy to Cuba and got a makeover. Here we have picadillo sauce over bell pepper noodles. The soft, fragrant sauce has raisins for sweetness and olives for saltiness, which meld together in this enticing dish. The green bell pepper noodles are crisp and refreshing, and enhance the richness of the stew's seasonings. The whole thing can be made ahead, making it ideal for weekly meal planning.

1 tablespoon extra-virgin olive oil

3 *green bell peppers, spiralized with* BLADE A

Salt and pepper

¾ cup chopped white onion

2 garlic cloves, minced

1½ pounds 93% lean ground turkey

1 bay leaf

1 cup canned tomato sauce

½ teaspoon ground cinnamon

1 teaspoon ground cumin

1 teaspoon chili powder

½ teaspoon cayenne pepper

1 teaspoon dried oregano

¼ cup golden raisins

⅓ cup chopped stuffed pimiento olives, plus 1½ tablespoons olive juice from the jar

1 Heat the olive oil in a large skillet over medium-high heat. When the oil is shimmering, add the bell peppers and season with salt and pepper. Cook for 5 minutes or until al dente. Transfer to a medium bowl and set aside.

2 Immediately add the onion and garlic to the skillet and cook for 5 minutes or until the onion is softened. Add the turkey and cook for 10 minutes or until browned, breaking it up with a wooden spoon as it cooks. Add the bay leaf, tomato sauce, cinnamon, cumin, chili powder, cayenne, and oregano. Season with salt and pepper and stir to combine. Reduce the heat to medium-low, cover, and simmer for about 10 minutes.

3 Uncover the pan and stir in the raisins, olives, and olive juice. Cover again and simmer for 5 minutes more. Remove and discard the bay leaf.

4 Divide the bell pepper noodles among four bowls and top with the picadillo sauce.

Replace half the turkey with crumbled Spanish (dry-cured) chorizo for some extra (and authentic) spice!

Quick Steak and Bell Pepper Stir-Fry

≋≋ | Dairy-Free
≋≋ | Low-Cal
    | Saves Well

TIME TO PREP 20 minutes
TIME TO COOK 20 minutes
SERVES 4

NUTRITIONAL INFORMATION
Calories: 260
Fat: 16 g
Sodium: 516 mg
Carbohydrate: 12 g
Fiber: 1 g
Sugar: 7 g
Protein: 18 g

ALSO WORKS WELL WITH
Zucchini

When I was growing up, whenever we ordered Chinese takeout, my father's go-to was pepper steak with broccoli. I would always steal some bites, enjoying the salty sauce coating the thin, juicy pieces of steak. By using bell pepper noodles here, you cut down on prep time and create a more substantial meal. And just like classic takeout, this dish saves well in the refrigerator and might even be better as leftovers the next day.

Salt and pepper

2 cups small broccoli florets

1 tablespoon oyster sauce

2 tablespoons low-sodium soy sauce

1 teaspoon rice vinegar

¼ cup low-sodium chicken broth

2 tablespoons coconut oil

8 ounces flank or skirt steak, thinly sliced against the grain

1 tablespoon sesame oil

¼ teaspoon red pepper flakes

4 scallions, diced, white and dark green parts kept separate

3 garlic cloves, thinly sliced

¼ teaspoon grated fresh ginger

2 tablespoons chopped fresh ginger

1 red bell pepper, spiralized with BLADE A, noodles trimmed

1 orange bell pepper, spiralized with BLADE A, noodles trimmed

1 jalapeño, thinly sliced

1 Bring a medium pot of lightly salted water to a boil over high heat. Add the broccoli and cook for 3 minutes, then drain and set aside.

2 Meanwhile, whisk together the oyster sauce, soy sauce, vinegar, and broth in a small bowl.

3 Heat the coconut oil in a large skillet over medium-high heat. Season the steak with salt and pepper. When the oil has melted, add the steak to the pan in a single layer and cook until browned on both sides and nearly cooked through, 6 to 7 minutes. Set aside on a plate to rest for 5 minutes.

4 Add the sesame oil to the same skillet. When the oil is shimmering, add the red pepper flakes, broccoli, scallion whites, garlic, and ginger and cook, stirring, until fragrant, about 1 minute. Add the bell pepper noodles and jalapeño and cook for about 5 minutes or until the noodles soften.

5 Return the steak to the skillet and pour over the sauce. Cook, tossing occasionally, until the sauce has thickened, 3 to 5 minutes. Garnish with the dark green parts of the scallions and serve.

Bell Pepper Taco Skillet

Gluten-Free
Dairy-Free (opt.)
Saves Well

TIME TO PREP 25 minutes
TIME TO COOK 35 minutes
SERVES 4

NUTRITIONAL INFORMATION
Calories: 346
Fat: 21 g
Sodium: 143 mg
Carbohydrate: 21 g
Fiber: 7 g
Sugar: 7 g
Protein: 10 g

ALSO WORKS WELL WITH
Sweet Potato, Jícama

This Mexican-themed meal is sure to become one of your most craved dishes—the melted cheese, savory beef, and seasoned bell pepper noodles are irresistible. With an easy cleanup too, what's not to love? Whether you're having a margarita party or looking for a fun, fresh dinner idea, this dish comes together quickly and shows off those classic flavors that make Mexican food so desirable. While any kind of bell pepper will work here, go for varied colors and embrace that fiesta spirit. And you have my permission to eat this straight out of the skillet!

For the fajita seasoning

¼ teaspoon cayenne pepper

1 teaspoon chili powder

¼ teaspoon garlic powder

½ teaspoon paprika

½ teaspoon smoked paprika

½ teaspoon onion powder

¼ teaspoon ground cumin

¼ teaspoon salt

¼ teaspoon dried oregano

1 large ear of corn, husked

Salt and pepper

½ pound lean ground beef

3 large garlic cloves, minced

½ teaspoon dried oregano

1 tablespoon extra-virgin olive oil

1 small yellow onion, sliced

2 large bell peppers (I used yellow and red), cored, spiralized with BLADE A

2 Roma (plum) tomatoes, seeded and chopped

¾ cup Mexican blend cheese

1 avocado, thinly sliced

1 tablespoon chopped fresh cilantro

1 Mix together all the fajita seasoning ingredients in a small bowl.

2 Place the corn in a medium pot and add water to cover and a pinch of salt. Bring to a boil, cook for 2 to 3 minutes until fork-tender, and drain.

3 While the corn cooks, place a 12-inch skillet (cast iron, if you have it) with a lid over medium heat. When water flicked onto the skillet sizzles, add the beef. Season with salt and black pepper. Add the garlic and oregano and cook for 10 minutes or until the meat is browned, breaking it up with the back of a spoon as it cooks. Remove it from the skillet and set aside.

4 Add the olive oil to the skillet and heat over medium-high heat. When the oil is shimmering, add the onion and bell peppers and cook for 5 minutes or until the vegetables begin to soften.

5 Return the beef to the pan and add the tomatoes and 1 tablespoon of the fajita seasoning. Toss together and cook for 2 to 3 minutes. Using a knife, slice the corn kernels straight off the cob into the skillet. Sprinkle the cheese over the top and cover. Cook for 5 to 7 minutes or until the cheese melts.

6 Uncover the skillet and garnish with the avocado slices and cilantro. Serve immediately.

To make this dish vegetarian, replace the meat with about ½ cup each of black beans and kidney beans.

Roasted Bell Pepper Chicory Salad

with Anchovy–White Bean Dressing and Soft-Baked Eggs

Gluten-Free
Dairy-Free

TIME TO PREP 10 minutes
TIME TO COOK 15 minutes
SERVES 4

NUTRITIONAL INFORMATION
Calories: 340
Fat: 16 g
Sodium: 130 mg
Carbohydrate: 40 g
Fiber: 9 g
Sugar: 8 g
Protein: 17 g

True to my Italian roots, I love roasted peppers—as snacks, in sandwiches, over pastas, as antipastos, and, of course, in salads. This seemingly fancy salad comes together easily and really fills you up. The soft-baked eggs melt into the bitter chicory greens for a bright, creamy bite with full-flavored, garlicky anchovy dressing. If you're not gluten-free, pair it with toasted sourdough bread.

For the salad

2 red bell peppers, spiralized with **BLADE A**, noodles trimmed

2 orange bell peppers, spiralized with **BLADE A**, noodles trimmed

½ teaspoon garlic powder

Salt and pepper

4 whole large eggs

4 cups chicory

For the dressing

2 olive oil–packed anchovy fillets, minced

1 garlic clove, minced

2 teaspoons sherry vinegar

3 tablespoons extra-virgin olive oil

¼ cup chopped fresh flat-leaf parsley

Juice of ½ lemon

1 (15-ounce) can cannellini beans, rinsed and drained

Salt and pepper

1 Preheat the oven to 450 degrees. Line a large baking sheet with parchment paper. Lay out the red and orange bell pepper noodles on the baking sheet, spacing them apart, and season with the garlic powder, salt, and pepper. Roast for 20 minutes or until wilted, tossing once halfway through.

2 Meanwhile, place the eggs in a small pot and add water to cover by ¼ inch. Cover the pot and bring the water to a boil over high heat. As soon as it's boiling, turn off the heat and let the eggs sit, covered, for 7 minutes. Drain and rinse with cold water until cool enough to handle, then peel, halve lengthwise, and set aside.

3 Meanwhile, make the dressing. Whisk together the anchovies, garlic, vinegar, olive oil, parsley, and lemon juice in a medium bowl. Add the beans and toss to coat. Season with salt and black pepper.

4 Transfer the bell pepper noodles to a large bowl, add the chicory, and toss. Pour over the dressing and toss to coat.

5 Divide the bell pepper–chicory mixture among four plates and top each with two egg halves.

Anchovies—you either love 'em or you hate 'em. If you're part of the latter contingency, simply omit them and add ¼ cup pitted and sliced kalamata olives for a similarly salty and rich taste.

Summer Ratatouille

Ratatouille isn't just an animated Disney movie about a rat that can cook—it's also a traditional Provençal dish. Summertime vegetables are stewed to enhance their flavors before they're baked to tasty perfection. Spiralizing the vegetables reduces the prep time and adds a new texture. While traditional ratatouilles call for each vegetable to cook separately, this quick version simplifies those steps for an easy, breezy summer meal.

Vegan
Vegetarian
Gluten-Free
Paleo
Dairy-Free
Low-Cal
One Pot
Saves Well

TIME TO PREP 25 minutes
TIME TO COOK 35 minutes
SERVES 4

NUTRITIONAL INFORMATION
Calories: 172
Fat: 9 g
Sodium: 957 mg
Carbohydrate: 24 g
Fiber: 6 g
Sugar: 16 g
Protein: 5 g

- 2 tablespoons extra-virgin olive oil
- 2 large garlic cloves, pressed
- ¼ teaspoon red pepper flakes
- 1 *Vidalia onion, peeled, spiralized with BLADE A, noodles trimmed*
- 2 *red bell peppers, spiralized with BLADE A, noodles trimmed*
- 1 *medium zucchini, spiralized with BLADE D, noodles trimmed*
- 1 *medium yellow squash, spiralized with BLADE D, noodles trimmed*
- 1 cup packed julienned Italian eggplant
- Salt and pepper
- 1 (28-ounce) can whole peeled tomatoes, with juices
- 1 bay leaf
- 1 tablespoon fresh oregano leaves
- ¼ cup packed fresh basil, finely chopped

1 Heat the olive oil in a large pot over medium heat. When the oil is shimmering, add the garlic, red pepper flakes, and onion and cook until the onion is softened, about 5 minutes.

2 Add the bell pepper, zucchini, and squash noodles and the eggplant. Season with salt and pepper and cook until the vegetables are softened, about 10 minutes.

3 Add the tomatoes and their juices to the pot, crushing them with your hands. Stir in the bay leaf and oregano and further break apart the tomatoes using a wooden spoon. Increase the heat to high and bring to a boil, then reduce the heat to low and simmer until the vegetables are tender, 10 to 15 minutes. Take care not to overcook them, or they'll be mushy.

4 Stir in the basil and heat for 1 minute. Remove the bay leaf before serving.

Foil Pouch Sea Bass

Sea bass has such a delicate flavor that it doesn't need to be cooked with much more than fresh herbs and olive oil. The spiralized bell peppers soften as their flavors develop with the caper, lemon, and parsley–infused juices from the fish. With everything layered together in a foil pouch, cleanup couldn't be easier, making this meal a great weeknight dinner.

Gluten-Free
Paleo
Dairy-Free
Low-Cal

TIME TO PREP 20 minutes
TIME TO COOK 15 minutes
SERVES 4

NUTRITIONAL INFORMATION
Calories: 300
Fat: 21 g
Sodium: 263 mg
Carbohydrate: 13 g
Fiber: 4 g
Sugar: 6 g
Protein: 18 g

ALSO WORKS WELL WITH
Zucchini, Kohlrabi, Jícama

3 tablespoons extra-virgin olive oil

2 yellow bell peppers, spiralized with BLADE A, noodles trimmed

2 orange bell peppers, spiralized with BLADE A, noodles trimmed

Salt and pepper

4 (3-ounce) sea bass fillets

2 shallots, minced

4 teaspoons minced garlic

Juice of 1 lemon

¼ cup halved cherry tomatoes

1 tablespoon drained capers

2 tablespoons chopped fresh parsley, for garnish

If you don't use foil in your household, parchment paper works well, too. Try brushing egg wash over the edges to seal the packets closed.

1 Preheat the oven to 425 degrees. Tear off four 18-inch lengths of foil. Generously brush ½ tablespoon of the olive oil in the center of each sheet.

2 In a large bowl, toss together the yellow and orange bell pepper noodles. Mound them in the center of each foil sheet and season with salt and pepper. Season the sea bass fillets with salt and pepper and place one on top of the bell pepper noodles on each foil sheet. Sprinkle the shallots and garlic over the fish, dividing them evenly.

3 In a small bowl, combine the lemon juice, cherry tomatoes, capers, and remaining 1 tablespoon olive oil to make the sauce. Pull the sides of the foil up around the fish and drizzle over the sauce. Fold in the edges of the foil to make sealed packets.

4 Arrange the packets on a baking sheet and bake for 12 to 15 minutes or until the sea bass is cooked through and opaque. Open the packets carefully (the steam is very hot), garnish the fish with the parsley, and serve directly from the packets.

Broccoli

Yes—broccoli! Most people are surprised when they hear that broccoli can be spiralized. Doing so is a great way to use the stem in addition to the florets to minimize waste and maximize your vegetable intake. You've probably seen broccoli slaw around, which uses julienned broccoli stems. Broccoli slaw is *okay*, but imagine using noodles that elevate the texture and turn that dish into a full-fledged pasta alternative. Now imagine what else you can make!

Broccoli noodles are sturdy and therefore resilient, so they can be cooked pretty much any way. I most enjoy them boiled, as they fill up with water and take on the consistency of whole wheat pasta, similar to what happens with spiralized carrots. Just be sure to pick out broccoli stems that are large enough. At the very least, stems should be 1½ to 2 inches in width and 3 to 4 inches in length for best results. Trick of the trade: Ask your local farmers to save more of the stem the next time they harvest the broccoli. They'll be flattered you asked!

NUTRITIONAL BENEFITS: Broccoli is a good source of lutein, a powerful antioxidant that also supports eye health. It's also packed with phytochemicals, which help the body detoxify, and fiber, which aids digestion.

PREPARATION AND STORAGE: Slice the stem off the broccoli head, preserving as much of it as possible. Trim the sides of the broccoli stem as much as you can without compromising its width, removing any thick pieces that stick out. Slice the ends off to leave flat, even surfaces. Store in an airtight container in the refrigerator for up to 5 days. Broccoli noodles can also be frozen for up to 8 months for future use.

BEST BLADES TO USE
- Blade D (if you're using a 3-blade spiralizer, use blade C)

BEST COOKING METHODS
- Boil for 2 to 3 minutes
- Sauté over medium-high heat for 5 to 7 minutes
- Bake at 425 degrees for 10 minutes

Grams's Tuna and Macaroni Salad

Gluten-Free
Dairy-Free
Low-Cal

TIME TO PREP 10 minutes

TIME TO COOK 10 minutes plus
1 hour to chill

SERVES 2 to 4

NUTRITIONAL INFORMATION
Calories: 154
Fat: 1 g
Sodium: 289 mg
Carbohydrate: 12 g
Fiber: 3 g
Sugar: 5 g
Protein: 26 g

ALSO WORKS WELL WITH
Zucchini, Kohlrabi, Jícama

Any time my parents have the family over for a summer barbecue, my Grams brings her tuna and macaroni salad, and it's always a welcome treat. It might be the ratio of tuna to noodle or the exact amount of salt she uses—all I know is that it's addictive. Family recipes like this one are tough to re-create without the magic touch of a loving grandmother, but I've tried my hardest. I swapped in avocado fayonnaise for the mayonnaise in the tuna, and instead of macaroni pasta, I used boiled broccoli noodles for a lower-calorie and -carb option. While I still love the original, this spiralized one is second best. Maybe my grandkids will try to re-create it one day!

For the salad
Salt
2 broccoli stems, spiralized with **BLADE D,** noodles trimmed
2 (3-ounce) cans tuna in water, drained
½ cup diced celery

For the fayonnaise
½ large ripe avocado, mashed (½ cup)
1 teaspoon Dijon mustard
Salt and white pepper
1 teaspoon fresh lemon juice
¼ teaspoon garlic powder

1 Bring a medium pot filled halfway with salted water to a boil over high heat. When the water is boiling, add the broccoli noodles and cook for 3 minutes or until al dente. Drain and pat dry thoroughly.

2 Meanwhile, whisk together all the ingredients for the fayonnaise in a large bowl until combined.

3 Add the cooked broccoli noodles, tuna, and celery to the bowl with the fayonnaise. Season generously with salt and toss to combine thoroughly. For the best flavor, refrigerate for at least 1 hour before serving.

Grams doesn't do this, but you may want to add in a teaspoon of chopped dill into the fayonnaise for extra flavor.

Sun-Dried Tomato, Chicken, and Broccoli Pasta

At my first job out of college, I spent most of my lunch breaks at the local grocery store salad bar, packing as much as I could fit into their provided containers. This particular salad bar prepared a chilled sun-dried tomato and broccoli bow-tie pasta that was smothered in a garlicky Parmesan sauce. I still remember looking forward to my lunches just for that pasta! Now I've made an Inspiralized version, using broccoli noodles in place of those bow ties. While I haven't looked back since starting Inspiralized, I do sometimes think about those salad bar lunches . . .

Gluten-Free
Dairy-Free (opt.)
Low-Cal
Saves Well

TIME TO PREP 10 minutes
TIME TO COOK 15 minutes
SERVES 4

NUTRITIONAL INFORMATION
Calories: 240
Fat: 8 g
Sodium: 172 mg
Carbohydrate: 11 g
Fiber: 3 g
Sugar: 4 g
Protein: 32 g

ALSO WORKS WELL WITH
Zucchini, Butternut Squash, Sweet Potato, Turnip, Bell Pepper

Salt and pepper

2 cups broccoli florets

2 broccoli stems, spiralized with **BLADE D**, noodles trimmed

1 tablespoon extra-virgin olive oil

1 pound skinless, boneless chicken breast, cut into 1-inch pieces

1 teaspoon garlic powder

2 garlic cloves, minced

1 tablespoon minced shallot

½ cup chopped sun-dried tomatoes (dried, not packed in oil)

¼ teaspoon red pepper flakes

¼ cup grated Parmesan cheese

To make this dish vegetarian, replace the chicken with a 14-ounce can of chickpeas, rinsed and drained.

1 Bring a medium pot filled halfway with salted water to a boil over high heat. When the water is boiling, add the broccoli florets and broccoli noodles and cook for 3 minutes or until al dente. Drain and pat dry thoroughly.

2 Meanwhile, heat the olive oil in a large skillet over medium heat. Season the chicken with the garlic powder, salt, and black pepper. When the oil is shimmering, add the chicken and cook for 3 to 5 minutes per side or until browned on the outside and no longer pink inside. Transfer to a plate.

3 To the same pan, add the garlic, shallot, sun-dried tomatoes, and red pepper flakes. Cook for 1 minute or until the shallot is translucent. Stir in the broccoli florets, broccoli noodles, and chicken and cook for 1 minute, tossing continuously to coat the florets in the oil.

4 Remove the skillet from heat, add the Parmesan, and toss to combine. Divide among four bowls and serve.

Shrimp Tom Kha
with Broccoli Noodles

Gluten-Free
Dairy-Free
One Pot

TIME TO PREP 15 minutes
TIME TO COOK 20 minutes
SERVES 4

NUTRITIONAL INFORMATION
Calories: 317
Fat: 17 g
Sodium: 951 mg
Carbohydrate: 13 g
Fiber: 2 g
Sugar: 6 g
Protein: 28 g

ALSO WORKS WELL WITH
Zucchini, Kohlrabi, Turnip,
Daikon Radish, Chayote

Tom kha is a spicy and sour hot soup made with coconut milk that's most popular in Thailand and Laos. Luckily, you don't need to be in Southeast Asia to enjoy its enticing flavors. The broccoli noodles in their spiralized form are durable enough to stand up to the thick coconut milk, becoming infused with the flavors of the lemongrass and chile. Each chopstick-full is more delightful than the last!

- 4 cups low-sodium chicken broth
- 1 (1-inch) piece fresh ginger or galangal, peeled and sliced
- Zest of ½ lime
- 1 (15-ounce) can full-fat coconut milk
- 2 cups broccoli florets
- 2 *broccoli stems, spiralized with BLADE C, noodles trimmed*
- 1 fresh lemongrass stalk, roughly cut into 2-inch pieces
- 12 ounces mushrooms (cremini or button), stemmed and sliced
- 10 ounces shrimp, peeled and deveined
- 1½ tablespoons fish sauce (I like Red Boat)
- 1½ tablespoons fresh lime juice
- 4 hot red chiles, thinly sliced
- ¼ cup fresh cilantro leaves, for garnish

1 Combine the broth, ginger, and lime zest in a medium saucepan and bring to a simmer over medium heat. Reduce the heat to low and simmer for 10 minutes.

2 Add the coconut milk, broccoli florets, broccoli noodles, lemongrass, and mushrooms and return the heat to medium. Cook for 5 minutes or until the mushrooms are softened. Add the shrimp and cook until pink, opaque, and completely cooked through, 3 to 5 minutes.

3 Stir in the fish sauce and lime juice. Remove the pan from the heat, discard the lemongrass, and divide the soup among four bowls. Garnish with the red chile slices and cilantro.

Galangal is a common ingredient in Thai food that's similar in look to ginger but extra fiery in taste. If you can't find it or prefer your Tom Kha with less heat, ginger will work just fine.

Butternut Squash

Taking one look at butternut squash, you'd think it would be a nightmare to spiralize—it's large, heavy, and tough, and has an awkward, bulbous bottom. And it's a pain to cut up with a knife! But butternut squash is one of the easiest vegetables to spiralize and yields a plentiful amount of noodles. Just one of these medium veggies can feed up to four people, depending on the dish! Its delicate sweetness makes it one of my favorites to eat in the winter.

When you're picking yours out, ripeness matters—a squash that isn't ripe enough will be too tough to slice, even with the spiralizer, and it won't taste as great, either. A ripe squash should be a dull orange color with no shiny skin or major blemishes. Choose one that has a longer neck, since that's the part that yields noodles. As for the round bottom, I like to slice it into chunks, roast them, and save them in the refrigerator to toss into salads and pasta dishes, or even to snack on!

NUTRITIONAL BENEFITS: This squash contains a high amount of dietary fiber, making it heart-healthy. It's packed with potassium, which contributes to bone health, and vitamin B_6, which boosts your immune system and metabolism.

PREPARATION AND STORAGE: Peel the squash using a vegetable peeler. Slice off the bulbous end, maintaining as much of the long neck as possible. Slice the other end off to leave a flat, even surface. If the squash is longer than 6 inches, halve it crosswise for better leverage. Store in an airtight container in the refrigerator for up to 5 days. Butternut squash noodles can also be frozen for up to 8 months for future use.

BEST BLADES TO USE
- Blade A
- Blade B
- Blade C
- Blade D

BEST COOKING METHODS
- Roast at 400 degrees for 8 to 10 minutes

Butternut Squash Rice and Beans

Vegan
Vegetarian
Gluten-Free
Dairy-Free
Low-Cal
Saves Well

TIME TO PREP 15 minutes
TIME TO COOK 40 minutes
SERVES 6

NUTRITIONAL INFORMATION
Calories: 259
Fat: 5 g
Sodium: 1012 mg
Carbohydrate: 52 g
Fiber: 18 g
Sugar: 8 g
Protein: 15 g

ALSO WORKS WELL WITH
Sweet Potato, Jícama

I'll never forget the first time I went to Puerto Rico with Lu to visit his family. It was Thanksgiving, and I had no idea what to expect. I already knew his relatives were loving, warm, and kind people. But I didn't know what Thanksgiving dinner would be like, which was the important matter at hand. Would there be cranberry sauce? Sweet potatoes? Stuffing? Nope! We had a true Puerto Rican holiday—and it was delicious. Most memorably, there was a huge vat of rice and beans, which I devoured (along with about four slices of flan). Every Latin culture prepares its rice and beans differently, but this spiralized version is how Lu and I do it in our house.

1 tablespoon extra-virgin olive oil

1 medium yellow onion, finely diced

½ green bell pepper, finely diced

2 celery stalks, finely diced

2 large garlic cloves, minced

Salt and pepper

3 (15-ounce) cans red kidney beans, rinsed and drained

1 (15-ounce) can diced tomatoes

1 tablespoon tomato paste

1 teaspoon dried thyme

1 teaspoon dried oregano

1 teaspoon smoked paprika

½ teaspoon chili powder

¼ cup low-sodium vegetable broth, plus more as needed

1 *large butternut squash, peeled, spiralized with* BLADE D, *then riced (see page 16)*

2 tablespoons chopped fresh cilantro

6 lime wedges, for serving

1 Heat the olive oil in a large skillet with a lid over medium heat. When the oil is shimmering, add the onion, bell pepper, celery, and garlic. Season with salt and pepper and cook until softened, about 7 minutes.

2 Meanwhile, combine half the beans and half the tomatoes in a food processor and pulse until just about pureed.

3 Add the tomato paste to the vegetables in the skillet and stir to coat. Add the blended bean mixture, the remaining beans and canned tomatoes with their juices, the thyme, oregano, paprika, and chili powder. Reduce the heat to low, cover, and cook for 30 minutes, stirring every 5 minutes. If the liquid reduces too much and the mixture dries out, add broth, 1 tablespoon at a time, to keep the beans moist.

4 Add the butternut squash rice and the broth, cover, and cook for 5 to 7 minutes more or until the rice softens.

5 Stir in the cilantro and serve with lime wedges.

Pumpkin-Rosemary Alfredo
with Crispy Prosciutto

Gluten-Free
Paleo
Dairy-Free
Saves Well

TIME TO PREP 25 minutes
TIME TO COOK 20 minutes
SERVES 4

NUTRITIONAL INFORMATION
Calories: 451
Fat: 29 g
Sodium: 1185 mg
Carbohydrate: 32 g
Fiber: 6 g
Sugar: 9 g
Protein: 22 g

ALSO WORKS WELL WITH
Sweet Potato, Beet,
Rutabaga, Carrot

The beginning of fall is like the end of Cinderella's ball—everything turns into pumpkins: pumpkin raviolis, pumpkin lattes, carved pumpkins in window displays and on stoops, and towers of canned pumpkin at the grocery store. While you could certainly roast your own pumpkin and make this sauce from scratch, there's no need—canned puree is perfect and certainly not hard to find! Just make sure you don't buy pumpkin *pie filling*. The flavor of the prosciutto in combination with the rosemary and nutmeg in this dish are perfectly autumnal over the butternut squash noodles. The coconut milk ensures a bold sauce that's much lighter on the calories and fat than your typical Alfredo.

1 large or 2 medium butternut squashes, peeled, spiralized with BLADE D, noodles trimmed

Salt and pepper

8 thin slices of prosciutto

1 tablespoon minced shallot

2 small garlic cloves, minced

Pinch of red pepper flakes

1 (15-ounce) can pumpkin puree

1½ teaspoons fresh rosemary, chopped

1 heaping cup coconut cream (see page 19)

½ teaspoon ground nutmeg

1 tablespoon chopped fresh parsley, for garnish

1 Preheat the oven to 400 degrees. Line a baking sheet with parchment paper and lay out the butternut squash noodles, spacing them apart. Season with salt and black pepper and bake for 8 to 10 minutes or until al dente.

2 Place the prosciutto in a large skillet in a single layer, then cook over medium heat for 5 to 7 minutes or until crispy, flipping once. Transfer to a paper towel–lined plate to drain.

3 Let the skillet cool for about 2 minutes, then add the shallot, garlic, and red pepper flakes and cook, stirring frequently, for 30 seconds or until fragrant, taking care not to burn. Add the pumpkin puree and rosemary and season with salt and black pepper. Cook for 2 to 3 minutes or until warmed through. Add the coconut cream and nutmeg. Stir to combine and cook the sauce for 5 minutes more to allow the flavors to meld.

4 Divide the butternut squash pasta among four bowls and top with the sauce and two slices of prosciutto each. Garnish with the parsley.

Butternut Squash Ravioli
with Sage and Toasted Pine Nuts

Vegetarian
Gluten-Free
Low-Cal

TIME TO PREP 10 minutes
TIME TO COOK 25 minutes
SERVES 4 (3 ravioli per serving)

NUTRITIONAL INFORMATION
Calories: 83
Fat: 7 g
Sodium: 28 mg
Carbohydrate: 4 g
Fiber: 1 g
Sugar: 1 g
Protein: 3 g

ALSO WORKS WELL WITH
Sweet Potato, Zucchini

While no one can mess with my grandfather's raviolis with tomato sauce, this savory and slightly sweet spiralized version is stunning. A simple ricotta-Parmesan filling seasoned with nutmeg lets the butternut squash do the talking. The light sage sauce flows over the ravioli, and the toasted pine nuts add a nutty, classic crunch. This dish will impress any guest—it certainly makes for a creative dinner!

For the filling
½ teaspoon fresh lemon juice
¼ teaspoon ground nutmeg
¾ cup ricotta cheese
2 tablespoons grated Parmesan cheese
Salt and pepper

For the ravioli
1 medium butternut squash, peeled and prepped
2 tablespoons extra-virgin olive oil
8 fresh sage leaves
¼ cup pine nuts

Want to change it up? Replace the ricotta and Parmesan with goat cheese for a different, slightly richer flavor.

1 Make the filling. In a medium bowl, combine all the filling ingredients and mix well. Set aside.

2 Make the ravioli. Slice the squash lengthwise to create a slit, taking care not to pierce any farther than its center. Spiralize using **BLADE A**. Select 24 slices of squash, saving any additional for another use.

3 Heat 1 tablespoon of the olive oil in a large skillet over medium heat. When the oil is shimmering, add the sage and fry for about 5 minutes, then transfer to a paper towel–lined plate to drain. Add the butternut squash slices in a single layer, working in batches if necessary, and cook for 5 minutes per side or until fork-tender. Transfer to a large piece of foil or parchment and set aside.

4 Carefully wipe the pan clean and add the remaining 1 tablespoon olive oil over medium heat. When the oil is shimmering, crumble in the fried sage, then transfer the sauce to a small bowl. Immediately add the pine nuts to the pan and toast, stirring, until golden brown, 3 to 5 minutes. Add to the bowl with the sauce.

5 To serve, lay out three butternut squash slices on each plate. Using a knife or the back of a spoon, spread 2 tablespoons of the cheese mixture over each slice and then top with another slice. Drizzle the sage–pine nut sauce on top to finish.

Butternut Squash Noodles

with Almond Ricotta and Coconut Bacon

Vegan
Vegetarian
Gluten-Free
Paleo
Dairy-Free

TIME TO PREP 20 minutes plus
16 hours for the almond ricotta
TIME TO COOK 20 minutes
SERVES 6

NUTRITIONAL INFORMATION
Calories: 317
Fat: 25 g
Sodium: 192 mg
Carbohydrate: 21 g
Fiber: 7 g
Sugar: 5 g
Protein: 9 g

ALSO WORKS WELL WITH
Sweet Potato, Beet

I try out all the food trends—every single one of them, from matcha lattes to bone broth. This is partly because I'm a food blogger, but also because curiosity gets the best of me! Some trends are better left as trends (*ahem*, cricket powder), but others make their way into my kitchen as staples. Almond ricotta and coconut bacon are fantastic vegan alternatives that I found this way. The consistency and flavor of both are shockingly comparable to the originals, making for delicious butternut squash pasta without the processed components. I bet you'll end up adopting them, too! Note that making almond ricotta takes some time: you need to soak the almonds overnight, then puree and strain the mixture for 8 hours. Make it ahead of time and store it in an airtight container in the refrigerator for up to 5 days. Of course, you could also treat yourself and use real, whole milk ricotta.

For the almond ricotta

- 2 cups raw blanched almonds, soaked in filtered water overnight, rinsed, and drained
- 1 cup filtered water
- Salt and pepper
- ½ teaspoon herbes de Provence

For the coconut bacon

- ½ tablespoon maple syrup
- 1 tablespoon liquid smoke (I like the hickory flavor, but use whatever you prefer)
- 1 tablespoon tamari or reduced-sodium soy sauce
- 1 cup unsweetened coconut flakes (not shredded)
- Salt

For the butternut squash

- 1 *large butternut squash, peeled, spiralized with* BLADE C
- 1 tablespoon olive oil
- Salt and pepper

1 Make the almond ricotta. In a high-speed blender or food processor, combine the soaked almonds and water. Puree until mostly smooth, with some texture but no large chunks remaining. Place a fine-mesh strainer or colander over a bowl and line with cheesecloth. Add the almond mixture and drain for 8 hours. Discard any liquid that collects in the bowl. Transfer the ricotta to it and season with salt, pepper, and the herbes de Provence.

2 Make the coconut bacon. Preheat the oven to 350 degrees. Line two baking sheets with parchment paper.

3 In a medium bowl, whisk together the maple syrup, liquid smoke, and tamari. Add the coconut flakes and stir to coat. Season with salt, then spread the coconut flakes over a prepared baking sheet, spacing them apart. Bake for about 10 minutes.

recipe continues

4 Meanwhile, make the butternut squash. Lay out the butternut squash noodles on the other prepared baking sheet, spacing them apart. Drizzle over the olive oil and massage it into the noodles with your fingers. Season with salt and pepper.

5 After the coconut has roasted for 10 minutes, remove it and flip the pieces. Return it to the oven, add the butternut squash noodles, and bake together for about 10 minutes more or until the bacon is crispy and the squash is al dente.

6 Divide the noodles among six plates. Top each serving with almond ricotta and sprinkle with the coconut bacon.

While this dish itself is special, it features two foods that are super versatile: vegan bacon and vegan ricotta. Long story short: double those parts of this recipe, then creatively repurpose them! I love a smear of the almond ricotta on toast with the coconut bacon sprinkled on top.

Pear, Pomegranate, and Roast Turkey Salad
with Butternut Squash and Maple-Sesame Vinaigrette

Dairy-Free (opt.)
Saves Well

TIME TO PREP 25 minutes
TIME TO COOK 10 minutes
SERVES 4

NUTRITIONAL INFORMATION
Calories: 477
Fat: 25 g
Sodium: 836 mg
Carbohydrate: 33 g
Fiber: 8 g
Sugar: 13 g
Protein: 34 g

ALSO WORKS WELL WITH
Sweet Potato

In the days after a Thanksgiving feast, there's nothing better than leftovers. But turkey and cranberry sauce sandwiches can get boring pretty fast—and can quickly pack on the holiday pounds. This spiralized butternut squash and pear salad with a sweet vinaigrette is a novel break from the traditional. It's even hearty enough for the Thanksgiving table itself—and works great whenever you're craving the flavors of fall!

For the salad

- 1 *medium butternut squash, peeled, spiralized with **BLADE B**, noodles trimmed*
- **Cooking spray**
- **Salt and pepper**
- 1 **large Asian pear**
- 1 **(5-ounce) container baby spinach**
- ¾ **cup pomegranate seeds**
- ½ **cup roughly chopped pecans**
- ½ **cup crumbled goat cheese**
- 1 **pound roasted turkey, carved**

For the vinaigrette

- 1 **tablespoon maple syrup**
- 1 **tablespoon extra-virgin olive oil**
- 1 **tablespoon sesame oil**
- 2 **tablespoons apple cider vinegar**
- 1 **teaspoon white sesame seeds**
- 1 **tablespoon soy sauce**
- **Pepper to taste**
- 1 **garlic clove, minced**

1 Preheat the oven to 400 degrees. Line a baking sheet with parchment paper. Spread out the butternut squash noodles on the baking sheet, spacing them apart. Coat lightly with cooking spray and season with salt and pepper. Roast for 10 to 12 minutes or until al dente.

2 Meanwhile, make the vinaigrette. Whisk together all the ingredients for the vinaigrette in a small bowl.

3 Spiralize the pear with **BLADE D** and place it in a large bowl. Add the spinach, pomegranate seeds, pecans, and goat cheese. Add the roasted squash noodles, drizzle with the vinaigrette, and toss to coat. Top with the turkey pieces. Divide the salad among four plates and serve immediately.

No leftover Thanksgiving turkey? No problem. Buy a rotisserie chicken and shred the meat using forks or tongs.

Winter Lasagna
with Brussels Sprouts and Chicken Sausage

Gluten-Free
Saves Well

TIME TO PREP 20 minutes
TIME TO COOK 60 minutes
SERVES 4 to 6

NUTRITIONAL INFORMATION
(for 1 of 6 servings)
Calories: 365
Fat: 22 g
Sodium: 505 mg
Carbohydrate: 23 g
Fiber: 5 g
Sugar: 5 g
Protein: 23 g

ALSO WORKS WELL WITH
Sweet Potato, Rutabaga

In middle and high school, I played two sports: lacrosse and soccer. One of my favorite parts of being on both teams was the pasta dinners. The night before a game, we'd all gather at one of the players' parents' home to carb-load and store energy for the next day. Needless to say, I ate my fair share of penne bakes, stuffed shells, and, of course, lasagna. After all, lasagna is the best way to feed a hungry crowd! In this dish, I replaced the pasta's refined carbohydrates for complex ones by using butternut squash. As it roasts in the oven, the vegetable's natural sugars release, resulting in subtly sweet layers and gorgeous orange pops of color. This squash will please everyone—from picky spouses to a team of growing teenagers.

1 medium butternut squash, peeled and prepped

1½ teaspoons extra-virgin olive oil

6 fresh sage leaves

4 chicken sausage links, casings removed

6 cups Brussels sprouts

3 garlic cloves, minced

¼ teaspoon red pepper flakes

1 large shallot, minced

Salt and pepper

1½ cups ricotta cheese

⅓ cup grated Parmesan cheese

1 large egg, beaten

1 cup shredded Gruyère cheese

1 Preheat the oven to 425 degrees.

2 Slice the squash lengthwise to create a slit, taking care not to pierce any farther than its center. Spiralize using **BLADE A**.

3 Heat the olive oil in a large skillet over medium heat. When the oil is shimmering, add the sage leaves and cook until crispy, about 5 minutes. Transfer to a paper towel–lined plate to drain. Immediately add the sausage to the same skillet and cook, breaking up the meat with a wooden spoon as it cooks, until browned, 5 to 7 minutes.

4 Meanwhile, in a food processor, pulse the Brussels sprouts until mostly shredded. When the sausage is browned, add the Brussels sprouts, garlic, red pepper flakes, and shallot and season with salt and black pepper. Cook for 2 to 3 minutes or until the Brussels sprouts are wilted. Remove the pan from the heat.

recipe continues

5 In a medium bowl, whisk together the ricotta, Parmesan, and egg.

6 Arrange a layer of butternut squash slices in the bottom of a 4.2-quart casserole dish, overlapping them as needed to create a complete layer. Add a layer of the Brussels sprout and sausage mixture, then add a layer of the ricotta-Parmesan mixture. Repeat these three layers, then top with the remaining butternut squash slices. Finish with the Gruyère.

7 Cover the lasagna with foil and bake for 40 to 45 minutes or until the squash is easily pierced with a fork and the cheese has melted.

8 Remove the lasagna from the oven, remove the foil, and immediately crumble over the sage. Set aside to rest for 5 minutes, then carefully slice and serve.

This recipe is ideal for meal planning, as it freezes well. To reheat, bake at 425 degrees for 20 minutes or until warmed through, then slice into portions.

Teriyaki Mini Meatballs
over Roasted Scallions and Butternut Squash Noodles

Dairy-Free
Saves Well

TIME TO PREP 30 minutes
TIME TO COOK 25 minutes
SERVES 4

NUTRITIONAL INFORMATION
Calories: 352
Fat: 21 g
Sodium: 429 mg
Carbohydrate: 22 g
Fiber: 3 g
Sugar: 9 g
Protein: 21 g

ALSO WORKS WELL WITH
Zucchini, Kohlrabi, Turnip,
Sweet Potato, Daikon Radish

When I'm stumped on what to make for dinner, I usually defer to some adaptation of spiralized spaghetti and meatballs. I love creating and trying out new flavor combinations, and this teriyaki version has fast become a favorite. The Asian tastes are a nice change from traditional Italian style, and the butternut squash noodles' sweetness complements the salty soy and warm sesame in the sauce. And when they're mini, they're just cuter!

For the teriyaki sauce
- ¼ cup soy sauce
- 1 tablespoon rice vinegar
- 1½ teaspoons grated fresh ginger
- 1 garlic clove, pressed and minced
- 1 tablespoon sesame oil
- 1 tablespoon honey
- 1 teaspoon hot sauce, or a pinch of red pepper flakes

For the meatballs
- 1 pound lean ground turkey
- 1 tablespoon minced shallot
- 1 teaspoon finely minced garlic
- 2 tablespoons soy sauce
- 1 tablespoon sesame oil
- 1 teaspoon white sesame seeds
- 8 scallions
- 1 large butternut squash, peeled, spiralized with BLADE D, noodles trimmed
- Salt and pepper

1 Preheat the oven to 450 degrees. Line two baking sheets with parchment paper.

2 Make the teriyaki sauce: Whisk together all the ingredients for the teriyaki sauce in a small bowl.

3 In a large bowl, combine the turkey, shallot, garlic, and 1 tablespoon of the soy sauce. Form the mixture into twelve 1-inch meatballs and place them on a prepared baking sheet. Brush them with about half of the teriyaki sauce, reserving the remainder.

4 In a shallow dish, mix together the sesame oil, remaining 1 tablespoon soy sauce, and the white sesame seeds. Dunk the scallions into the mixture, turning to coat, and place them on the baking sheet with the meatballs. Bake for 10 minutes. Lay out the squash noodles on the other baking sheet, spacing them apart. Add salt and pepper.

5 Remove the meatballs and scallions from the oven, flip them over, and brush with teriyaki sauce. Return to the oven and add the squash noodles. Roast together for 10 minutes or until the meatballs are cooked through and the noodles are wilted and al dente.

6 Divide the noodles among four plates and top each with three meatballs and two roasted scallions.

Oven-Fried Avocado Tacos
with Chipotle Cream

≋ Vegetarian
≋ Gluten-Free
Paleo
Dairy-Free
Low-Cal

TIME TO PREP 30 minutes
TIME TO COOK 15 minutes
SERVES 4 (3 tacos per serving)

NUTRITIONAL INFORMATION
Calories: 120
Fat: 8 g
Sodium: 24 mg
Carbohydrate: 9 g
Fiber: 3 g
Sugar: 2 g
Protein: 3 g

ALSO WORKS WELL WITH
Jícama, Zucchini, Chayote

If you've never had fried avocado, allow me the honor of introducing you—I think you'll be fast friends. Fried avocado is my weakness (along with buttermilk pancakes and soft-baked chocolate chip cookies), but here I've created a gluten-free, oven-fried version that is just as tasty on the tongue, but lighter on the hips. Seasoned butternut squash noodles and chipotle cream tie these vegetarian tacos all together, making for an irresistible, spiralized taco night.

For the chipotle cream

2 chipotle peppers in adobo sauce with 1 teaspoon sauce

½ cup coconut cream (see page 19)

2 tablespoons fresh lime juice

For the oven-fried avocado

½ cup almond flour

1 teaspoon garlic powder

1 teaspoon onion powder

1 teaspoon sweet paprika

2 large eggs, beaten

1 heaping cup unsweetened shredded coconut

2 ripe avocadoes

For the noodles

1 medium butternut squash, peeled, spiralized with BLADE C, noodles trimmed

1 tablespoon extra-virgin olive oil

1 teaspoon ground cumin

1 teaspoon smoked paprika

Salt and pepper

12 large Bibb lettuce leaves

½ heaping cup fresh cilantro leaves, for garnish

12 thinly sliced lime wedges, for serving

1 Preheat the oven to 400 degrees. Line two baking sheets with parchment paper.

2 Make the chipotle cream. In a food processor, combine all the ingredients for the chipotle cream and pulse until creamy. Taste and add salt to taste.

3 Make the oven-fried avocado. Set up your dredging station. In a small bowl, combine the almond flour and the garlic powder, onion powder, and paprika. In a second small bowl, beat the eggs. In a third small bowl, add the shredded coconut. Place the bowls side by side.

4 Halve the avocadoes and carefully remove the pits. Cut each half into three slices crosswise, then halve the slices horizontally to make 24 slices total.

5 Dip the avocado slices in the almond flour mixture, shaking off any excess. Then dip them in the egg mixture, allowing any excess to drip off. Finally dip them in the coconut mixture, turning to coat well and pressing to adhere. Place on one of the prepared baking sheets, spacing them apart. Transfer to the oven.

recipe continues

6 Make the noodles. As soon as the avocado goes into the oven, lay out the butternut squash noodles on the second baking sheet and toss with oil and season with cumin, smoked paprika, salt, and pepper. Toss to coat, then space apart. Place in the oven and bake together with the avocado for about 8 minutes. Flip the avocado and continue baking together for 2 to 4 minutes more, or until the noodles are al dente and the avocado is lightly golden.

7 Assemble the tacos. Place 12 whole Bibb lettuce leaves on a clean, dry surface and top each with a small handful of butternut squash noodles, dividing them evenly. Add two pieces of avocado each, drizzle with the chipotle cream, and garnish with the cilantro. Serve with lime wedges.

Make it a taco bowl! Chop up the lettuce and mix it in with the butternut squash noodles as a base. Then add the other ingredients on top.

Butternut Squash Noodles

with Butter Beans and Sun-Dried Tomato Cream Sauce

Vegan
Vegetarian
Gluten-Free
Dairy-Free
Low-Cal

TIME TO PREP 20 minutes
TIME TO COOK 20 minutes
SERVES 4

NUTRITIONAL INFORMATION
Calories: 184
Fat: 4 g
Sodium: 260 mg
Carbohydrate: 28 g
Fiber: 6 g
Sugar: 5 g
Protein: 5 g

ALSO WORKS WELL WITH
Rutabaga, Sweet Potato, Turnip, Broccoli, Celeriac

It can be tough for me to plan my meals ahead because I often get recipe ideas and become so consumed with excitement that I have to try them out immediately—I'm like a crazy professor scribbling on the chalkboard. But there is one thing I do always make ahead and keep on hand: pasta sauces! Especially with the more time-consuming ones, prepping in advance makes eating healthy weeknight meals much more realistic and manageable, since I can just throw a sauce on any spiralized vegetable. This sun-dried tomato cream sauce is one of my favorites. It's freezer-friendly, too. In fact, you may want to double it when you make this recipe—you're going to want to keep some extra on hand for your future spiralized creations!

1 large butternut squash, peeled, spiralized with BLADE C

Cooking spray

Salt and pepper

1 teaspoon olive oil

2 garlic cloves, minced

2 teaspoons minced shallot

½ cup chopped drained oil-packed sun-dried tomatoes

½ cup coconut cream (see page 19)

¼ teaspoon red pepper flakes

¼ teaspoon dried basil

¼ teaspoon dried oregano

½ cup low-sodium vegetable broth

1 cup canned butter beans, rinsed and drained

2 tablespoons chopped fresh parsley

1 Preheat the oven to 400 degrees. Line a baking sheet with parchment paper and lay out the butternut squash noodles, spacing them apart. Spray with cooking spray and season with salt and black pepper. Bake for 8 to 10 minutes or until al dente.

2 Meanwhile, heat the olive oil in a large skillet over medium-high heat. When the oil is shimmering, add the garlic and shallot and cook for 1 minute or until fragrant. Add the sun-dried tomatoes, coconut cream, red pepper flakes, basil, and oregano and season with salt and black pepper. Increase the heat to high and bring to a boil, then reduce the heat to medium-low and simmer for 2 minutes to develop the flavors.

3 Transfer the sauce to a food processor or high-speed blender. Add the broth and pulse until creamy. Taste and adjust the seasoning to your preference.

4 Return the skillet to medium-high heat and add the sauce, beans, and parsley. Cook, stirring, for 1 to 2 minutes to heat through. Divide the pasta among four bowls and top with the sauce and beans.

Cabbage

Spiralizing a cabbage yields days (maybe even weeks!) worth of cabbage, making it ideal for Sunday-night meal planning. Spiralizing won't yield noodles like you're used to seeing, but rather, it's an easier, quicker, and more enjoyable way to shred cabbage. No more laborious knife slicing— just load it onto the spiralizer and spin.

If you think you're underwhelmed by cabbage, hold on. This veggie is super underrated; I love its texture and versatility. I promise that once you try the recipes here, you'll think it's worthy of a chapter in this book and a place on your plate.

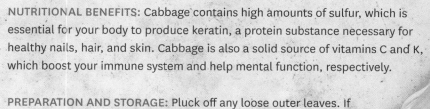

NUTRITIONAL BENEFITS: Cabbage contains high amounts of sulfur, which is essential for your body to produce keratin, a protein substance necessary for healthy nails, hair, and skin. Cabbage is also a solid source of vitamins C and K, which boost your immune system and help mental function, respectively.

PREPARATION AND STORAGE: Pluck off any loose outer leaves. If necessary, slice off the ends to leave flat, even surfaces. Store in an airtight container in the refrigerator for up to 1 week. Spiralized cabbage can also be frozen for up to 8 months for future use.

BEST BLADES TO USE
- Blade A

BEST COOKING METHODS
- Raw
- Blanch
- Steam or boil for 3 minutes
- Sauté over medium-high heat for 5 minutes

Crunchy Bok Choy and Cabbage Salad

In my opinion, there's no better salad bar than the one at Whole Foods. The sheer volume of creative and delicious options is impressive. Their chefs are constantly inventing new pastas salads that instantly become favorites. In the summer of 2015, it was their Paleo Crunchy Cabbage Salad. It's meant to be a filling side, but you can easily top it with your favorite protein, like baked tofu or grilled chicken, and turn it into a complete meal. This spiralized re-creation is both refreshing and profoundly flavorful. It's the dish that got me so excited over cabbage in the first place!

Vegetarian
Gluten-Free
Paleo
Dairy-Free
Low-Cal
No Cook
Saves Well

TIME TO PREP 20 minutes

TIME TO COOK 5 minutes

SERVES 4

NUTRITIONAL INFORMATION
Calories: 236
Fat: 19 g
Sodium: 430 mg
Carbohydrate: 14 g
Fiber: 3 g
Sugar: 6 g
Protein: 6 g

For the dressing
- 3 tablespoons sesame oil
- 2 tablespoons rice vinegar
- 1 teaspoon honey
- Juice of ½ lemon
- Salt

For the salad
- 6 cups chopped bok choy
- 1 *napa cabbage, spiralized with* BLADE A
- ¼ cup sliced scallions
- ½ cup sliced raw almonds
- ½ teaspoon white sesame seeds
- ½ teaspoon black sesame seeds

1 Make the dressing. In a large bowl, whisk together all the ingredients for the dressing.

2 Make the salad. Add all the ingredients for the salad to the bowl with the dressing. Toss to combine thoroughly and place in the refrigerator to marinate for at least 20 minutes or until the cabbage has softened.

Spanish Cabbage Stew
with Cod and Saffron

⌇⌇ Gluten-Free
⌇⌇ Paleo
　　 Dairy-Free
　　 Low-Cal

TIME TO PREP 25 minutes
TIME TO COOK 40 minutes
SERVES 2

NUTRITIONAL INFORMATION
Calories: 242
Fat: 8 g
Sodium: 752 mg
Carbohydrate: 18 g
Fiber: 4 g
Sugar: 9 g
Protein: 23 g

Inspired by Spanish cuisine's use of saffron and light tomato sauces, this dish is definitely one for date night. It plates beautifully and fills the kitchen with an inviting, exotic fragrance. The cabbage soaks up the sauce and meshes well with the simple, flaky cod. Plus, all the vegetables used here are spiralized, so preparation is quick, allowing you to feel more relaxed in the kitchen. This stew satisfies, but is light enough to leave room for dessert, another glass of wine, dancing—or all of the above!

½ cup low-sodium vegetable broth

Pinch of saffron (about 20 small threads)

1 tablespoon extra-virgin olive oil

½ *small white onion, peeled, spiralized with* **BLADE A**, *noodles trimmed*

1 large garlic clove, minced

1 *red bell pepper, spiralized with* **BLADE A**, *noodles trimmed*

3 *cups spiralized (* **BLADE A** *) green cabbage*

¼ teaspoon red pepper flakes

1 (14.5-ounce) can diced tomatoes, with juices

¼ teaspoon ground cumin

1 teaspoon ground paprika

Salt and pepper

2 (3- to 4-ounce) skinless pieces of cod

1 tablespoon minced fresh parsley, for garnish

~~~~~~~~~~~~~~~~~~~~~~~~~~~~~~~~~~~~

For an extra kick of flavor, swap in smoked paprika instead of regular, and add a pinch of cayenne pepper.

~~~~~~~~~~~~~~~~~~~~~~~~~~~~~~~~~~~~

1 Bring the broth to a simmer in a small pot over high heat. Add the saffron and transfer to a small cup or bowl. Set aside for 10 minutes to allow the flavor to infuse.

2 Heat the olive oil in a large skillet with a lid over medium heat. When the oil is shimmering, add the onion noodles and cook until tender, about 5 minutes. Add the garlic and bell pepper noodles and cook until slightly softened, about 2 minutes. Add the cabbage and cook until slightly softened, about 5 minutes. Add the saffron-infused broth, red pepper flakes, tomatoes and their juices, cumin, paprika, and salt and black pepper to taste.

3 Increase the heat slightly and simmer, stirring often, until the tomatoes have cooked down slightly and the mixture is fragrant, about 10 minutes. Reduce the heat to low, cover the skillet, and simmer for 10 minutes more.

4 Season the cod with salt and black pepper and place the pieces on top of the stew, nestling them in. Cover and cook for about 7 minutes or until the fish is opaque and cooked through.

5 Divide the cod between two bowls. Portion out the cabbage stew, pouring it on top of the cod. Garnish with the parsley.

Spicy Cabbage and Carrot Detox Soup

Gluten-Free
Paleo
Dairy-Free
One Pot
Low-Cal
Saves Well

TIME TO PREP 20 minutes
TIME TO COOK 35 minutes
SERVES 4

NUTRITIONAL INFORMATION
Calories: 98
Fat: 4 g
Sodium: 713 mg
Carbohydrate: 14 g
Fiber: 4 g
Sugar: 7 g
Protein: 4 g

We've all been there. Whether it's a holiday party with one too many sprinkle cookies or that extra slice of birthday cake in the office, you're left feeling sluggish and slothlike. While it's important to live life to its fullest, it's just as important to balance that out. Enter detox soup. While most detox soups are flavorless and dull, this spicy cabbage and carrot version will leave your taste buds satisfied and your body on its way to a full recovery.

1 tablespoon extra-virgin olive oil

1 white or yellow onion, peeled, spiralized with BLADE A, noodles trimmed

1 large carrot, peeled, spiralized with BLADE D, noodles trimmed

1 large garlic clove, minced

1½ teaspoons minced serrano chile

⅛ teaspoon ground cumin

⅛ teaspoon ground turmeric

⅛ teaspoon ground ginger

1 small savoy or green cabbage, spiralized with BLADE A (about 6 cups)

1 (15-ounce) can whole peeled tomatoes, crushed with your hands

4 cups low-sodium chicken broth

Salt and pepper

1 Heat the olive oil in a stockpot over medium heat. When the oil is shimmering, add the onion and carrot noodles, the garlic, serrano, cumin, turmeric, and ginger. Cook, stirring, until the onion is softened, about 7 minutes.

2 Add the cabbage, tomatoes and their juices, and broth. Season with salt and black pepper and stir well. Bring to a boil, then reduce the heat to low and cover the pot. Simmer for 20 to 25 minutes or until the cabbage is cooked through and softened. Serve hot.

To make this soup vegan, use vegetable broth instead of chicken broth.

Cabbage Buddha Bowl
with Chickpea-Avocado Mash and BBQ Tahini

Vegan
Vegetarian
Gluten-Free
Dairy-Free
No Cook

TIME TO PREP 15 minutes
TIME TO COOK 5 minutes
SERVES 2

NUTRITIONAL INFORMATION
Calories: 450
Fat: 31 g
Sodium: 523 mg
Carbohydrate: 42 g
Fiber: 17 g
Sugar: 8 g
Protein: 12 g

Buddha bowls are the most efficient way to cram as many superfoods and nourishing ingredients into a meal as you can—plus, they're fun to build. All you have to do is think of everything you'd like to eat at that moment, throw it all in a bowl, then tie the whole thing together with a complementary sauce or dressing. In this cabbage bowl, every bite is chock-full of flavors and textures. It's an enjoyable way to eat up all these healthy ingredients!

For the dressing

1½ tablespoons tahini

3 tablespoons apple cider vinegar

1 tablespoon barbecue sauce (I like Tessemae's Matty's BBQ Sauce)

1 tablespoon extra-virgin olive oil

Salt and pepper

For the Buddha bowl

1 cup canned chickpeas, rinsed and drained

1 very ripe avocado

¼ teaspoon paprika

1 tablespoon fresh lemon juice

Salt and pepper

1 small red cabbage, spiralized with BLADE A (about 2 cups)

2 cups shredded kale leaves

1 Make the dressing. Place all the ingredients for the dressing and 1 tablespoon water in a food processor and pulse until creamy. Add more water if needed to achieve the desired consistency. Taste and adjust the seasoning to your preferences.

2 In a medium bowl, combine the chickpeas and avocado and roughly mash with a potato masher or the back of a fork until mostly smooth but with some chunks remaining. Season with the paprika, lemon juice, salt, and pepper.

3 Assemble the Buddha bowls. Divide the cabbage and kale between two bowls and top with equal dollops of the chickpea-avocado mash. Drizzle the dressing over the top and serve.

Carrot

Traditionally, carrots have been served as mundane crudités, or prettily but simply roasted whole, or just julienned and tossed into salads. Why not make them into noodles and rice?

Carrots are beautiful and colorful, with a sweet, earthy flavor. They're my favorite noodle to boil, as they fluff up, absorbing liquid, and are sturdy enough to hold up to thick sauces like a Bolognese or a slow-cooker vegetable stew. Carrot noodles work famously in soups, infusing their healthy flavors into broths.

It can be tough to find a carrot thick enough for spiralizing—many are thin and long. For the best experience, look for those that are at least 1½ inches in diameter. Be careful, though: many large carrots can be GMOs, so check with your grocer or farmer to make sure the vegetable is organic or simply non-GMO.

NUTRITIONAL BENEFITS: Carrots are rich in beta-carotene, which helps with vision—it's even been shown to protect against macular degeneration and cataracts. Carrots are also high in vitamin A, which has antiaging properties to help you glow from the inside out.

PREPARATION AND STORAGE: Peel the carrot and slice off both ends to leave flat, even surfaces. Before loading the carrot onto the spiralizer, be sure neither end is thinner than 1 inch. Store in an airtight container in the refrigerator for up to 1 week. Spiralized carrots can also be frozen for up to 8 months for future use.

BEST BLADES TO USE

- Blade D

BEST COOKING METHODS

- Raw
- Boil or steam for 2 to 3 minutes
- Sauté over medium-high heat for 5 to 7 minutes
- Roast at 425 degrees for 6 to 10 minutes

Roasted Carrot Noodles
with Smoked Salmon, Avocado, and Creamy Herb Dressing

Gluten-Free
Paleo
Dairy-Free

TIME TO PREP 15 minutes
TIME TO COOK 15 minutes
SERVES 4

NUTRITIONAL INFORMATION
Calories: 402
Fat: 34 g
Sodium: 441 mg
Carbohydrate: 13 g
Fiber: 6 g
Sugar: 4 g
Protein: 14 g

ALSO WORKS WELL WITH
White Potato, Golden Beet,
Broccoli

This protein-packed dish showcases the saltiness of the smoked salmon and the sweetness that emerges as the carrots roast, enhancing the simplicity of the herb dressing. Tiny yet powerful hemp hearts make for a crunchy, nutty bite that's nutritionally dense. Delicate but robust, this dish checks off all the flavor and nutrition boxes.

3 large carrots, peeled, spiralized with **BLADE D**, noodles trimmed

4 teaspoons extra-virgin olive oil

Salt and pepper

2 ripe avocados

8 ounces smoked salmon, sliced

1 tablespoon hemp hearts, for garnish

For the dressing

1 large pasteurized egg yolk

¼ teaspoon garlic powder

1 garlic clove, minced

1 tablespoon fresh lemon juice

2 tablespoons red wine vinegar or sherry vinegar

¼ cup olive oil

¼ cup packed fresh dill

¼ cup packed fresh parsley

2 tablespoons chopped fresh chives

Salt and pepper

1 Preheat the oven to 375 degrees. Line a baking sheet with parchment paper and lay out the carrot noodles, spacing them apart. Drizzle with the olive oil and season with salt and pepper. Roast for 15 minutes or until al dente.

2 Meanwhile, make the dressing. In a food processor, combine the egg yolk, garlic powder, fresh garlic, lemon juice, and vinegar and pulse until smooth. Add the olive oil, dill, parsley, and chives and process again, adding water if necessary, 1 tablespoon at a time, until the dressing has the consistency of heavy cream. Season with salt and pepper.

3 Peel and pit the avocados. Cut each half into four slices.

4 Divide the carrot noodles among four plates. Top with smoked salmon, then avocado. Drizzle the dressing over the top and garnish with the hemp hearts.

If you're not a fan of smoked salmon, try poached instead.

Garlic-Miso Soup
with Carrot Noodles, Seaweed, and Tofu

When I was in high school, I worked at a Japanese restaurant on Friday and Saturday nights. As hostess, part of my role was to help prepare takeout orders, which more often than not included miso soup with seaweed and tiny precious squares of tofu floating in it. I spent so many hours ladling the delightfully simple soup into to-go containers that every time I smell seaweed and miso together, I'm transported back there. This recipe is my version of that memory. I added carrot noodles to pull it together into a full meal, plus garlic for added health benefits.

Vegan
Vegetarian
Gluten-Free
Dairy-Free
Low-Cal

TIME TO PREP 10 minutes
TIME TO COOK 25 minutes
SERVES 4

NUTRITIONAL INFORMATION
Calories: 121
Fat: 3 g
Sodium: 888 mg
Carbohydrate: 14 g
Fiber: 3 g
Sugar: 6 g
Protein: 9 g

ALSO WORKS WELL WITH
Zucchini, Daikon Radish, Turnip

1 teaspoon olive oil

2 teaspoons minced garlic

6 cups low-sodium vegetable broth

1 tablespoon miso paste

½ cup dried wakame seaweed

12 ounces extra-firm tofu, drained (see Tip) and cubed

1 tablespoon reduced-sodium soy sauce or tamari

2 carrots, peeled, spiralized with BLADE D, noodles trimmed

Cracked pepper

1 Heat the olive oil in a large stockpot over medium-high heat. When the oil is shimmering, add the garlic and cook for 30 seconds or until fragrant. Add the broth and 4 cups water. Increase the heat to high and bring to a boil.

2 Transfer ½ cup of the boiling mixture to a small bowl. Add the miso paste and whisk rapidly to dissolve. Return the miso mixture to the pot. Reduce the heat to medium-low.

3 Add the seaweed, tofu, soy sauce, and carrot noodles to the pot. Season with pepper and simmer for 5 to 7 minutes more or until the carrot noodles are al dente. Serve immediately.

To drain tofu, halve the block crosswise, then sandwich both rectangles between paper towels on a plate. Place another plate or heavy object on top and set aside for at least 5 minutes.

Mom's Matzo Ball Soup
with Carrot Noodles

Vegetarian
Dairy-Free
Low-Cal

TIME TO PREP 15 minutes
TIME TO COOK 45 minutes
SERVES 4

NUTRITIONAL INFORMATION
Calories: 234
Fat: 12 g
Sodium: 73 mg
Carbohydrate: 26 g
Fiber: 1 g
Sugar: 5 g
Protein: 6 g

I know, I know—this recipe calls for a boxed matzo ball mix. Well, that's why it's called Mom's Matzo Ball Soup—because she used the mix! This soup was one of my favorite dinners, and I always requested it when I felt sick. Even though I grew up in an Italian household, it was the ultimate comfort food. What was so special, if it just comes from a mix? Mom made the broth from scratch and always added extra carrots to fill us up. My recipe tweaks the original just slightly, using carrot noodles instead of diced carrots.

For the matzo balls

- 2 large eggs, beaten
- 2 tablespoons vegetable oil
- 1 5 ounce packet matzo ball mix (Mom always uses Manischewitz brand)

For the soup

- 1 large yellow onion, quartered
- ½ head garlic, cloves peeled
- 2 large carrots, plus 1 large carrot, peeled, spiralized with BLADE D, noodles trimmed
- 3 celery stalks
- 4 sprigs of flat-leaf parsley
- 1½ teaspoons whole black peppercorns
- ¼ teaspoon salt, plus more as needed
- 1 tablespoon chopped fresh dill
- Pepper

This broth recipe is a great base for any vegetable-based soup. Use it and reuse it!

1 Make the matzo balls. In a medium bowl, whisk together the eggs and oil. Add the matzo ball mix and stir to fully combine. Refrigerate for 15 minutes.

2 Meanwhile, bring a large pot of salted water with a lid to a boil over high heat.

3 Form the chilled matzo ball mixture into eight ¾-inch balls. Drop them into the boiling water, cover, and reduce the heat to low. Simmer for 20 to 25 minutes or until the balls are fluffed up and firm. Remove with a slotted spoon and set aside.

4 Meanwhile, make the soup. In a separate large pot with a lid, combine the onion, garlic, carrots, celery, parsley, peppercorns, and salt. Add enough water to cover the ingredients by 1 inch. Bring to a boil over high heat, then reduce the heat to medium-low, cover, and simmer for 30 minutes.

5 After 15 minutes, remove the vegetable solids from the broth with a slotted spoon and discard. Increase the heat to medium-high and return to a simmer. Add the carrot noodles and cook for 5 minutes or until al dente.

6 To serve, ladle the carrot noodle soup into four bowls and top each with two matzo balls. Sprinkle the soup with dill. Season with salt and pepper and serve immediately.

Za'atar Chickpeas
over Radicchio and Carrot

Vegetarian
Gluten-Free
Dairy-Free (opt.)
Low-Cal

TIME TO PREP 20 minutes

SERVES 4

NUTRITIONAL INFORMATION
Calories: 300
Fat: 19 g
Sodium: 498 mg
Carbohydrate: 26 g
Fiber: 9 g
Sugar: 2 g
Protein: 9 g

If the atmosphere and vibe of a restaurant or bar is captivating, I think the food tastes slightly better. Whenever I walk into a space that has been gorgeously designed, I'm already in awe and excited for my dining experience. I found this to be true with Barbounia, one of my favorite Mediterranean restaurants in New York City. For my first meal there (of many), I ordered a classic Greek salad that was sprinkled with za'atar, an ancient Middle Eastern seasoning that serves up woodsy and nutty notes and notably includes the spice sumac. Whether it was the décor or the za'atar, that meal left an impression. If you're anything like me, you'll want to sprinkle it on everything—grilled naan bread, meats, or fish, or on a spiralized veggie salad!

For the salad

1 (15-ounce) can chickpeas, rinsed and drained

1 tablespoon za'atar

2 teaspoons extra-virgin olive oil

4 cups sliced radicchio

1 *large carrot, peeled, spiralized with* BLADE C, *noodles trimmed*

1½ tablespoons crumbled feta cheese

For the dressing

¼ cup extra-virgin olive oil

1 teaspoon minced shallot

2 tablespoons fresh lemon juice

2 teaspoons minced fresh parsley

Salt and pepper

1 Preheat the oven to 400 degrees. Line a baking sheet with parchment paper.

2 In a small bowl, combine the chickpeas, za'atar, and olive oil. Toss to combine and spread the mixture out on the prepared baking sheet. Bake for 30 to 35 minutes or until the chickpeas are crisp, shaking the pan halfway through.

3 When the chickpeas are done, make the dressing. In a large bowl, whisk together all the ingredients for the dressing.

4 Add the radicchio and carrot noodles to the dressing and toss to combine. Divide the salad among four plates and top with the chickpeas and feta.

Za'atar isn't hard to find, but you can make your own version at home if you like. Combine 1 teaspoon each of fresh oregano, sumac, ground cumin, and sesame seeds and season with salt.

Slow-Cooker Spiced Lentils and Cauliflower
over Carrot Rice

Vegetarian
Gluten-Free
Paleo
Dairy-Free
Low-Cal
Saves Well

TIME TO PREP 30 minutes
TIME TO COOK 4 hours
SERVES 8

NUTRITIONAL INFORMATION
Calories: 273
Fat: 1 g
Sodium: 224 mg
Carbohydrate: 41 g
Fiber: 18 g
Sugar: 8 g
Protein: 14 g

ALSO WORKS WELL WITH
Sweet Potato, Butternut
Squash, Celeriac, Turnip,
Beet

One of the things I enjoy most about living Jersey City is that it's ethnically diverse. There are always interesting cultural events happening around town and, of course, many different types of cuisines. On my first trip to a now-favorite Indian restaurant called Mantra, I asked the waiter to bring me their "best dish." He returned with a spiced lentil stew with cauliflower. I was blown away by the depth and variety of flavor in each bite, and loved the texture of the softened lentils and velvety cauliflower. This spiralized version is my way of sharing a little piece of Jersey City with you.

2 cups brown lentils

1 onion, diced

2 garlic cloves, minced

1½ teaspoons minced fresh ginger

2½ to 3 tablespoons red curry paste

1½ teaspoons garam masala

2 bay leaves

½ teaspoon ground turmeric

½ teaspoon ground cumin

½ teaspoon salt

¼ teaspoon cayenne pepper (or less, if you don't like spice!)

1 (14.5-ounce) can crushed tomatoes

1 tablespoon tomato paste

3 cups low-sodium vegetable broth

4 cups chopped cauliflower florets

8 large carrots, peeled, spiralized with BLADE D, then riced (see page 16)

¼ cup coconut cream (see page 19)

Large handful of fresh cilantro, for garnish

1 Rinse the lentils and place them in a large slow cooker. Add the onion, garlic, ginger, curry paste, garam masala, bay leaves, turmeric, cumin, salt, and cayenne. Stir to combine thoroughly.

2 Add the canned tomatoes, tomato paste, broth, and cauliflower. Stir well to combine, making sure the lentils are mostly submerged. Cover and cook on High for 3½ hours.

3 Stir in the carrot rice and cook together until the lentils and carrot rice are soft but not mushy, about 30 minutes more.

4 Remove the bay leaves and stir in the coconut cream. Divide the mixture among eight bowls and garnish with cilantro.

This recipe makes 8 servings, but if you are making it to save for future use and want just a few servings immediately, spiralize only 1 large carrot per desired serving.

Celeriac

At first glance, celeriac (also known as celery root) is gnarly looking—it's hairy, knobby, and bulbous. While it may never win a vegetable beauty pageant, it has the same wonderful flavors as its cousins carrot, parsley, and parsnip.

The root of the celery stalks you're used to seeing, eating, and cooking with, celeriac definitely carries hints of that taste. It's herbal and slightly smoky in a way that balances out robust sauces and heavy proteins. It also works well in lighter dishes, offering a refreshing bite. Before I started spiralizing, I had only seen celeriac prepared as a mash, roasted with other root vegetables, or tossed raw into salads and slaws. You'll find much more creative interpretations here!

Although it takes a few minutes to peel and prep the vegetable to be spiralized, it yields an abundance of noodles. When you're shopping, opt for a medium celeriac for best results.

NUTRITIONAL BENEFITS: Celeriac is high in dietary fiber, potassium, magnesium, and vitamin B_6. Thus, it has potent anti-inflammatory powers, leaves you feeling fuller longer, and keeps your metabolism revved. It's low on the glycemic index, making it a great pasta alternative that won't spike your blood sugar levels, nourishing and satisfying you instead.

PREPARATION AND STORAGE: Slice off any large hairy knobs and peel entirely. Then slice off each end to leave flat, even surfaces. Store in an airtight container for up to 5 days in the refrigerator. Spiralized celeriac can also be frozen for up to 8 months for future use.

BEST BLADES TO USE
- Blade A
- Blade B
- Blade C
- Blade D

BEST COOKING METHODS
- Raw
- Sauté over medium-high heat for 5 to 7 minutes
- Boil for 3 minutes
- Roast at 425 degrees for 10 minutes

Stuffed Cabbage Rolls
with Celeriac Rice and Adzuki Beans

Vegan
Vegetarian
Gluten-Free
Dairy-Free
Saves Well

TIME TO PREP 25 minutes

TIME TO COOK 1 hour

SERVES 4 to 6
(2 to 3 rolls per serving)

NUTRITIONAL INFORMATION
(for 1 of 6 servings)
Calories: 307
Fat: 11 g
Sodium: 515 mg
Carbohydrate: 42 g
Fiber: 14 g
Sugar: 10 g
Protein: 13 g

ALSO WORKS WELL WITH
Butternut Squash, Sweet
Potato, Kohlrabi, Turnip

Halupki is an Eastern European stuffed-cabbage dish. Traditionally, the cabbage is filled with beef and rice, covered with a sweet, thin tomato sauce, and baked. This vegetarian version swaps in beans for the beef and spiralized celeriac rice for the regular stuff. This dish yields twelve fluffy, gorgeous cabbage rolls that can be frozen, so make a batch and warm them up for future dinners.

1 large head green cabbage, cored

1½ tablespoons extra-virgin olive oil

½ yellow onion, diced

3 garlic cloves, minced

½ red bell pepper, diced

½ green bell pepper, diced

Salt and pepper

1 *large celeriac, peeled, spiralized with* BLADE D, *then riced (see page 16)*

1 (15-ounce) can adzuki beans, drained and rinsed

1 cup coarsely ground walnuts

1 (14.5-ounce) can tomato sauce

1 teaspoon garlic powder

1 cup low-sodium vegetable broth

¼ cup minced fresh parsley, for garnish

1 Preheat the oven to 375 degrees.

2 Fill a large pot halfway with water and bring it to a boil. Add the cabbage and cook for 2 to 3 minutes, then, using a spoon or tongs, peel away 12 whole large leaves and transfer them to a kitchen or paper towel. Pat dry. Chop the remaining cabbage.

3 Heat 1 tablespoon of the olive oil in a large skillet over medium-high heat. When the oil is shimmering, add the onion, garlic, and bell peppers and season with salt and pepper. Cook for 5 minutes or until the onions are softened. Add the celeriac rice, beans, and walnuts and stir to combine. Cook for 5 minutes or until the rice is softened. Remove the pan from the heat and set aside.

4 Combine the tomato sauce and garlic powder in a medium pot. Season with salt and pepper. Bring to a simmer over medium-high heat, then reduce the heat to maintain a simmer and cook for 5 minutes to develop the flavors.

5 Cover the bottom of a 9 x 13-inch baking dish with the chopped cabbage. Pour over 1 cup of the tomato

sauce. Lay out one whole cabbage leaf on a clean, dry surface and cut out the thick stem in the center in a V shape, keeping the leaf intact. Place about ¾ cup of the celeriac rice filling in the center. Fold both sides over the filling and roll up. Place the roll seam-side down in the baking dish. Repeat with the remaining leaves and filling.

6 Pour the broth over the rolls, then pour over the remaining sauce. Bake for 45 minutes or until the celeriac rice is cooked through and softened. Garnish with parsley before serving.

Chicken and Celeriac Rice Soup

Gluten-Free
Paleo
Dairy-Free
Low-Cal
Saves Well

TIME TO PREP 15 minutes
TIME TO COOK 45 minutes
SERVES 4

NUTRITIONAL INFORMATION
Calories: 244
Fat: 14 g
Sodium: 1010 mg
Carbohydrate: 12 g
Fiber: 2 g
Sugar: 3 g
Protein: 18 g

ALSO WORKS WELL WITH
Turnip

Chicken and rice soup comes in a second for Most Comforting Soup of All Time (after chicken noodle, of course). This lighter version uses celeriac rice in place of regular rice, giving you the same consistency without the high glycemic index and calorie count. The chicken cooks in the broth, infusing it with a salty and deeply savory flavor. If I'm feeling under the weather or just need a quick pick-me-up, this soup always does the trick.

½ heaping cup diced red onion

1 large carrot, finely diced

2 garlic cloves, minced

Small pinch of red pepper flakes

Salt and pepper

1 tablespoon fresh thyme, or 1 teaspoon dried

1 tablespoon fresh oregano, or 1 teaspoon dried

4 skin-on, bone-in chicken thighs (about 1¼ pounds)

2 bay leaves

6 cups low-sodium chicken broth

1 *large celeriac*

1 tablespoon minced fresh parsley

This recipe freezes well, so make a big batch to keep on hand for the winter.

1 In a large stockpot with a lid, combine the onion, carrot, garlic, and red pepper flakes and season with salt and black pepper. Cook over medium heat for 3 to 5 minutes or until the onion is softened and mostly translucent. Add the thyme and oregano and stir until combined, about 30 seconds.

2 Add the chicken thighs and bay leaves. Pour in the broth and 2 cups water. Increase the heat to medium-high, cover, and bring to a boil. Reduce the heat to medium-low and simmer for 30 minutes.

3 While the chicken cooks, peel the celeriac and spiralize with blade D. Working in batches, if necessary, pulse the noodles in a food processor until ricelike.

4 Remove the chicken from the broth. Remove and discard the skin, then pull off and shred the meat, reserving the bones and any juices. Return the bones to the pot and add the celeriac rice. Simmer, uncovered, for 10 minutes more or until the rice is softened.

5 Remove and discard the bones and bay leaves. Add the shredded chicken to the soup and season with salt and black pepper. Cook for 5 minutes more, then stir in the parsley and serve.

Celeriac Spaghetti and Vegetarian Meatballs

Vegetarian
Dairy-Free
Saves Well

TIME TO PREP 30 minutes
TIME TO COOK 1 hour
SERVES 4

NUTRITIONAL INFORMATION
Calories: 317
Fat: 13 g
Sodium: 655 mg
Carbohydrate: 40 g
Fiber: 13 g
Sugar: 8 g
Protein: 13 g

When you think of spaghetti and meatballs, do you think of *Lady and the Tramp*? I definitely do, and thanks to the endless noodle possibilities spiralizing presents, that scene can be re-created infinitely. These meatballs were inspired by and adapted from the Veggie Balls from the Meatball Shop in New York City, a restaurant with a build-your-own type of menu. They have plenty of veggie sides to create a more wholesome meal. Perhaps one day, one of them will be spiralized? A girl can dream.

½ cup dried brown lentils, rinsed

1 bay leaf

8 ounces white mushrooms, trimmed and roughly chopped

2 tablespoons extra-virgin olive oil

¼ teaspoon red pepper flakes

2 garlic cloves, minced

½ cup low-sodium vegetable broth

1 tablespoon soy sauce

½ cup rolled oats

¼ teaspoon dried basil

¼ teaspoon dried oregano

¼ teaspoon dried parsley

¼ teaspoon dried rosemary

Salt and pepper

1 large or 2 medium celeriacs

1½ cups jarred tomato basil sauce (I like Victoria Fine Foods)

1½ tablespoons minced fresh parsley

1 Preheat the oven to 350 degrees. Line a baking sheet with parchment paper.

2 In a small saucepan, combine the lentils, bay leaf, and 1 cup water. Bring to a boil over high heat, then reduce the heat to low and simmer for 20 to 30 minutes, slightly overcooking the lentils. Remove from heat, drain, and set aside to cool for about 5 minutes. Remove and discard the bay leaf.

3 Transfer the lentils to a food processor, add the mushrooms, and pulse until roughly chopped.

4 Heat 1 tablespoon of the olive oil in a large skillet over medium-high heat. When the oil is shimmering, add the red pepper flakes and garlic and cook, stirring continuously, for 30 seconds or until fragrant. Stir in the lentil-mushroom mixture and cook for 3 to 5 minutes or until browned. Stir in the broth, soy sauce, oats, basil, oregano, dried parsley, and rosemary. Cook until the liquid has been completely absorbed. Season with salt and black pepper. Remove the pan from the heat and set aside to cool for about 5 minutes.

recipe continues

5 Using your hands, form the mixture into about twelve 1½-inch balls. Place on the prepared baking sheet, spacing them apart. Bake for 40 minutes or until golden brown.

6 While the meatballs cook, peel your celeriac and spiralize with **BLADE D**, then trim the noodles.

7 Wipe the skillet from the meatball mixture clean and heat the remaining 1 tablespoon olive oil over medium heat. When the oil is shimmering, add the celeriac noodles and season with salt and pepper. Cook for about 7 minutes, then pour over the tomato sauce and toss to coat the noodles. Cook for 2 to 3 minutes more or until the sauce is heated through and the noodles are al dente.

8 Using tongs, divide the celeriac among four bowls and top each with three meatballs. Pour over the remaining sauce from the pan. Garnish with the parsley and serve.

Try using a basil pesto instead of the tomato sauce for a totally new version of this dish.

Buffalo Wings
with Celeriac Slaw

Gluten-Free

TIME TO PREP 15 minutes
TIME TO COOK 45 minutes
SERVES 4

NUTRITIONAL INFORMATION
Calories: 358
Fat: 22 g
Sodium: 214 mg
Carbohydrate: 15 g
Fiber: 2 g
Sugar: 5 g
Protein: 28g

For all those people who reach first for the carrots and celery sticks when the Buffalo wings come out on football Sunday, this recipe is for you. Whenever I go out to a bar with Lu to watch a game, he usually orders them, and they always come with ranch slaw. Yummy, but not the healthiest. I've taken matters into my own hands and created a slimmed-down wings recipe. A plentiful side of spiralized slaw that uses a Greek yogurt–based dressing over celeriac noodles invokes the same refreshing bite of celery. Game time ready!

For the wings

- 1 pound skin-on, bone-in chicken wings
- 1 tablespoon extra-virgin olive oil
- 1.5 teaspoons garlic powder
- Salt and pepper
- 2 to 3 tablespoons hot sauce (I like Frank's or Tessemae's)

For the slaw

- 1 cup nonfat plain Greek yogurt
- 1 teaspoon fresh lemon juice
- 1 tablespoon red wine vinegar
- 1 teaspoon Dijon mustard
- 1 tablespoon chopped fresh parsley
- 2 teaspoons chopped fresh chives
- ½ teaspoon garlic powder
- ½ teaspoon onion powder
- Salt and pepper
- *1 large celeriac, peeled and prepped*
- *1 large carrot, peeled, spiralized with* **BLADE D**

1 Make the wings. Preheat the oven to 400 degrees. Place a wire rack on top of a baking sheet.

2 Put the chicken in a medium bowl. Drizzle the olive oil over and rub it into the wings with your fingers. Season generously with garlic powder, salt, and pepper. Place the wings on the rack and bake for 45 minutes or until the skin is crispy and the chicken is cooked through. Transfer the wings to a clean medium bowl, add the hot sauce, and toss thoroughly to coat.

3 Meanwhile, make the slaw. In a large bowl, stir together all the ingredients for the slaw except the celeriac and carrot. Taste and adjust the seasoning to your preferences. Slice the celeriac halfway through lengthwise to create a slit, being careful not to pierce any farther than its center. Spiralize with **BLADE C** and add to the bowl with the dressing. Add the carrots and toss thoroughly to combine. Refrigerate until ready to serve.

4 Serve the celeriac slaw alongside the Buffalo wings.

Try this slaw alongside a spicy fish dish or a burger.

Chayote

Chayote, also known as vegetable pear, is a Spanish squash that grows plentifully in Mexico and other Latin American countries; fortunately, it has become available in the United States, too. It yields perfect spirals and can hold up to most preparation methods. This veggie has a crisp, mild flavor just like zucchini, so the two can often be used interchangeably, but unlike zucchini, chayotes don't release much moisture, making them a better fit for warm sauces.

Although it's edible, some people are sensitive to the skin of chayote and peel it prior to spiralizing. But this is totally optional and mainly a consistency preferences.

If you live in an area where this perennial vegetable is readily available, pick up some and experiment all year long!

NUTRITIONAL BENEFITS: Chayote is very low in calories, making it ideal if you're trying to lose or maintain your weight and for cholesterol reduction. It's also a rich source of folates, which help metabolic function.

PREPARATION AND STORAGE: Peel if desired. Otherwise, just spiralize as is or slice off the thinnest end to leave a flat, even surface for better leverage. Store in an airtight container over paper towels or napkins in the refrigerator for up to 5 days.

BEST BLADES TO USE
- Blade C
- Blade D

BEST COOKING METHODS
- Raw
- Boil for 2 minutes
- Sauté over medium heat for 2 to 3 minutes

Slow-Cooker Carnitas Soup
with Chayote Noodles

Gluten-Free
Paleo
Dairy-Free
Saves Well

TIME TO PREP 20 minutes
TIME TO COOK 5 to 8 hours
SERVES 8

NUTRITIONAL INFORMATION
Calories: 442
Fat: 16 g
Sodium: 1012 mg
Carbohydrate: 18 g
Fiber: 5 g
Sugar: 8 g
Protein: 55 g

ALSO WORKS WELL WITH
Zucchini, Kohlrabi, Jícama

Slow cooking effortlessly intensifies any dish. By stewing for several hours, basic flavors become strong and full-bodied. The spices and seasonings in this dish infuse the meat, and in turn, all that goodness seeps into the simple broth. The chayote offers a nice crunch and a refreshing pause from the powerful depth of this spiced soup.

For the carnitas
- 1 tablespoon chili powder
- 2 teaspoons ground cumin
- 2 teaspoons dried oregano
- 1½ teaspoons onion powder
- 1 teaspoon cayenne pepper
- Salt and pepper
- 1 (4-pound) boneless pork shoulder, excess fat trimmed
- 4 garlic cloves, pressed
- 1½ cups fresh orange juice
- Juice of 1 lime

For the soup
- 4 chayotes, peeled and prepped
- 1½ tablespoons extra-virgin olive oil
- 1 medium white or yellow onion, diced
- 3 garlic cloves, minced
- 2 jalapeños or serrano chiles, seeded and finely diced
- 12 cups low-sodium chicken broth
- 2 avocados, sliced
- Juice of 4 small limes
- 1½ cups roughly chopped fresh cilantro leaves
- Salt and pepper

1 Make the carnitas. In a small bowl, combine the chili powder, cumin, oregano, onion powder, cayenne, and salt and black pepper to taste. Season the pork with the spice mixture, rubbing it in thoroughly on all sides.

2 Place the pork, garlic, orange juice, and lime juice in your slow cooker. Cover and cook on Low for 8 hours or on High for 5 hours.

3 Remove the pork shoulder from the slow cooker and shred the meat, trimming and discarding any excess fat. Return the shredded pork and its juices to the pot and season with salt and black pepper. Cover and keep warm for 30 minutes to further soften the meat.

4 Meanwhile, make the soup. Spiralize the chayotes with **BLADE D** and trim the noodles.

5 Heat the olive oil in a large saucepan over medium-high heat. When the oil is shimmering, add the onion and sauté for 2 minutes or until softened. Add the garlic and jalapeños and cook for 30 seconds or until fragrant. Add the broth and chayote noodles, increase the heat to high, and bring to a boil. Reduce the heat to low and simmer. Add the avocados, lime juice, and cilantro and cook for 2 to 3 minutes to deepen the flavors. Season with salt and black pepper.

6 Ladle the soup into eight bowls and top each with about ½ cup of the carnitas.

If you want this soup soon or don't have a slow cooker, order carnitas tacos from your favorite local Mexican restaurant. While you wait for them to arrive, make the soup. Simply take the meat from the tacos and stir it into the broth. Or you can even substitute shredded rotisserie chicken instead of pork.

Chayote Tex-Mex Bowls
with Tomatillo Sauce

Vegan
Vegetarian
Gluten-Free
Dairy-Free

TIME TO PREP 25 minutes
TIME TO COOK 20 minutes
SERVES 2

NUTRITIONAL INFORMATION
Calories: 407
Fat: 21 g
Sodium: 365 mg
Carbohydrate: 52 g
Fiber: 18 g
Sugar: 14 g
Protein: 13 g

ALSO WORKS WELL WITH
Zucchini, Kohlrabi, Jícama

One way to stay on track with your healthy eating while dining out is to ask for simple changes that don't make extra work for the chef. If it's minor, your waiter or waitress will be less hesitant to ask for the change since it won't slow down the kitchen. Whenever I see a burrito on the menu, I ask for it naked, meaning ditch the wrap and serve the burrito filling alone or over a bed of greens. This Tex-Mex bowl is like a naked burrito over chayote noodles. The mild squash holds the tomatillo sauce well and stands up to all the various flavors here.

2 medium tomatillos, husked and washed well

1 tablespoon fresh lime juice

2 teaspoons diced jalapeño, plus 1 small jalapeño, seeded and minced

2 tablespoons chopped white onion

¼ cup packed fresh cilantro, plus more for garnish

Salt

1 ear of corn

1½ tablespoons extra-virgin olive oil

1 garlic clove, minced

½ small red onion, diced

1 green bell pepper, diced

¼ teaspoon ground cumin

¼ teaspoon chili powder

½ teaspoon dried oregano

Pepper

¾ cup black beans, rinsed and drained

2 chayotes, spiralized with BLADE D, noodles trimmed

½ avocado, sliced

1 tablespoon roasted shelled pepitas, for garnish

1 Place the tomatillos in a medium saucepan and add water to cover. Bring the water to a boil over high heat and cook for about 10 minutes or until the tomatillos turn light green. Drain and transfer to a food processor. Add the lime juice, diced jalapeño, white onion, cilantro, and salt to taste and blend until combined but still chunky, with the consistency of salsa. Taste and adjust the seasoning to your preferences with more salt or lime juice.

2 Place the corn in the same saucepan and add water to cover and a pinch of salt. Cover the pan and bring the water to a boil over medium-high heat, then reduce the heat to medium and simmer for 3 to 5 minutes or until the corn is easily pierced with a fork. Remove the corn and slice the kernels off into a medium bowl.

3 Heat 1 tablespoon of the olive oil in a large skillet over medium heat. When the oil is shimmering, add the garlic, minced jalapeño, red onion, and bell pepper. Add the cumin, chili powder, and oregano and season with salt and black pepper. Cook for 3 to 5 minutes or until the vegetables just soften but still have a crunch. Add the corn and black beans and cook for 1 minute more to warm through. Transfer the mixture to a large bowl.

4 Wipe the skillet clean and heat the remaining ½ tablespoon olive oil over medium-high heat. When the oil is shimmering, add the chayote noodles and cook for 3 minutes or until al dente.

5 Divide the noodles between two bowls. Add the vegetable and black bean mixture. Top with avocado slices and pour the tomatillo sauce over the top. Garnish with cilantro and the pepitas.

Blackened Tilapia
over Chayote-Mango Pasta Salad

Gluten-Free
Paleo
Dairy-Free
Low-Cal

TIME TO PREP 25 minutes
TIME TO COOK 10 minutes
SERVES 4

NUTRITIONAL INFORMATION
Calories: 271
Fat: 9 g
Sodium: 406 mg
Carbohydrate: 29 g
Fiber: 6 g
Sugar: 18 g
Protein: 23 g

ALSO WORKS WELL WITH
Zucchini, Jícama

Being from the Caribbean, Lu loves tropical flavors—he goes crazy for anything that comes with mango. I've made him swordfish with mango-avocado salsa, zucchini pasta cooked with mango and coconut flakes, and this tilapia recipe, which is probably his favorite. The spicy blackened fish gets along fabulously with the sweet mango and refreshing chayote and bell pepper. With fresh herbs like cilantro and mint, you'll have to check out your window to make sure you're not at the beach!

For the salad
- 1 large chayote, spiralized with BLADE D, noodles trimmed
- 1 red bell pepper, spiralized with BLADE A, noodles trimmed
- 1 ripe mango, sliced into matchsticks
- 1 cup chopped tomato
- ½ cup diced red onion
- 2 tablespoons finely chopped fresh cilantro
- 2 tablespoons finely chopped fresh mint
- Juice of 1 lime
- 2 teaspoons extra-virgin olive oil
- ¼ teaspoon cayenne pepper
- Salt and pepper

For the seasoning
- 4 teaspoons paprika
- 1 teaspoon cayenne pepper
- 2 teaspoons dried oregano
- 2 teaspoons garlic powder
- 2 teaspoons onion powder
- 2 teaspoons ground cumin

- 4 (3-ounce) tilapia fillets
- 1 tablespoon extra-virgin olive oil

1 Make the salad. Place all the ingredients for the salad in a large bowl. Gently toss to combine and marinate in the refrigerator until ready to serve.

2 Make the seasoning. In a small bowl, mix together all the spices for the seasoning. Rub it into both sides of the tilapia fillets.

3 Heat the olive oil in a large skillet over medium-high heat. When the oil is shimmering, add the tilapia. Cook for 3 minutes per side or until the fish is opaque and flakes easily with a fork.

4 Divide the chayote salad among four plates and top each with a tilapia fillet, pouring any pan juices over the top.

Cucumber

Most of the time, cucumbers are dunked into dips, sliced for a sandwich, or diced and tossed into salads. Not a whole lot to them . . . until now! Cucumber noodles can be used as a stand-alone noodle alternative, but they also work as a crunchy addition to trendy bowl meals.

Since cucumbers are composed primarily of water, they're wonderful for hydration, but they start to release that liquid the moment they are spiralized. Be sure to pat them dry thoroughly before using them in a recipe, and avoid cooking them. However you choose to incorporate your cucumber noodles, they're sure to be more exciting than ever before.

NUTRITIONAL BENEFITS: Cucumbers help you stay hydrated, which is essential for your body to run optimally and can help flush out unwanted toxins. They also contain skin-clearing magnesium, potassium, and silicon. That's why so many beauty products are cucumber scented or fortified!

PREPARATION AND STORAGE: Avoid peeling; simply slice off the ends to leave flat, even surfaces. Store in an airtight container over paper towels in the refrigerator for 2 to 3 days.

BEST BLADES TO USE
- Blade A
- Blade B
- Blade C
- Blade D

BEST COOKING METHODS
- Raw

Turkey, Spinach, and Hummus Cucumber Noodle Roll-Ups

Gluten-Free
Dairy-Free
Low-Cal
No Cook

TIME TO PREP 15 minutes
TIME TO COOK 5 minutes
SERVES 2 (2 roll-ups per serving)

NUTRITIONAL INFORMATION
Calories: 64
Fat: 2 g
Sodium: 219 mg
Carbohydrate: 4 g
Fiber: 1 g
Sugar: 1 g
Protein: 7 g

ALSO WORKS WELL WITH
Zucchini, Apple

I distinctly (and lovingly!) remember my mother fixing me "turkey roll-ups" for after-school snacks. I loved dipping them into mustard and munching on them while telling her about my day. Now I've re-created that childhood memory into something a little more grown-up. The spinach and crunchy cucumber noodles add texture and vitamins, and the hummus packs in more protein and flavor. Whether you're looking for a snack for your children or something to pack for yourself at the office, these roll-ups are satisfying and, most important, fun to eat.

4 slices of deli turkey (I like Applegate Farms)

4 tablespoons hummus

2 teaspoons hemp hearts (optional)

1 cup packed baby spinach leaves

1 *medium seedless cucumber, spiralized with* **BLADE D**, *noodles trimmed and pat dry*

Hot sauce, for serving

1 Lay out the turkey slices on a clean, dry surface. Spread 1 tablespoon of the hummus on each and top evenly with hemp hearts. On the short side end farthest from you, add about ¼ cup of the spinach leaves to each, then top with about ¼ cup of the cucumber noodles.

2 Roll it all up like a burrito. Secure with a toothpick if needed and drizzle with or dip into hot sauce.

You'll immediately love these roll-ups and want to make them over and over again. To keep things interesting, try using other types of deli meat and smears. I like them with pastrami and mustard.

California Roll Sushi Bowl
with Ginger-Carrot Dressing

Dairy-Free
Low-Cal

TIME TO PREP 25 minutes
TIME TO COOK 10 minutes
SERVES 4

NUTRITIONAL INFORMATION
Calories: 300
Fat: 16 g
Sodium: 445 mg
Carbohydrate: 22 g
Fiber: 7 g
Sugar: 11 g
Protein: 13 g

ALSO WORKS WELL WITH
Carrot

If you've never tried a sushi bowl, you're in for a treat. They deliver all the same great flavors as your sushi favorites, but they think outside the box—or the roll. What's even better about bowls is that you can create your own bites. Fork up more avocado in one and more kani in the next. The fluffy daikon rice and crunchy cucumber noodles make this dish more filling than traditional sushi rolls. I chose the classic California roll here because its ingredients are readily available at most grocery stores, but if you like something else better, deconstruct it into your own spiralized sushi bowl!

For the dressing

- 2 tablespoons extra-virgin olive oil
- 2 teaspoons grated fresh ginger
- ¼ cup rice vinegar
- 1 tablespoon low-sodium soy sauce
- 1 teaspoon honey
- 1 carrot (4 ounces), peeled and finely grated

For the sushi bowl

- 1 *large daikon radish, peeled, spiralized with* BLADE D, *then riced (see page 16) and drained*
- 4 scallions, sliced
- 1 teaspoon rice vinegar
- 1 *large cucumber, spiralized with* BLADE C, *noodles trimmed*
- 1 sheet nori (dried seaweed), cut into thin strips
- 12 ounces kani (crabmeat), cut into ¼-inch pieces and halved
- 1 avocado, sliced
- 4 teaspoons toasted white sesame seeds

1 Make the dressing. In a food processor, combine all the ingredients for the dressing and pulse until creamy.

2 In a medium bowl, combine the daikon rice, scallions, and rice vinegar.

3 Divide the seasoned daikon rice among four bowls and top each with equal amounts of the cucumber noodles, nori, kani, avocado, and sesame seeds. Drizzle over the dressing and serve.

Lamb-Feta Burgers
with Greek Cucumber Noodle Salad

Gluten-Free

TIME TO PREP 25 minutes
TIME TO COOK 15 minutes
SERVES 4

NUTRITIONAL INFORMATION
Calories: 413
Fat: 30 g
Sodium: 499 mg
Carbohydrate: 15 g
Fiber: 3 g
Sugar: 4 g
Protein: 22 g

ALSO WORKS WELL WITH
Zucchini, Chayote, Beet

You probably already know that your first line of defense when ordering healthfully at a restaurant is answering "Salad, please" when asked "Fries or a side salad?" Sadly, that measly pile of lettuce never quite competes with those crispy, mouthwatering fries. When you're at home, you can change all that. Instead of serving burgers with a predictable salad, change it up with spiralized noodles! These cucumber noodles are hydrating, crunchy, and filling, and won't leave your fingertips oil-slicked. This Greek-flavored lamb burger is lightly stuffed with feta, which complements the tangy cucumber noodles. Plus, since you swapped fries for cucumbers, there's room for a little dessert. That's my kind of compromise!

For the burgers

- 1 pound lean ground lamb
- 3 tablespoons chopped fresh parsley
- ½ teaspoon ground cumin
- ½ teaspoon dried oregano
- ½ teaspoon paprika
- ½ teaspoon garlic powder
- ½ cup crumbled feta
- Salt and pepper

For the dressing

- 1½ teaspoons dried oregano
- 1 teaspoon garlic powder
- Pinch of red pepper flakes
- 1 tablespoon red wine vinegar
- 1 tablespoon olive oil
- Salt and pepper

For the cucumber salad

- 2 seedless cucumbers, spiralized with BLADE C, noodles trimmed and patted dry
- ½ cup diced red onion
- 1 cup halved cherry tomatoes
- 1 cup packed baby spinach
- ⅓ cup pitted kalamata olives, halved
- ½ cup diced red bell pepper
- ¼ cup canned chickpeas, drained and rinsed
- 1 tablespoon extra-virgin olive oil
- 4 large romaine lettuce leaves, for serving (optional)

recipe continues

1 Make the lamb burgers. In a large bowl, combine all the ingredients for the burgers and, using your hands, mix thoroughly. Form the mixture into four patties and set them on a plate. Refrigerate for 10 minutes.

2 Meanwhile, make the dressing. In a large bowl, whisk together the oregano, garlic powder, red pepper flakes, vinegar, and olive oil for the dressing. Taste and add salt and black pepper to your preferences.

3 Add all the ingredients for the cucumber salad to the bowl with the dressing and toss to combine.

4 Heat the olive oil in a large skillet over medium-high heat. When the oil is shimmering, add the burgers, working in batches if necessary, and cook for 3 to 4 minutes per side for medium doneness.

5 Serve each burger on a romaine lettuce leaf, if desired, with a side of the cucumber noodle salad.

The burgers in this recipe can be served on romaine, but if you like, add a bun, or just top the salad with the burger and dig in with a fork!

Chicago-Style Carrot Dogs
with Spiralized Pickles

〰〰 Vegetarian
〰〰 Vegan
〰〰 Dairy-Free
Low-Cal
Saves well

TIME TO PREP 20 minutes
TIME TO COOK 45 minutes
SERVES 4

NUTRITIONAL INFORMATION
Calories: 203
Fat: 2 g
Carbohydrates: 39 g
Sodium: 1070 mg
Protein: 6 g
Sugar: 13 g

ALSO WORKS WELL WITH
Zucchini

I first visited Chicago to run a half marathon. While I was definitely excited (and totally nervous), I was also thinking about the food. Chicago is famous for its food scene, so I was anticipating some great meals. How would Chicago-style pizza compare to New York's? What about their hot dogs? It's tough for me to admit, but Chicago-style hot dogs are just more impressive—they have crunchy veggie toppings and seem more meal-like, with onions, peppers, tomatoes, and other garnishes like relish and pickles. I made them vegan with these carrot dogs, and spiralized the pickle to get more in every bite. After all, a pickle's just a cucumber, right? Now, as for pizza . . . I'll always prefer a New York slice!

4 thick carrots

2 tablespoons liquid smoke (I like the hickory flavor)

2 tablespoons soy sauce

1 tablespoon maple syrup

¼ teaspoon onion powder

¼ teaspoon garlic powder

Pepper

4 hot dog buns (see note below)

2 vine tomatoes, sliced into 8 wedges

8 peperoncinos or sport peppers

Yellow mustard

½ cup small diced white onion

Sweet relish

2 kosher dill pickles, spiralized with BLADE D, noodles trimmed

When selecting a bun, check the ingredients list for sneaky, processed components like milk or preservatives. I love Alvarado Street Bakery's Sprouted Hot Dog Buns.

1 Preheat the oven to 425 degrees.

2 Prepare the carrots. Peel them, carefully rounding the edges to create a shape that resembles a hot dog.

3 In a small bowl, whisk together the liquid smoke, soy sauce, maple syrup, onion powder, and garlic powder. Place the carrots in a shallow baking dish and pour over the liquid mixture. Toss to coat, massaging the marinade into the carrots. If you have the time, marinate for at least 2 hours.

4 Season the marinated carrots with pepper and place on a baking sheet, reserving the marinade. Transfer to the oven and roast for 45 to 50 minutes or until fork tender. Every 20 minutes, brush the carrots with the reserved marinade.

5 Place the roasted carrot dogs in hot dog buns. On one side of each, add 2 tomato wedges. On the other side, add the peppers. Squirt yellow mustard on top in a zigzag. Top with about 2 tablespoons of white onion and a dollop of sweet relish. Finish with the spiralized pickles and serve.

Jícama

Native to Latin America, jícama is a crunchy, slightly starchy, sweet, and nutty vegetable. I love cooking with jícama because it's so mild in flavor that it works as the base for almost all types of dishes, although it's typically only used in slaws or salads. It's refreshingly crisp and low in calories. Jícama is especially popular in the summertime, but you can incorporate it into meals year-round.

Jícamas tend to be large and heavy, and sometimes have a waxy exterior. Always look for one with firm outer skin, which indicates proper ripeness. Avoid any jícamas that are spongy or have soft spots—those are overripe. Using a regular peeler will do the trick, but might require some elbow grease. Once peeled, you'll immediately be able to smell its freshness; if it has a sour or soapy smell, it's overripe and won't spiralize well (or taste good).

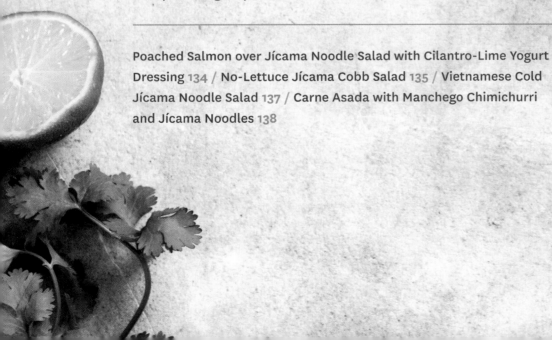

NUTRITIONAL BENEFITS: Jícama is low in calories and high in vitamin C and dietary fiber, making it ideal for weight loss and maintenance.

PREPARATION AND STORAGE: Peel jícama completely. If you have a larger jícama, for the sake of leverage, slice off each side to leave flat, even surfaces, until you have a thinner, more rectangular vegetable that's no more than 6 inches wide. Store in an airtight container in the refrigerator for up to 5 days.

BEST BLADES TO USE
- Blade B
- Blade C
- Blade D

BEST COOKING METHODS
- Raw
- Roast at 400 degrees for 10 to 20 minutes
- Boiled or steamed

Poached Salmon
over Jícama Noodle Salad with Cilantro-Lime Yogurt Dressing

~~~ | Gluten-Free
~~~ | Low-Cal
~~~

TIME TO PREP 10 minutes
TIME TO COOK 20 minutes
SERVES 4

NUTRITIONAL INFORMATION
Calories: 218
Fat: 1 g
Sodium: 198 mg
Carbohydrate: 21 g
Fiber: 8 g
Sugar: 6 g
Protein: 31 g

ALSO WORKS WELL WITH
Kohlrabi, Golden Beet,
Zucchini

Martha Stewart taught me how to poach salmon. Well, she didn't personally show me, but I watched her demonstrate it online in a video. That counts, right? It's an easy, clean way to cook fish and meat. The salmon will flake effortlessly with a fork, and in this salad it is very elegant. The cilantro-lime yogurt dressing captures the fish's gentle flavors, while the crunchy jícama lends a refreshing bite. And after you master it, you can tell people Ali Maffucci taught *you* how to poach salmon.

For the salmon
- 1 carrot, cut into 1-inch pieces
- 1 celery stalk, cut into 1-inch pieces
- ½ small white onion
- ½ lemon, cut into ½-inch-thick rounds
- Salt
- 4 (4-ounce) skinless salmon fillets

For the dressing
- 1 cup nonfat plain Greek yogurt
- ½ cup chopped fresh cilantro
- 1 tablespoon apple cider vinegar
- ¼ teaspoon garlic powder
- Juice of 1 large lime
- Salt and pepper

For the salad
- 1 large or 2 small jícamas, peeled, spiralized with BLADE C, noodles trimmed
- 1 large jalapeño, thinly sliced into rounds, for garnish
- 1 cup microgreens, for garnish

1 In a large, deep skillet or heavy stockpot, combine the carrot, celery, onion, and lemon. Add enough water to cover, about 6 cups, then salt the water. Bring to a boil over high heat, then reduce the heat to medium, cover, and simmer for about 8 minutes.

2 Season the salmon on both sides with salt and gently place in the pot, being sure the liquid just covers the fish. Reduce the heat to medium-low, cover, and gently poach the salmon for about 5 minutes or until opaque. Using a slotted spatula, remove the salmon from the liquid and set aside. Discard the poaching liquid and solids.

3 Meanwhile, make the dressing. In a small bowl, whisk together all the ingredients for the dressing. Taste and adjust the seasoning to your preference. Set aside.

4 Divide the jícama noodles among four plates, top each with a salmon fillet, and generously dollop the salad with the dressing. Garnish with the jalapeño and microgreens.

In the summer, grill the salmon with lemon wedges on top.

No-Lettuce Jícama Cobb Salad

 | Gluten-Free
Dairy-Free

TIME TO PREP 20 minutes
TIME TO COOK 10 minutes
SERVES 2

NUTRITIONAL INFORMATION
Calories: 369
Fat: 24 g
Sodium: 453 mg
Carbohydrate: 27 g
Fiber: 11 g
Sugar: 10 g
Protein: 13 g

ALSO WORKS WELL WITH
Zucchini, Cucumber, Kohlrabi

When I'm at a sports bar and want to order something moderately healthy, I always go for the Cobb salad—it's packed with veggies, but also comes with classic bar food toppings like bacon and cheese. It's a good compromise! This spiralized version ditches the lettuce for jícama noodles, and uses turkey bacon, no cheese, and a clean dressing. Biting into a jícama noodle is much more thrilling than chewing on the same old lettuce, especially if you're sitting next to a friend who's splurging on the burger and fries. It's all about moderation and training your taste buds to crave whole foods.

For the salad
- 4 turkey bacon slices
- 1 small jícama, peeled, spiralized with BLADE D, noodles trimmed
- 1 hard-boiled egg, quartered
- ½ cup halved cherry tomatoes
- ¼ cup quartered pitted black olives
- ½ avocado, sliced

For the dressing
- 2 tablespoons red wine vinegar
- 2½ teaspoons Dijon mustard
- Salt and pepper
- ½ tablespoon minced fresh chives
- 2 tablespoons finely minced shallot
- 2 tablespoons extra-virgin olive oil

1 Place the turkey bacon in a large nonstick skillet. Cook over medium-high heat, flipping over once, for about 10 minutes or until crispy and browned. Transfer to a paper towel–lined plate to drain and cool.

2 Divide the jícama between two plates and top evenly with the egg, tomatoes, olives, and avocado. Crumble 2 slices of the turkey bacon over each plate.

3 Make the dressing. In a small bowl, whisk together the vinegar, mustard, and salt and pepper to taste. Stir in the chives and shallot. Gradually whisk in the oil to make a smooth dressing.

4 Drizzle the dressing over the salads and serve immediately.

To soften the jícama a bit, marinate it in half the dressing for 15 minutes in the refrigerator. Then divide it between two plates, top with the rest of the ingredients, and pour the remaining vinaigrette over the top.

Vietnamese Cold Jícama Noodle Salad

Gluten-Free
Paleo
Dairy-Free
Low-Cal
No Cook
Saves Well

TIME TO PREP 30 minutes
TIME TO COOK 5 minutes
SERVES 4

NUTRITIONAL INFORMATION
Calories: 236
Fat: 14 g
Sodium: 1145 mg
Carbohydrate: 26 g
Fiber: 9 g
Sugar: 11 g
Protein: 4 g

ALSO WORKS WELL WITH
Golden Beet, Zucchini

Cold noodle salads are great to have on hand during the week, especially when you have leftover cooked proteins. This one is great served with leftover grilled chicken, tofu, frozen shrimp, or even some chilled steak. But if you don't eat meat and love your veggies, then look no further—even on its own, this dish is packed with flavor, color, and heart-healthy ingredients like ginger, cashews, and fresh herbs.

For the dressing

- 3 tablespoons fresh lime juice
- 3 tablespoons fish sauce (I like Red Boat)
- 1 garlic clove, sliced
- 1 (½-inch) piece fresh ginger, peeled and sliced
- 1 tablespoon rice vinegar
- 1 tablespoon honey
- 2 small Thai chiles, seeded and thinly sliced, or 1 or 2 serrano chiles
- 3 tablespoons avocado oil or other neutral oil

For the salad

- 1 large seedless cucumber
- 1 medium to large jícama, peeled, spiralized with **BLADE D**, noodles trimmed
- 1 large carrot, peeled, spiralized with **BLADE D**, noodles trimmed
- 4 scallions, thinly sliced
- 4 red radishes, thinly sliced into rounds
- ¼ cup fresh cilantro leaves
- ¼ cup Thai basil or regular basil leaves, thinly sliced
- ¼ cup chopped roasted unsalted cashews
- Lime wedges, for serving

1 Make the dressing. In a food processor, combine all the ingredients for the dressing and pulse until smooth.

2 Make the salad. Halve the cucumber crosswise, then slice each half lengthwise to create a slit, being careful not to pierce any farther than its center. Spiralize both halves with **BLADE A**, then pat the noodles dry and place them in a large bowl. Add the jícama, carrot, scallions, radishes, cilantro, and basil. Pour the dressing over the salad and toss thoroughly to combine.

3 Divide the salad among four plates and garnish with the cashews. Serve with lime wedges.

When preparing the jícama, spiralize slowly and use light pressure to make a thinner noodle, typical of this Vietnamese salad. See the tip on page 15.

Carne Asada

with Manchego Chimichurri and Jícama Noodles

This recipe has some moving pieces, but the timing is seamless—everything finishes cooking at the same time! While the steak marinates, prepare all the other ingredients. By the time the steak is finished, all that's left to do is top the dishes with the succulent carne asada. The jícama noodles hold the manchego chimichurri well, giving the dish the full-bodied flavor of fresh herbs and nutty manchego cheese.

Gluten-Free

TIME TO PREP 1½ hours
TIME TO COOK 20 minutes
SERVES 4

NUTRITIONAL INFORMATION
Calories: 421
Fat: 29 g
Sodium: 145 mg
Carbohydrate: 14 g
Fiber: 6 g
Sugar: 3 g
Protein: 26 g

ALSO WORKS WELL WITH
Kohlrabi, Zucchini, Sweet Potato

For the marinade

- 2 garlic cloves
- ⅓ cup packed fresh cilantro leaves
- Zest of 1 lime
- Juice of 2 limes
- ¼ cup extra-virgin olive oil
- 1 tablespoon chili powder
- 1 teaspoon ground cumin
- 1 teaspoon dried oregano
- ¼ teaspoon cayenne pepper
- 1½ pounds flank steak

For the chimichurri

- ½ cup packed fresh flat-leaf parsley
- ½ teaspoon dried oregano
- ½ cup packed fresh cilantro
- 2 medium garlic cloves, minced
- ½ diced seeded serrano chile or jalapeño
- 2 tablespoons diced white onion
- 1½ tablespoons red wine vinegar
- 2 tablespoons extra-virgin olive oil
- ¼ cup diced manchego cheese

- 1 *large jícama*
- 2 beefsteak tomatoes

1 Make the marinade. In a food processor, combine all the ingredients for the marinade and pulse until smooth. Taste and add salt to your preference.

2 Transfer the marinade to a large resealable plastic bag and add the steak, turning it to coat. Marinate the steak in the refrigerator for at least 1 hour, turning occasionally. Remove it from the refrigerator and let rest at room temperature for at least 15 minutes.

3 Meanwhile, make the chimichurri. In a food processor, combine all the ingredients for the chimichurri and pulse until creamy. Taste and add salt and pepper to your preference.

4 Peel the jícama, spiralize with **BLADE C**, and trim the noodles. Transfer to a large bowl. Dice the tomatoes and add to the jícama. Pour three-quarters of the chimichurri on top, toss to combine, and set aside.

5 Heat a grill pan or large skillet over medium-high heat. When the pan is hot, add the steak and sear for about 4 minutes per side for medium-rare or 6 minutes per side for medium-well. Transfer to a carving or cutting board and let rest for 3 to 5 minutes. Slice the steak thinly (about ¼-inch slices) against the grain.

6 Divide the jícama-tomato mixture among four plates. Top each serving with the carne asada, drizzle with the remaining chimichurri, and pour over any leftover juices from the steak. Serve immediately.

Kohlrabi

Kohlrabi is sometimes known as the "alien turnip," but don't let its odd shape deter you—it's one of the easiest vegetables to spiralize. They are either purple or green on the outside, but both have a similar cream-yellow-colored flesh with the texture of a radish and the slight sweetness of jícama, as well as a hint of cucumber and broccoli. This overall mildness makes them super versatile for spiralized cooking.

The bulb of a kohlrabi sprouts a bundle of greens that also can be cooked along with the flesh. When choosing a kohlrabi for spiralizing, try to find one with unblemished leaves and a bulb that does not appear cracked or overgrown. If you get one in your CSA box, just flip to this chapter and discover what you can do with this seemingly intimidating but delightful vegetable.

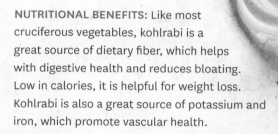

NUTRITIONAL BENEFITS: Like most cruciferous vegetables, kohlrabi is a great source of dietary fiber, which helps with digestive health and reduces bloating. Low in calories, it is helpful for weight loss. Kohlrabi is also a great source of potassium and iron, which promote vascular health.

PREPARATION AND STORAGE: Peel the kohlrabi bulb. If it has uneven round ends, slice off the ends to leave flat, even surfaces. Store in an airtight container in the refrigerator for up to 5 days.

BEST BLADES TO USE
- Blade A
- Blade B
- Blade C
- Blade D

BEST COOKING METHODS
- Raw
- Boil or steam
- Sauté over medium heat for 5 minutes
- Roast at 400 degrees for 15 minutes

Kohlrabi Spaghettini Aglio e Olio

Vegetarian
Dairy-Free (opt.)
Gluten-Free
Low-Cal
Saves Well

TIME TO PREP 20 minutes
TIME TO COOK 10 minutes
SERVES 4

NUTRITIONAL INFORMATION
Calories: 104
Fat: 9 g
Sodium: 51 mg
Carbohydrate: 5 g
Fiber: 3 g
Sugar: 2 g
Protein: 4 g

ALSO WORKS WELL WITH
Zucchini

Spaghettini, by definition, is a pasta strand that is thinner than spaghetti but thicker than vermicelli. Since this noodle is so fine, it's best served with a simple olive oil and garlic sauce, like an *aglio e olio* ("garlic and oil" in Italian). When we were studying abroad and visiting friends in Italy, my friends and I often found ourselves out late at night, drunk off wine and laughter, gathered around a massive vat of spaghettini! This easy pasta dish works for every occasion, whether a late-night meal or a quick vegetarian dinner.

2 tablespoons extra-virgin olive oil

2 medium kohlrabies, peeled, spiralized with BLADE D, noodles trimmed

Salt and pepper

4 medium garlic cloves, sliced into rounds

¼ to ½ teaspoon red pepper flakes

¼ cup chopped fresh flat-leaf parsley

4 tablespoons grated Parmigiano-Reggiano cheese

1 Heat 1 tablespoon of the olive oil in a large nonstick skillet over medium-high heat. When the oil is shimmering, add the kohlrabi noodles. Season with salt and pepper and cook for about 5 minutes or until al dente. Transfer to a plate.

2 Turn off the heat and let the skillet cool for about 2 minutes. Return the heat to medium-high and add the remaining 1 tablespoon olive oil, the garlic, and the red pepper flakes. Cook for about 2 minutes or until the garlic is golden, taking care not to brown or burn it. Remove the skillet from heat, add the kohlrabi noodles and parsley, and season generously with salt and pepper. Toss thoroughly to combine.

3 Divide the pasta among four bowls and top each with 1 tablespoon of the cheese.

Grate some lemon zest over the pasta to add a tangy, refreshing accent.

General Tso's Cauliflower
with Kohlrabi Rice

Vegetarian
Dairy-Free
Low-Cal

TIME TO PREP 15 minutes
TIME TO COOK 45 minutes
SERVES 4

NUTRITIONAL INFORMATION
Calories: 214
Fat: 11 g
Sodium: 134 mg
Carbohydrate: 28 g
Fiber: 7 g
Sugar: 16 g
Protein: 5 g

ALSO WORKS WELL WITH
Butternut Squash, Golden
Beet, Jícama

I definitely believe in moderation when it comes to food, but some dishes are just so nutritionally bad that after embarking on a healthy journey and nourishing yourself, you don't want to do that to your body. General Tso's is one of those foods for me, but with this spiralized, lightened-up version, I can take the classic Chinese dish off that no-no list. Thanks to arrowroot powder—a gluten-free thickening agent commonly used in healthy cooking—and the crunchy, sturdy nature of cauliflower, these General Tso's cauliflower bites have all the flavors of the original without the deep-frying, flour, cornstarch, or sugar. The kohlrabi rice soaks up all the sauce, making this dish a true takeout fake-out.

1 small head cauliflower, cut into florets

1 tablespoon extra-virgin olive oil

Salt and white pepper (use black pepper if you don't have white)

3 scallions, sliced, white and green parts kept separate

2 medium kohlrabies, peeled, spiralized with BLADE D, then riced (see page 16)

1 tablespoon sesame oil

3 tablespoons dark soy sauce

2 teaspoons rice vinegar

2 tablespoons honey

1 cup low-sodium vegetable broth

1 tablespoon coconut oil

2 teaspoons finely minced fresh ginger

2 garlic cloves, finely minced

5 whole dried red chile peppers, halved

1 tablespoon arrowroot powder, mixed with 1 tablespoon water

1 tablespoon white sesame seeds

recipe continues

1 Preheat the oven to 450 degrees. Line a baking sheet with parchment paper. Place the cauliflower on the baking sheet and drizzle with the olive oil. Using your hands, massage the oil into the cauliflower. Space the florets apart, season with salt and white pepper, and bake for 20 to 25 minutes or until golden brown, flipping once halfway through. Remove and set aside.

2 Place a large skillet over medium-high heat. When water flicked onto the skillet sizzles, add the white parts of the scallions and cook for 1 minute or until fragrant. Add the kohlrabi rice and season with salt. Cook for 5 minutes or until al dente. Divide the kohlrabi rice among four serving plates and set aside.

3 Meanwhile, in a small bowl, stir together the sesame oil, soy sauce, vinegar, honey, and vegetable broth and set aside.

4 In the same skillet you used for the kohlrabi rice, heat the coconut oil over medium heat. When the oil has melted, add the ginger, garlic, and chiles and stir. Add the soy sauce mixture, increase the heat to high, and bring to a boil. Reduce the heat to low and simmer the sauce for 1 minute. Add the arrowroot powder mixture and whisk continuously until the sauce thickens. Add the cauliflower and scallion greens and cook, stirring and spooning the sauce over the cauliflower as you stir, for 5 minutes or until the cauliflower is heated through and completely coated in the sauce.

5 Add the cauliflower to the plated kohlrabi rice. Garnish with sesame seeds.

This dish doesn't save well for more than 1 day in the refrigerator, so if you're making it for only yourself and want leftovers, halve the recipe to make two servings.

Spicy Kohlrabi Tortilla Soup
with Shrimp

When I'm at a restaurant, I rarely order soup—they tend to be overloaded with sodium and contain hidden processed ingredients like sugar. But whenever I see tortilla soup on the menu, I can't resist—it's always perfectly spicy, crunchy from the tortilla strips, and packed with vegetables. This spiralized version replaces the tortilla strips with crispy kohlrabi noodles and adds shrimp for extra protein and flavor.

Gluten-Free
Dairy-Free
One Pot
Saves Well

TIME TO PREP 15 minutes
TIME TO COOK 20 minutes
SERVES 4 to 6

NUTRITIONAL INFORMATION
Calories: 384
Fat: 11 g
Sodium: 1155 mg
Carbohydrate: 39 g
Fiber: 15 g
Sugar: 10 g
Protein: 36 g

ALSO WORKS WELL WITH
Zucchini, Jícama

- 1 *medium kohlrabi, peeled and prepped*
- 1 tablespoon extra-virgin olive oil
- 1 small white or yellow onion, diced
- 1 large garlic clove, minced
- 1 large jalapeño, seeded and finely diced
- 1 teaspoon chili powder
- 1 teaspoon dried oregano
- ½ teaspoon ground cumin
- ¼ teaspoon smoked paprika
- 6 cups low-sodium vegetable broth or chicken broth
- 1 (14.5-ounce) can fire-roasted diced tomatoes
- 1 (14.5-ounce) can black beans, rinsed and drained
- 1 pound frozen medium shrimp, thawed, peeled, and deveined
- 1 avocado, sliced
- Juice of 2 small limes
- 1 cup roughly chopped fresh cilantro leaves
- Salt and pepper

1 Slice the kohlrabi halfway through lengthwise to create a slit, being careful not to pierce any farther than its center. Spiralize with **BLADE D** and set aside.

2 Heat the olive oil in a large pot over medium-high heat. When the oil is shimmering, add the onion and cook for 3 to 5 minutes or until softened. Add the garlic and jalapeño and cook for 30 seconds or until fragrant. Add the chili powder, oregano, cumin, and paprika and stir to combine.

3 Add the broth, tomatoes, and beans to the pot. Increase the heat to high and bring to a boil, then reduce the heat to medium-low and add the shrimp, avocado, and lime juice to the pot. Cook for 5 minutes more or until the shrimp are pink, cooked through, and opaque.

4 Stir in the cilantro and kohlrabi noodles. Season with salt and pepper and simmer for 30 seconds more. Ladle the soup into bowls and serve.

Fried Green Tomatoes
with Avocado Ranch Kohlrabi

Vegetarian
Gluten-Free
Paleo
Dairy-Free

TIME TO PREP 20 minutes
TIME TO COOK 10 minutes
SERVES 4

NUTRITIONAL INFORMATION
Calories: 421
Fat: 31 g
Sodium: 132 mg
Carbohydrate: 30 g
Fiber: 13 g
Sugar: 12 g
Protein: 15 g

ALSO WORKS WELL WITH
Jícama, Zucchini

One of the best parts about dating someone is introducing him or her to something they may have never heard of, done, or tried—something you love. On a trip to Napa Valley with Lu a month after our wedding, we sat down at the acclaimed restaurant Farmstead, and one of the daily specials was fried green tomatoes. Having gone to college in North Carolina, I have eaten my fair share of fried green tomatoes, but Lu had never tried them. Obviously, I insisted we order them! As we dipped the tomatoes in the decadent aioli that accompanied them, nothing else mattered in the world except for our next bite—they were *that* good! In an effort to make a healthier version, I dusted the tomatoes in almond flour and replaced the dipping sauce with an avocado ranch–dressed kohlrabi salad.

For the dressing
- 1 ripe avocado
- 1 cup plain unsweetened almond milk
- 3 tablespoons fresh lemon juice
- 2 teaspoons red wine vinegar
- 1 teaspoon garlic powder
- 1½ teaspoons minced fresh dill
- 2 teaspoons minced fresh parsley
- 1 teaspoon onion powder
- 1 teaspoon paprika
- Salt (I use about ¼ teaspoon)
- Black pepper

- 2 *medium kohlrabies, peeled and prepped*
- 2 large eggs
- 1 cup almond flour
- 1 teaspoon onion powder
- ¼ teaspoon paprika
- ½ teaspoon garlic powder
- ¼ teaspoon cayenne pepper
- Salt and black pepper
- 2 tablespoons plus 1 teaspoon coconut oil
- 4 green tomatoes, thinly sliced (about ¼ inch thick)

1 Make the dressing. In a food processor, combine all the ingredients for the dressing and pulse until creamy. Taste and adjust the seasoning to your preference.

2 Slice the kohlrabies halfway through lengthwise to create a slit, being careful not to pierce any farther than their centers. Spiralize with **BLADE C** and transfer the noodles to a large bowl. Add the dressing and toss to combine. Refrigerate until ready to serve.

3 Set up your dredging station. In a shallow medium bowl, beat the eggs. On a large plate, mix together the almond flour, onion powder, paprika, garlic powder, and cayenne. Season with salt and black pepper. Set the dishes side by side.

4 Heat 2 teaspoons of the coconut oil in a large skillet over medium-high heat. When the oil has melted, dip a few tomato slices in the egg and allow any excess to drip back into the bowl. Transfer to the almond flour mixture, pressing to coat. Place in the skillet in a single layer and fry for 3 to 4 minutes per side or until golden brown. Repeat with the remaining tomato slices, using 2 teaspoons of oil per batch.

5 Serve about four tomato slices with about 1 cup of avocado-ranch kohlrabi.

For a salty kick, sprinkle the kohlrabi salad with roasted pepitas or sunflower seeds.

Chicken Mole
with Kohlrabi Rice

∿∿ Gluten-Free
∿∿ Paleo
      Dairy-Free (opt.)
      Saves Well

TIME TO PREP 20 minutes
TIME TO COOK 25 minutes
SERVES 4

NUTRITIONAL INFORMATION
Calories: 460
Fat: 16 g
Sodium: 424 mg
Carbohydrate: 28 g
Fiber: 8 g
Sugar: 17 g
Protein: 54 g

ALSO WORKS WELL WITH
Sweet Potato, Rutabaga,
Jícama

I've always appreciated the richness, fragrance, and beauty of mole, a sauce used in Mexican cuisine. There are many different types, but this recipe showcases mole poblano, a dark red version served over meat. The story goes that nuns in a convent needed to whip up something quickly for a visiting archbishop, so they rummaged through the kitchen and made a sauce from whatever ingredients they could find, mainly chile peppers, spices, and chocolate. Yes, chocolate! Here we use 70% cacao, which gives the sauce a deep flavor and color while counteracting the heat of the peppers. The kohlrabi rice is simply prepared, letting the mole-bathed chicken do all the talking.

- 1 tablespoon plus 3 teaspoons extra-virgin olive oil
- 4 skinless, boneless chicken breasts
- Salt and pepper
- 2 garlic cloves, minced
- ½ yellow onion, diced
- 1 (6-ounce) can tomato paste
- 1 large chipotle chile in adobo, finely chopped, plus 1 teaspoon adobo sauce
- 2 tablespoons golden raisins
- 1 ounce dark chocolate (at least 70% cacao), finely chopped

- 1 teaspoon ground cinnamon
- 1 teaspoon ground cumin
- ½ teaspoon chili powder
- ½ teaspoon ground coriander
- 1½ cups low-sodium chicken broth
- 2 medium kohlrabies, peeled, spiralized with *BLADE D*, then riced (see page 16)
- 2 tablespoons chopped fresh cilantro
- 1 tablespoon fresh lime juice
- 2 tablespoons crumbled cotija cheese, for garnish (optional)

1 Heat 1 tablespoon of the olive oil in a medium skillet over medium heat. Season the chicken with salt and pepper on both sides. When the oil is shimmering, add the chicken and cook for 3 to 5 minutes per side or until golden brown on the outside and cooked through. Transfer to a plate and tent with foil to keep warm.

2 In the same skillet, heat 2 teaspoons of the oil over medium heat. When the oil is shimmering, add the garlic and onion and cook, stirring frequently, for 3 to 5 minutes or until the onion is softened. Stir in the tomato paste and the chipotle chile and adobo and cook, stirring continuously, for about 1 minute or until combined.

3 Stir in the raisins, chocolate, cinnamon, cumin, chili powder, coriander, and broth. Season with salt. Increase the heat to medium-high and bring the sauce to a strong simmer. Reduce the heat to low and simmer, stirring occasionally, for 5 to 7 minutes or until slightly reduced.

4 Return the chicken to the skillet, including any collected juices. Simmer for 3 to 5 minutes or until the chicken is warmed through and coated well with the sauce.

5 Meanwhile, prepare the rice. Heat the remaining 1 teaspoon oil in a large skillet over medium heat. When the oil is shimmering, add the kohlrabi rice and season with salt and pepper. Cook for 5 minutes or until al dente. Stir in the cilantro and lime juice and stir.

6 To serve, divide the rice among four plates. Add one chicken breast to each and spoon the mole sauce over the top. Garnish with cotija, if desired.

It's important to use a high-quality chocolate bar here to avoid any unwanted bitterness or staleness. Heck, if you're eating chocolate, might as well make it good.

Onion

Before the spiralizer became as popular and widely used as it is today, it was called a "vegetable slicer," as it easily cuts and shreds most produce. What's one of the most tedious veggies to take a knife to? The onion! Whenever I use the spiralizer at cooking classes or demos, I get the most *ooh*s and *ahh*s when I spiralize an onion. The tool effortlessly slices through the onion, producing bountiful curly cuts in mere seconds. It's quicker and easier than using a knife—and more tear-free.

Onions are used as the base in many types of dishes. If nothing else, I encourage you to ditch the knife and use the spiralizer to slice your onions, whether you're preparing a creative recipe from this book or merely making a salad.

NUTRITIONAL BENEFITS: Onions help promote the flow of vitamin C in the body, which supports immunity. Raw onions also encourage the production of the good cholesterol, HDL.

PREPARATION AND STORAGE: Peel the onion and slice off both ends to leave flat, even surfaces. Store in an airtight container in the refrigerator for 2 to 3 days.

BEST BLADES TO USE
- Blade A

BEST COOKING METHODS
- Raw
- Bake at 425 degrees for 15 to 20 minutes

Kale and Quinoa Salad
with Pickled Onions and Caesar Dressing

Vegetarian
Gluten-Free
Dairy-Free
Low-Cal
No Cook

TIME TO PREP 2 hours
TIME TO COOK 15 minutes
SERVES 4

NUTRITIONAL INFORMATION
Calories: 218
Fat: 5 g
Sodium: 461 mg
Carbohydrate: 34 g
Fiber: 5 g
Sugar: 11 g
Protein: 10 g

Quick-pickling onions is an excellent party trick to have in your back pocket. They work well on top of burgers and hot dogs and in tacos, curries, and salads. Their tartness and tanginess add dimension and appeal to any dish. Pickling also takes the bite out of sharp red onions—and the longer you let them sit, the more flavorful they become. This seasonal winter kale salad is loaded with vitamin C–packed pomegranate, protein-laden quinoa, and a dairy-free Caesar dressing, all topped with ground flaxseed for a crunchy, nutty taste.

For the pickled onions

- ½ cup apple cider vinegar
- 1 tablespoon honey
- 1½ teaspoons kosher salt
- 1 red onion, peeled, spiralized with BLADE A, noodles trimmed

- ½ cup quinoa

For the dressing

- ¼ cup raw cashews, soaked for at least 2 hours (preferably overnight) and drained
- ¼ cup plain unsweetened almond milk
- 1 large garlic clove
- 1½ teaspoons fresh lemon juice
- 2 teaspoons nutritional yeast
- ½ teaspoon Dijon mustard
- Salt and pepper

- 4 cups finely chopped curly kale leaves
- ½ cup pomegranate seeds
- 2 teaspoons ground flaxseed

1 Make the pickled onions. In a resealable container, whisk together the vinegar, honey, and salt. Add onion and set aside to pickle at room temperature for at least 1 hour, or overnight in the refrigerator.

2 Make the quinoa. Place the quinoa and 1 cup water in a small pot, cover, and bring to a boil over high heat. Uncover, reduce the heat to low, and simmer for 10 to 15 minutes, adding more water as needed until the quinoa fluffs up and is tender. When the water has evaporated and the quinoa is fluffy, transfer to a bowl and refrigerate.

3 Meanwhile, make the dressing. Place all the ingredients for the dressing in a high-speed blender or food processor and pulse until creamy. Taste and adjust the seasoning to your preferences.

4 Put the chilled quinoa, kale, and pomegranate seeds in a large bowl. Drizzle the Caesar dressing over the salad and toss to combine thoroughly. Divide the salad among four plates. Top with pickled onions and sprinkle with the flaxseed.

Make the pickled onions and dressing the day before to simplify preparation and increase their flavor.

Wedge Salad
with Caramelized Onions, Mushroom Bacon, and Greek Yogurt–Balsamic Dressing

Vegetarian
Gluten-Free

TIME TO PREP 15 minutes
TIME TO COOK 30 minutes
SERVES 4

NUTRITIONAL INFORMATION
Calories: 362
Fat: 26 g
Sodium: 335 mg
Carbohydrate: 29 g
Fiber: 8 g
Sugar: 16 g
Protein: 10 g

The wedge salad is a steakhouse classic—it is its own institution. Traditionally served with blue cheese dressing and bacon bits, it's definitely one of the tastiest salads, but not the most waistline-friendly. I've transformed the wedge salad into a mostly wholesome version, starring caramelized onions, a Greek yogurt dressing, and mushroom bacon. This vegan bacon is made entirely from sliced mushrooms with sweet-smoky seasonings. It crisps up in the oven, yielding crunchy pieces that truly taste like the real thing.

For the mushroom bacon
- 2 tablespoons olive oil
- 2 tablespoons liquid smoke
- 2 tablespoons sesame oil
- ¼ teaspoon garlic powder
- ¼ teaspoon paprika
- 4 teaspoons maple syrup
- Salt and pepper
- 8 ounces king oyster (also sold as trumpet royale) mushrooms, cut lengthwise into ½-inch pieces

For the dressing
- ¼ cup nonfat plain Greek yogurt
- 3 tablespoons balsamic vinegar
- 2 teaspoons Dijon mustard
- 1 tablespoon honey
- Salt and pepper

For the salad
- 2 romaine lettuce heads, rinsed, ends chopped off, and halved lengthwise
- 2 tablespoons extra-virgin olive oil
- Salt and pepper
- 1 onion, peeled, spiralized with BLADE A, noodles trimmed
- ¼ teaspoon garlic powder
- 1 cup halved heirloom cherry tomatoes or seeded and diced Roma (plum) tomatoes
- ½ cup crumbled blue cheese

recipe continues

1 Preheat the oven to 350 degrees. Line a baking sheet with parchment paper.

2 Make the bacon. In a medium bowl, whisk together all the mushroom bacon ingredients except the mushrooms. Add the mushrooms and stir gently to coat. Spread out the mushrooms on the prepared baking sheet, spacing them apart. Bake for 10 minutes, then flip and bake for 10 minutes more or until browned, taking care not to burn them. Remove the mushrooms from the oven and place on a paper towel–lined plate to drain. The bacon will crisp up over the next 5 to 7 minutes.

3 Meanwhile, make the dressing. Place all the ingredients for the dressing in a food processor and blend until creamy. Taste and adjust the seasoning to your preferences.

4 Make the salad. Heat a grill pan or large skillet over medium-high heat. Brush the cut sides of the romaine lettuce with 1 tablespoon of the olive oil. Season lightly with salt and generously with pepper. When the pan is hot, add the romaine, cut-side down, working in batches if necessary. Grill for about 5 minutes or until lightly charred and marks appear, periodically pressing down with a spatula. Transfer each romaine half to a serving plate.

5 Heat the remaining 1 tablespoon oil in the same pan over medium-high heat. When the oil is shimmering, add the onion noodles and season with the garlic powder, salt, and pepper. Cook for 5 to 7 minutes or until caramelized and lightly browned. Remove the pan from the heat.

6 Scatter the onions, mushroom bacon, tomatoes, and blue cheese over the romaine halves and drizzle with the balsamic vinaigrette.

You can find premade mushroom bacon in some health food stores and online. Shiitake mushrooms work well here, too, if you can't find oyster mushrooms.

No-Cheese French Onion and Lentil Soup

Gluten-Free
Dairy-Free
One Pot
Saves Well

TIME TO PREP 15 minutes
TIME TO COOK 1 hour
SERVES 4 to 6

NUTRITIONAL INFORMATION
(for 1 of 6 servings)
Calories: 325
Fat: 8 g
Sodium: 145 mg
Carbohydrate: 44 g
Fiber: 7 g
Sugar: 6 g
Protein: 19 g

Okay, so this technically isn't a French onion soup—it doesn't have the signature cheesy giant crouton top. But this soup *is* all about everything else you find in that classic dish: gentle hints of thyme, caramelized onions, and a beef and wine stock that's robust and aromatic. A filling protein, the lentils here add more substance to this soup.

3 tablespoons extra-virgin olive oil

4 red onions, peeled, spiralized with **BLADE A***, noodles trimmed*

Salt and pepper

½ cup dry red wine

2 cups lentils, rinsed

2 bay leaves

6 cups low-sodium beef broth

1 teaspoon dried thyme

2 tablespoons chopped fresh parsley

1 Heat the olive oil in a large stockpot over medium heat. When the oil is shimmering, add the onion noodles and a pinch of salt. Cook, stirring, until the onions are translucent, about 5 minutes. Reduce the heat to medium-low and cook, stirring, until the onions have reduced to half their size and are browned and softened, 20 to 30 minutes.

2 Add the red wine to the onions, scraping up any browned bits from the bottom of the pot with a wooden spoon. Add the lentils, bay leaves, broth, and thyme. Season with salt and pepper, stir once, cover halfway, and simmer for 20 minutes or until the lentils are just cooked through. Taste and adjust the seasoning to your preferences.

3 Stir in the parsley and simmer for 1 minute to finish. Remove the bay leaves before serving.

If you're vegetarian, substitute vegetable broth for the beef broth. While the flavors will be less intense, the swap will still be delicious.

Almond-Crusted Lemon Sole

with Tomato, Sweet Onion, and Caper-Parsley Salad

Gluten-Free
Paleo
Dairy-Free

TIME TO PREP 15 minutes
TIME TO COOK 15 minutes
SERVES 4

NUTRITIONAL INFORMATION
Calories: 405
Fat: 29 g
Sodium: 386 mg
Carbohydrate: 15 g
Fiber: 4 g
Sugar: 7 g
Protein: 24 g

I've always loved fish—and if you'd ever tasted my mother's breaded lemon sole, you'd have always loved fish, too. The slightly crispy, golden brown breading combined with the tender, flaky, light white fish is magical. I would run to the table whenever I smelled fresh lemon and seafood in the kitchen—and now hopefully your loved ones will, too! This sweet onion and caper salad is my own personal touch, adding a refreshing complement.

For the fish

- 2 large eggs
- ½ cup almond meal
- 1 teaspoon garlic powder
- Salt and pepper
- 2 tablespoons extra-virgin olive oil
- 4 (3-ounce) skinless lemon sole fillets
- 4 large lemon wedges

For the salad

- 2 small Vidalia onions, peeled, spiralized with BLADE A, noodles trimmed
- 4 Roma (plum) tomatoes, cut lengthwise into ¼-inch-thick slices
- ¼ cup drained capers
- ½ cup chopped fresh parsley
- ¼ cup red wine vinegar
- ¼ cup fresh lemon juice
- 2 tablespoons plus 2 teaspoons extra-virgin olive oil
- Salt and pepper

1 Make the fish. Set up your dredging station. In a shallow medium bowl, beat the eggs. On a large plate, mix together the almond meal and garlic powder. Season with salt and pepper. Set the dishes side by side.

2 Heat the olive oil in a medium skillet over medium-high heat. Working with one fillet at a time, dip the sole into the egg, turn to coat, and allow any excess to drip back into the bowl. Dip the fish into the almond meal mixture, pressing to adhere. When the oil is shimmering, add the fish, working in batches if necessary, and cook for 3 minutes, then flip, squeeze over the lemon juice, and cook for 2 to 3 minutes more or until the fish is opaque and the crust is golden brown.

3 Make the salad. Place all the ingredients for the salad in a large bowl and toss to combine.

4 Serve the sole with the salad alongside.

Stir some finely chopped almonds into the almond meal before breading the sole for a crunchier texture.

Rosemary, Olive, and Onion Frittata
with Arugula Salad and Parmesan Vinaigrette

Vegetarian
Gluten-Free
Dairy-Free (opt.)
Low-Cal

TIME TO PREP 10 minutes
TIME TO COOK 25 minutes
SERVES 4 to 6

NUTRITIONAL INFORMATION
(for 1 of 6 servings)
Calories: 221
Fat: 16 g
Sodium: 293 mg
Carbohydrate: 5 g
Fiber: 1 g
Sugar: 1 g
Protein: 14 g

On rainy weekends, I've been known to spend an hour lying on my back with my hands extended up in the air, iPhone grasped, doing nothing other than 'sgramming—scrolling through Instagram, that is. Even when the weather is bad, there are somehow always pictures of chic women with perfect hair sitting in stilettos, packed into tiny restaurants in the West Village. Once I get over the fact that I'm at home and in sweatpants and totally unmotivated to get off the couch, I notice that they're almost always eating an elegant slice of frittata with the daintiest of salads to keep it company. This frittata is my way of having a little of that sophistication in my life, especially on my cherished relaxing weekends.

For the frittata
- 1 tablespoon olive oil
- *1 medium red onion, peeled, spiralized with BLADE A, noodles trimmed*
- Leaves from 1 sprig of rosemary
- ¼ teaspoon garlic powder
- Salt and pepper
- ½ cup pitted large black olives, quartered
- 9 egg whites plus 3 large eggs, beaten

For the dressing
- 2 tablespoons extra-virgin olive oil
- 1 tablespoon red wine vinegar
- 2 teaspoons grated Parmesan cheese
- Salt and pepper
- ⅛ teaspoon garlic powder
- ¼ teaspoon dried oregano
- 1 teaspoon fresh lemon juice
- Pinch of red pepper flakes

- 4 cups baby arugula

1 Preheat the oven to 375 degrees.

2 Heat the olive oil in a medium ovenproof skillet over medium-high heat. When the oil is shimmering, add the onion and season with the rosemary, garlic powder, salt, and pepper. Cook until softened, about 5 minutes. Stir in the olives, then pour over the eggs. Cook for 3 minutes to lightly set the eggs on the bottom, then transfer the pan to the oven and bake for 15 minutes. Pierce the frittata with a knife. If it comes out clean, it's done. If not, cook for 3 to 5 minutes more.

3 Meanwhile, make the dressing. Whisk together all the ingredients for the dressing in a medium bowl. Taste and adjust the seasoning to your preferences. Add the arugula and toss to combine.

4 Cut the frittata into slices and plate with some of the salad alongside.

Parsnip

When the temperatures drop and fall and winter produce starts to appear at farmer's markets and grocery stores, I always get excited for parsnips. I was first introduced to parsnips while staying with a friend's family in Windsor, England. My friend's mother made a root vegetable bake that included parsnips, and I was surprised by their pleasant, sweet taste. They've been in my diet ever since!

Parsnips are just a little bit sweet, but also pleasantly nutty, with a fibrous texture. The cold weather converts their starches into natural sugar, which introduces their signature flavor. Because their taste is so distinct, they should be used only with complementary flavors.

Sort of like carrots, but in an even more exaggerated way, all parsnips taper to a very thin end that isn't wide enough to be spiralized. To make the most of your produce, try to find one with the widest wide end possible. Be sure to choose a vegetable that's firm and has an ivory color.

NUTRITIONAL BENEFITS: Parsnips are packed with folate and potassium, both essential for cardiovascular health, and are also a solid source of vitamin C and dietary fiber.

PREPARATION AND STORAGE: Peel the parsnip. Slice off both ends to leave flat, even surfaces. Discard any part of the parsnip that is less than ½ inch in diameter, or use it in a nonspiralized recipe. Peeled or spiralized parsnips oxidize when exposed to air, so store them in a container filled with water with a little bit of lemon juice in the refrigerator for up to 2 days.

BEST BLADES TO USE
- Blade C
- Blade D

BEST COOKING METHODS
- Sauté over medium heat for 5 to 7 minutes
- Roast at 425 degrees for 10 to 15 minutes

Parsnip-Chive Waffles and Gluten-Free Oven-Fried Chicken

≋ | Gluten-Free
≋ | Paleo
≋ | Dairy-Free

TIME TO PREP 15 minutes
TIME TO COOK 50 minutes
SERVES 4

NUTRITIONAL INFORMATION
Calories: 494
Fat: 30 g
Sodium: 170 mg
Carbohydrate: 24 g
Fiber: 7 g
Sugar: 6 g
Protein: 31 g

ALSO WORKS WELL WITH
Sweet Potato, Rutabaga

Chicken and waffles is a commitment. Of course, it's a mind-blowingly delicious commitment—a soul food delicacy that I had the privilege of discovering when I lived in North Carolina during college. But that deep-fried chicken is greasy, and the waffle is nutritionally empty. This spiralized version is not only gluten-free, but it's also made with real, whole ingredients that offer the same richly indulgent flavors, while helping you with another commitment—to a healthy lifestyle!

For the chicken

- Cooking spray
- 2 large eggs
- ½ cup almond meal
- ¼ teaspoon dried thyme
- ¼ teaspoon cayenne pepper
- ¼ teaspoon paprika
- ¼ teaspoon onion powder
- ¼ teaspoon garlic powder
- Salt and pepper to taste
- 1½ pounds skin-on, bone-in chicken pieces (a mixture of thighs, breasts, and drumsticks), patted dry

For the waffles

- Cooking spray
- 3 large parsnips, peeled, spiralized with *BLADE C*, noodles trimmed
- ½ teaspoon garlic powder
- Salt and pepper
- 2 large eggs, beaten
- 3 tablespoons chopped fresh chives
- Maple syrup, for serving

recipe continues

1 Make the chicken. Preheat the oven to 375 degrees. Coat a wire rack with cooking spray and set it on a foil-lined baking sheet.

2 Set up your dredging station. Beat the eggs in a large bowl. Combine the almond meal, thyme, cayenne, paprika, onion powder, garlic powder, and salt and pepper on a large plate. Set the dishes side by side.

3 Working with one piece at a time, dip the chicken in the egg, allowing the excess to drip back into the bowl. Dredge the chicken in the seasoned almond meal, patting it into any crevices and pressing to adhere. As you bread each piece, set them on the prepared baking sheet on top of the rack. Bake until the chicken is cooked through, 20 to 30 minutes.

4 Meanwhile, make the waffles. Preheat a waffle iron. Wipe the skillet from the chicken clean and spray generously with cooking spray. Set over medium heat. When the skillet is hot, add the parsnip noodles and season with garlic powder, salt, and pepper. Cover and cook for 5 minutes or until the noodles are wilted. Transfer to a medium bowl. Add the eggs and chives to the bowl and toss to combine.

5 Coat the waffle iron with cooking spray and pack the parsnip mixture into four waffle cavities. Cook according to the manufacturer's instructions.

6 When the waffles are done, transfer them to four plates and top each equally with chicken pieces. Drizzle with maple syrup and serve.

These savory, nutty waffles work well with many different toppings. If you don't eat chicken or don't have the time to make it, try topping the waffle with mashed avocado, fried eggs, or some melted cheese. Heck, they're yummy by themselves, too!

Hearty Beef Stew
with Parsnip and Carrot Noodles

In the dead of winter, I crave everything slow roasted, oven baked, and steadily simmered. Temperatures drop and my appetite shifts—all I can think about are slow-cooker soups and hearty stews. This beef stew with spiralized parsnips and carrots is a great addition to anyone's cold weather–cooking repertoire. The nutty parsnips and sweet carrots are roasted to perfection and soak up the deep flavors of the slow-cooked beef. Curl up with a bowl of this and fall in love with the coziness of winter.

Gluten-Free
Dairy-Free
Low-Cal
Saves Well

TIME TO PREP 20 minutes
TIME TO COOK 1½ hours
SERVES 4

NUTRITIONAL INFORMATION
Calories: 213
Fat: 11 g
Sodium: 449 mg
Carbohydrate: 18 g
Fiber: 7 g
Sugar: 5 g
Protein: 15 g

ALSO WORKS WELL WITH
Sweet Potato, Rutabaga, Celeriac, Turnip, Butternut Squash

- 2 tablespoons extra-virgin olive oil
- 1 pound beef stew meat
- 2 garlic cloves, minced
- ½ red onion, diced
- ¼ teaspoon red pepper flakes
- 3 celery stalks, diced
- 3 tablespoons Worcestershire sauce
- 1 teaspoon dried thyme
- ½ teaspoon cayenne pepper
- Salt and pepper
- 4 cups low-sodium beef broth
- 1 (14-ounce) can diced tomatoes
- 2 bay leaves
- 3 large carrots, peeled, spiralized with BLADE D, noodles trimmed
- 3 large parsnips, peeled, spiralized with BLADE D, noodles trimmed
- Chopped fresh curly parsley, for garnish

The carrot and parsnip noodles can be frozen after they're cooked, so this entire dish can be made in advance and enjoyed all week long.

1 Preheat the oven to 400 degrees.

2 Heat 1 tablespoon of the olive oil in a Dutch oven or stockpot over medium heat. When the oil is shimmering, add the beef and cook until browned, 7 to 10 minutes. Using tongs, transfer the beef to a bowl, reserving any juices in the pot.

3 Add the garlic to the pot and cook for 30 seconds or until fragrant. Add the onion, red pepper flakes, and celery and cook for 2 minutes or until the vegetables are sweating. Return the beef to the pot. Stir in the Worcestershire sauce, thyme, and cayenne. Season with salt and black pepper and add the broth and tomatoes with their juices. Place the bay leaves on top. Cover, increase the heat to high, and bring to a boil. Reduce the heat to medium-low and simmer for 40 minutes. Remove the cover and simmer for 35 minutes more or until the stew has thickened.

4 Before serving, heat the remaining tablespoon of oil in a large skillet over medium heat. When the oil is shimmering, add the carrot and parsnip noodles, season with salt and pepper, and cook for 5 to 7 minutes or until al dente. Discard the bay leaves. Divide the noodles among four bowls and top each with beef stew. Garnish with parsley and serve.

Avocado "Toast"
with Cherry Tomato Jam

Gluten-Free
Paleo
Dairy-Free

TIME TO PREP 20 minutes
TIME TO COOK 45 minutes
SERVES 4

NUTRITIONAL INFORMATION
Calories: 352
Fat: 17 g
Sodium: 93 mg
Carbohydrate: 45 g
Fiber: 12 g
Sugar: 21 g
Protein: 8 g

ALSO WORKS WELL WITH
Sweet Potato, Rutabaga

Whoever invented avocado toast is an absolute genius—and should totally get paid royalties! With creamy, chunky fresh avocado mashed and smeared onto a thick, grainy toast, no wonder it's such a wildly popular dish. With so many variations of toppings, it's a different meal every time. My absolute favorite version is one that can only be found at Jack's Wife Freda in New York City. They use a wide, thick piece of sourdough bread that's lightly toasted and topped with cherry tomato jam. This spiralized version is a gluten-free, nutritious take, and it has made my home just a little bit trendier.

For the jam

1½ pounds cherry tomatoes, halved
2 tablespoons coconut sugar or honey
2 tablespoons apple cider vinegar
Juice of 1 lemon
½ teaspoon ground cinnamon
¼ teaspoon red pepper flakes
1 teaspoon salt
Pepper
¼ to ½ cup low-sodium vegetable broth (optional)

For the toast

Cooking spray
4 large parsnips, peeled, spiralized with BLADE D, noodles trimmed
Salt and pepper
3 large eggs, beaten
2 tablespoons olive oil
1 avocado, mashed
Sea salt
½ cup microgreens, for garnish (optional)

1 Make the jam. In a large saucepan, combine all the ingredients for the jam except the broth and bring to a boil over high heat. Reduce the heat to medium-low and simmer, stirring occasionally, for 45 minutes to 1 hour or until mixture thickens and is syrupy (with some chunks of tomatoes remaining). If the jam needs to cook longer to further break down the cherry tomatoes but most of the liquid has evaporated, add the broth as needed.

2 Meanwhile, make the toast. Place a large nonstick skillet over medium heat and coat with cooking spray. When water flicked onto the skillet sizzles, add the parsnip noodles and season with salt and pepper. Cook for 5 to 7 minutes or until softened and lightly browned. Transfer to a medium bowl and let cool for 1 to 2 minutes. Add the eggs and stir to coat.

3 Fill four ramekins halfway with the noodles. Cover each with a piece of foil or wax paper, pressing it down firmly onto the noodles to compress them. Refrigerate for at least 15 minutes to set.

recipe continues

4 In the same skillet in which you cooked the parsnips, heat 1 tablespoon of the olive oil over medium heat. When the oil is shimmering, add the parsnip buns two at a time, flipping each out of its ramekin into the skillet and patting the bottom until the bun falls out.

5 Cook for 3 minutes or until set, being sure to push in any stray noodles. Carefully flip and cook for 2 to 3 minutes more or until the buns are completely set and browned on both sides, pressing down with the back of a spatula. Repeat with the remaining buns, using the remaining 1 tablespoon olive oil.

6 Smear the buns with the mashed avocado, dividing it evenly. Season with sea salt and add a dollop of tomato jam. Garnish with microgreens, if desired.

If you don't have time to make the cherry tomato jam, you can use jarred instead. Just make sure it's no sugar added.

Parsnip Pasta
with Caramelized Leeks and Ham

Gluten-Free
Dairy-Free (Opt.)
Low-Cal
Saves Well

TIME TO PREP 10 minutes
TIME TO COOK 25 minutes
SERVES 4

NUTRITIONAL INFORMATION
Calories: 176
Fat: 3 g
Carbohydrates: 25 g
Sodium: 600 mg
Fiber: 6 g
Protein: 11 g
Sugar: 9 g

Using spiralized veggies as a pasta substitute is not only a less processed, cleaner alternative, it also adds flavor. While zucchini is on the low end of the flavor spectrum (it's a very mild-tasting vegetable), parsnips offer a nutty sweetness, placing them higher on that same spectrum. Here, the parsnips bring out the sweetness in ham, and the leeks add balance with their earthiness and offer a smooth, soft texture overall.

½ cup diced ham

2 cups sliced leeks

2 tablespoon minced shallots

Salt and pepper

3 large parsnips, peeled, spiralized with BLADE D, noodles trimmed

¼ cup grated Parmesan cheese

1 Heat a large skillet over medium-high heat. When water flicked onto the pan sizzles, add the ham. Cook for 7 to 10 minutes or until the ham starts to brown. Using a slotted spoon, transfer the ham to a plate and set aside.

2 Immediately add the leeks and shallots to the pan and season with salt and pepper. Cook for 5 minutes or until the leeks are wilted and almost caramelized. Set the leeks aside on the plate with the ham and add the parsnip noodles to the same pan. Season with salt and pepper. Cover and cook for 5 to 7 minutes or until al dente. Uncover and stir in the ham and leeks.

3 Remove the pan from the heat and stir in the Parmesan, tossing to combine. Divide the pasta into plates and serve immediately.

Broccoli Rabe and Sausage Parsnip Pasta

∼∼   Gluten-Free
∼∼   Dairy-Free (opt.)
  Low-Cal
  Saves Well

TIME TO PREP 15 minutes

TIME TO COOK 15 minutes

SERVES 4

NUTRITIONAL INFORMATION
Calories: 213
Fat: 11 g
Sodium: 449 mg
Carbohydrate: 18 g
Fiber: 7 g
Sugar: 5 g
Protein: 15 g

ALSO WORKS WELL WITH
Zucchini, Butternut Squash,
Celeriac, Rutabaga, Turnip

If I had a nickel for every time my grandfather served us broccoli rabe and sausage, this cookbook would be gold-plated. This combination is classically Italian, thanks to the undeniable spicy power of the sausage and the slightly bitter kick of the broccoli rabe. The parsnip noodles become the star of this dish, absorbing the sauce created by the olive oil and sausage juices. The Parmesan cheese ties everything together, bringing in a silky texture, a slightly salty taste, and a savory aroma. *Salute!*

1 bunch broccoli rabe

2 hot Italian sausage links, casings removed

½ teaspoon dried oregano

2 parsnips, peeled, spiralized with BLADE D,
   noodles trimmed

2 garlic cloves, minced

¼ teaspoon red pepper flakes

   Salt and pepper

½ cup low-sodium chicken broth

½ cup grated Parmesan cheese

1 tablespoon chopped fresh parsley

If you don't like the bitterness of broccoli rabe, try parboiling it after trimming. Bring a large pot filled halfway with water to a boil, add the broccoli rabe, cook for 3 minutes, then transfer to a bowl of ice water. Otherwise, broccolini or plain broccoli are great choices with similar textures.

1 Rinse the broccoli rabe and pat dry. Cut off most of the stems (the thickest parts). Using a vegetable peeler, pull some skin off the stems, and continue to until you hit the leaves. Chop into 1-inch pieces and set aside.

2 Place a large skillet over medium heat. When water flicked onto the skillet sizzles, add the sausage and oregano and cook, breaking up the meat with a wooden spoon, for 6 to 8 minutes or until browned and cooked through. Using tongs or a slotted spoon, transfer the sausage to a plate.

3 Immediately add the broccoli rabe, parsnip noodles, garlic, and red pepper flakes to the skillet. Season with salt and black pepper, then add the broth. Cook until the broth has reduced and the parsnip noodles are al dente, about 5 minutes.

4 Return the sausage to the skillet, add the cheese, and stir to combine. Remove from the heat and toss the ingredients to combine fully.

5 Divide among four plates, garnish with the parsley, and serve.

Pear

When I want a piece of fruit that's slightly less sweet and a bit softer and juicier, I always opt for a pear. The perfect winter fruit, pears have soft, buttery flesh and delicate skin. They come in many varieties, all unique in flavor, shape, and size. Some popular types include Bosc, green and red Anjou, Bartlett, Concorde, and Forelle. The easiest type of pear to spiralize with the highest noodle yield is the Asian pear, a round, light-brown type similar in shape to an apple. The best part is that it requires no preparation to spiralize, aside from snapping off the stem.

Pears are readily available in grocery stores year-round. When selecting one, make sure it's firm—not squishy, but also not rock hard. Overripe pears will turn into mush on the spiralizers; underripe will work, but they won't taste as flavorful or fresh.

NUTRITIONAL BENEFITS: Pears are touted as one of the highest-fiber fruits, fighting bloat and keeping cholesterol levels down. There's also an antioxidant in their skin that can help lower blood pressure and possibly even fight cancer.

PREPARATION AND STORAGE: Remove the stem prior to spiralizing. Peeled pears and pear noodles oxidize when exposed to air, so store them in a container filled with water with a little bit of lemon juice in the refrigerator for up to 2 days.

BEST BLADES TO USE
- Blade A
- Blade C
- Blade D

BEST COOKING METHODS
- Raw
- Bake at 350 degrees for 15 minutes

Grilled Halloumi, Lentils, and Arugula
with Roasted Fennel and Pear Noodles

Vegetarian
Gluten-Free

TIME TO PREP 20 minutes
TIME TO COOK 45 minutes
SERVES 4

NUTRITIONAL INFORMATION
Calories: 430
Fat: 29 g
Sodium: 642 mg
Carbohydrate: 28 g
Fiber: 6 g
Sugar: 7 g
Protein: 23 g

ALSO WORKS WELL WITH
Apple

My mother always tells me I make the best salads. A salad, to me, isn't a bunch of greens mixed together in a bowl. In my mind, it's a plate of freshly prepared ingredients that happen to sit atop a bed of greens. This recipe is a prime example—with roasted sweet fennel, crunchy pear noodles, filling lentils, and warm halloumi, there's so much to enjoy. After you try this dish, you'll never think of salads the same way again.

1 fennel bulb, chopped into wedges

1 tablespoon extra-virgin olive oil

1 tablespoon balsamic vinegar

½ teaspoon garlic powder

Salt and pepper

1 cup lentils, rinsed

For the dressing

3 tablespoons extra-virgin olive oil

2 tablespoons fresh lemon juice

1 teaspoon Dijon mustard

1 teaspoon honey

Cooking spray

8 ounces halloumi cheese, cut into 2-inch-long slices, about ¼ inch thick

1 *Bosc pear*

5 cups baby arugula

If you can't find halloumi cheese, feta works well, too.

1 Preheat the oven to 400 degrees. Line a baking sheet with parchment paper.

2 In a large bowl, toss together the fennel, olive oil, vinegar, and garlic powder. Transfer the wedges to the prepared baking sheet, season with salt and pepper, and bake for 30 minutes, flipping once halfway through, until the fennel begins to caramelize.

3 Meanwhile, place the lentils in a medium pot and add water to cover by 1 inch. Bring the water to a boil over high heat, then reduce the heat to low and simmer for 25 minutes or until tender. Drain, pat dry, and set aside.

4 While the lentils simmer, whisk together all the ingredients for the dressing in a large bowl.

5 Heat a grill pan or large skillet over medium-high heat and coat with cooking spray. When water flicked onto the pan sizzles, add the halloumi and grill for 2 to 3 minutes per side or until lightly charred and marks appear. Transfer to a plate.

6 When the fennel is done roasting, spiralize the pear with **BLADE D** and trim the noodles. Add the pear noodles, roasted fennel, and arugula to the bowl with the dressing and toss to coat. Divide the salad and lentils among four plates. Top with the grilled halloumi and serve immediately.

Chai-Spiced Pear Oatmeal

Vegan
Vegetarian
Gluten-Free
Dairy-Free
Low-Cal

TIME TO PREP 5 minutes
TIME TO COOK 20 minutes
SERVES 2

NUTRITIONAL INFORMATION
Calories: 244
Fat: 11 g
Sodium: 121 mg
Carbohydrate: 32 g
Fiber: 6 g
Sugar: 9 g
Protein: 6 g

ALSO WORKS WELL WITH
Apple

I'm imagining you in a gloriously chunky sweater on a cold, gently snowy day, hovering over the warmth of your stovetop, stirring these spiced pear noodles as you wait patiently for your morning oatmeal to fluff up. The chai flavors will fill your kitchen with coziness, and each bite will relax and nourish you. This oatmeal is like a snug blanket that will warm you even on the chilliest days.

¾ cup gluten-free rolled oats

1 teaspoon coconut oil

1 *Anjou pear, spiralized with* BLADE D, *noodles trimmed*

1½ cups plain unsweetened almond milk

¼ teaspoon pure vanilla extract

¼ teaspoon ground cinnamon

⅛ teaspoon ground cardamom

1 teaspoon maple syrup

2 tablespoons walnut halves

Cardamom is a key spice in chai. But if you don't have it in your pantry, that's okay—leave it out! This oatmeal can stand on its own even without it.

1 Bring 2 cups water to a boil in a medium saucepan over high heat. Add the oats and return to a boil, then reduce the heat to low and simmer for about 10 minutes or until all the water has been absorbed and the oatmeal is fluffy.

2 Meanwhile, heat the coconut oil in a medium skillet over medium-high heat. When the oil has melted, add the pear noodles, almond milk, vanilla, cinnamon, cardamom, and maple syrup. Stir to combine and simmer until the milk has evaporated and the sauce has thickened, about 15 minutes.

3 Meanwhile, place a small skillet over medium-high heat and add the walnuts. Toast, stirring, for 5 minutes or until fragrant. Remove from the pan.

4 Divide the oatmeal between two bowls and top with the pear mixture and the toasted walnuts.

Pear Noodle Bowl
with Maple-Roasted Acorn Squash and Pomegranate Dressing

Vegan
Vegetarian
Gluten-Free
Dairy-Free
Low-Cal

TIME TO PREP 15 minutes
TIME TO COOK 45 minutes
SERVES 4

NUTRITIONAL INFORMATION
Calories: 259
Fat: 7 g
Sodium: 5 mg
Carbohydrate: 50 g
Fiber: 8 g
Sugar: 21 g
Protein: 6 g

ALSO WORKS WELL WITH
Apple

Every autumn, I look forward to two things: the crispy colorful leaves on the ground and the large cold-weather squashes at the farmer's market. I always end up buying too many, because I get so excited when they first show up. They're decorative thanks to their large shape and gorgeous color, and I love displaying them in a bowl in my kitchen. In an attempt to save them from going bad, I always slice them up and roast them into velvety slivers. Having roasted squash on hand enables you to throw together a healthy and beautiful meal in a pinch, since the squash is full of hearty, filling dietary fiber. With the tastiness of pomegranate and pear added here, you might even think Mother Nature intended these seasonal ingredients to be eaten together.

1 acorn squash, quartered and seeded

2 teaspoons extra-virgin olive oil

4 teaspoons maple syrup

Salt and pepper

½ cup dry red quinoa, rinsed

For the dressing

¼ cup pomegranate juice

¼ cup extra-virgin olive oil

2 tablespoons apple cider vinegar

½ cup pomegranate seeds

1 teaspoon maple syrup

2 red Anjou pears, spiralized with BLADE D, noodles trimmed

¼ cup roughly chopped whole almonds

Other squashes work well here, too. Try butternut or delicata to switch things up.

1 Preheat the oven to 400 degrees. Line a baking sheet with parchment paper. Halve each squash quarter and lay them out on the baking sheet, spacing them apart. Drizzle with the olive oil and maple syrup, dividing them evenly over each slice. Season with salt and pepper. Roast for 35 to 40 minutes or until tender when pierced with a fork.

2 While the squash roasts, place the quinoa and 2 cups water in a medium pot. Cover and bring to a boil, then uncover, reduce the heat to medium-low, and cook for 15 minutes or until quinoa is fluffy. Transfer to a large bowl.

3 Make the dressing. Whisk together all the ingredients for the dressing in a small bowl.

4 Add the pear noodles and almonds to the bowl with the quinoa. Pour the dressing over the mixture and toss to combine thoroughly. Divide among four bowls and top each with two squash slices.

Cinnamon and Pecan Pear Noodle Pancakes

Vegetarian
Gluten-Free
Paleo
Dairy-Free
Low-Cal

TIME TO PREP 15 minutes
TIME TO COOK 20 minutes
SERVES 4

NUTRITIONAL INFORMATION
Calories: 155
Fat: 8 g
Sodium: 113 mg
Carbohydrate: 18 g
Fiber: 2 g
Sugar: 2 g
Protein: 4 g

ALSO WORKS WELL WITH
Apple

If you're ever just yearning for a stack of pancakes, my advice is to go for it. Life's too short to second-guess breakfast happiness! And this healthier version is sure to satisfy your hankering. These pancakes have a surprisingly sweet crunch, thanks to the pear noodles and chopped pecans. They're so good and good *for* you, you just may start craving them more often—and that's okay!

1⅓ cups gluten-free baking flour

1 teaspoon baking powder

½ teaspoon baking soda

1 teaspoon ground cinnamon

½ teaspoon sea salt

2 large eggs, beaten

¾ cup plain unsweetened almond milk

1 teaspoon pure vanilla extract

2 tablespoons coconut oil, melted and cooled to room temperature

1 *Anjou or Bosc pear*

¼ cup pecans, chopped

Cooking spray

Maple syrup, for serving

If you're short on time, use a gluten-free pancake mix to create the pancakes themselves and simply stir in the rest of the ingredients.

1 In a medium bowl, whisk together the flour, baking powder, baking soda, cinnamon, and salt. In a separate medium bowl, whisk together the eggs, almond milk, vanilla, and coconut oil. Fold the wet ingredients into the dry ingredients and stir together until smooth.

2 Spiralize the pear with **BLADE D** and break up the noodles with your hands. Add the pear noodles and pecans to the batter and mix to combine thoroughly.

3 Place a large skillet over medium heat and coat with cooking spray. When water flicked onto the skillet sizzles, ladle on the pancake batter—about ⅓ cup for 10 to 12 mini pancakes or ½ cup for four large pancakes—spreading it out with the back of the ladle to flatten. Cook for about 3 minutes. When the tops are bubbling and the edges are slightly dry, flip and cook for 3 minutes more, flattening with a spatula. Transfer the pancakes to serving plates and repeat with the remaining batter.

4 Drizzle maple syrup over the pancakes and serve.

Easy Pork Chops
with Shredded Brussels Sprout, Kale, and Pear Noodle Salad

Since my tastes can skew more toward the veg side and less toward the carnivore side, learning to cook meat properly was a process. One of Lu's favorites is the pork chop, so that was first on my list. I've found an easy and quick way to cook a pork chop simply but flavorfully. This crunchy, multidimensional salad, packed with nutrients from the leafy kale, healthy fats from the almonds, and soft, seasonal flavor from the sweet pear noodles and Brussels sprouts, is the perfect complement, and together they make a filling meal.

Gluten-Free
Paleo
Dairy-Free
Saves Well

TIME TO PREP 20 minutes
TIME TO COOK 15 minutes
SERVES 4

NUTRITIONAL INFORMATION
Calories: 390
Fat: 24 g
Sodium: 79 mg
Carbohydrate: 17 g
Fiber: 4 g
Sugar: 10 g
Protein: 29 g

ALSO WORKS WELL WITH
Apple

2 tablespoons plus 2 teaspoons extra-virgin olive oil

4 boneless pork chops

Salt and pepper

1 tablespoon maple syrup

3 tablespoons sliced blanched almonds

For the vinaigrette
2 tablespoons extra-virgin olive oil

1 tablespoon minced shallot

Salt and pepper

1 teaspoon honey

2 tablespoons apple cider vinegar

½ teaspoon Dijon mustard

6 ounces Brussels sprouts (about 2 cups), ends trimmed

1 *Bosc or Asian pear, spiralized with* **BLADE D**

1 cup finely chopped curly kale leaves

1 Preheat the oven to 400 degrees.

2 Heat 1 teaspoon of olive oil in a large ovenproof skillet over medium-high heat. Rub each pork chop with 1 teaspoon of the olive oil, then season generously with salt and pepper. When the oil is shimmering, add the pork chops and sear for about 3 minutes per side or until golden brown.

3 While the pork chops cook, whisk together the remaining 1 tablespoon oil and the maple syrup. Pour the mixture over the pork chops and transfer the pan to the oven. Roast until cooked through, 7 to 9 minutes (if using a meat thermometer, the pork chops should register 140 degrees at the thickest part). Transfer to a plate and let stand, undisturbed, for at least 5 minutes.

4 Place a medium skillet over medium-high heat. When water flicked onto the skillet sizzles, add the sliced almonds and toast, stirring frequently, until lightly browned and fragrant, about 3 minutes. Remove the almonds and set aside.

5 Make the vinaigrette. Whisk together all the ingredients for the vinaigrette in a large bowl. Taste and adjust the seasoning to your preferences.

6 Pulse the Brussels sprouts in a food processor until shredded and thoroughly chopped. Transfer to the bowl with the dressing and add the toasted almonds, pear noodles, and kale. Toss to combine thoroughly.

7 Divide the Brussels sprouts mixture among four plates and top each with a pork chop. Pour any pan juices over the top.

Radish

BI—that is, Before Inspiralizing—I exclusively consumed radishes raw in salads or pickled in sandwiches like banh mi. Now I love making radish rice, radish pasta, and radish noodle soups. I do still enjoy radishes in salads, but now they're totally different. As you'll quickly realize, or maybe already have, simply changing the shape of a vegetable alters the way it feels on the palate, due to its different surface area and texture.

There are many kinds of radishes. Black radishes have a spicy taste, pairing well with meats and hearty seafood and equalizing their flavors. Daikons have a mild taste. I love to spiralize brilliantly pink watermelon radishes, which tend to grow wider, making them perfect for spiralizing! It can be tough to find other radishes that are large enough to spiralize. Your best bet is to stick to black and daikon radishes, which typically grow abundantly. If you do find a large ruby radish, snag it!

NUTRITIONAL BENEFITS: Daikon is an effective diuretic, which aids digestion and cleanses the body and palate, helping to improve kidney function. Other radish varieties carry similar powers.

PREPARATION AND STORAGE: Peel the radish entirely. Slice the ends off to leave flat, even surfaces. Store in an airtight container in the refrigerator for 5 to 7 days.

BEST BLADES TO USE

- Blade A
- Blade C
- Blade D

BEST COOKING METHODS

- Raw
- Simmer or boil in a soup
- Sauté over medium heat for 5 to 7 minutes

Hot-and-Sour Soup
with Daikon Noodles

Vegetarian
Dairy-Free
One Pot
Low-Cal
Saves Well

TIME TO PREP 30 minutes
TIME TO COOK 15 minutes
SERVES 4

NUTRITIONAL INFORMATION
Calories: 110
Fat: 5 g
Sodium: 714 mg
Carbohydrate: 12 g
Fiber: 4 g
Sugar: 5 g
Protein: 8 g

ALSO WORKS WELL WITH
Zucchini, Turnip, Carrot

When I was growing up, my mother always ordered hot-and-sour soup whenever we got Chinese food. She claimed it cleared her sinuses and led to the eventual curing of any cold. While I'm not sure hot-and-sour soup has such magical medicinal powers, it's definitely one of the more flavorful, robust soups out there. With wispy eggs, salty broth, and soft simmered vegetables, this soup satisfies the senses. The daikon noodles transform this takeout staple into a hearty noodle soup.

1 **dried chile pepper, seeded and chopped**

4 cups **low-sodium chicken broth**

1 tablespoon **low-sodium soy sauce or tamari**

6 **dried shiitake mushrooms, rehydrated in hot water and thinly sliced**

1 **(6-ounce) can bamboo shoots, drained and cut into matchsticks**

¾ cup **firm tofu, drained and cut into matchsticks (see page 98)**

¼ teaspoon **ground white pepper**

¼ cup **white vinegar**

1 *large daikon radish, peeled, spiralized with* **BLADE D,** *noodles trimmed*

1 **large egg, lightly beaten**

1 teaspoon **sesame oil**

Salt

1 **scallion, thinly sliced**

1 Combine the chiles, broth, and soy sauce in a large stockpot with a lid and bring to a boil over high heat. Add the mushrooms and bamboo shoots. Reduce the heat to low, cover, and simmer for about 3 minutes or until the mushrooms are softened.

2 Add the tofu, white pepper, and vinegar, increase the heat to high, and return to a boil. Stir in the daikon noodles and cook for 3 minutes more or until al dente.

3 Turn off the heat and add the egg, stirring gently to create wisps. Stir in the sesame oil. Taste and season with salt, if needed.

4 Ladle the soup into four bowls and garnish with the scallions.

Black Radish and Orange Salad

with Radicchio and Salmon Cakes

Gluten-Free

TIME TO PREP 20 minutes
TIME TO COOK 10 minutes
SERVES 2

NUTRITIONAL INFORMATION
Calories: 323
Fat: 15 g
Sodium: 587 mg
Carbohydrate: 19 g
Fiber: 4 g
Sugar: 8 g
Protein: 28 g

ALSO WORKS WELL WITH
Carrot, Potato

This salad is a prime example of how spiralized veggies can be used to tactfully infuse textures and flavors into meals. If you were to add sliced black radishes to this salad, the bitterness would overpower the other flavors, rendering the meal somewhat unpalatable. But by spiralizing it instead, you're able to enhance the sweet orange and savory, fragrant salmon by adding a tart bite with each twirly strand.

For the salmon cakes
- ½ pound salmon fillet, skinless, cut into cubes
- 2 teaspoons Dijon mustard
- 1 small garlic clove, sliced
- ¼ teaspoon grated lemon zest
- 1 teaspoon fresh lemon juice
- 1 tablespoon minced fresh parsley
- 1 shallot, minced
- 1 tablespoon extra-virgin olive oil
- Salt and pepper

For the vinaigrette
- 2 tablespoons nonfat plain Greek yogurt
- 1 tablespoon extra-virgin olive oil
- 1 tablespoon red wine vinegar
- 1 tablespoon jarred small capers, drained
- ¼ teaspoon garlic powder
- 2 teaspoons fresh lemon juice
- 1 teaspoon Dijon mustard
- Salt and pepper

For the salad
- 1 black radish, peeled, spiralized with **BLADE D**, noodles trimmed
- 1 navel orange, peeled and chopped
- 4 cups chopped radicchio

1 Make the salmon cakes. Place the salmon, mustard, garlic, lemon zest and juice, and parsley in a food processor. Pulse just until the large pieces of salmon break down, taking care not to overpulse. Transfer the mixture to a medium bowl and stir in the shallot. Using your hands, form the mixture into four 2- to 3-inch patties.

2 Heat the olive oil in a large skillet over medium-high heat. When the oil is shimmering, add the salmon cakes in a single layer, working in batches if necessary. Season the tops with salt and pepper and cook for 2 to 3 minutes per side or until browned on the outside and cooked through.

3 Meanwhile, make the vinaigrette. Whisk together all the ingredients for the vinaigrette in a large bowl. Taste and adjust the seasoning to your preference. Add the radish noodles, orange, and radicchio. Toss to coat.

4 Divide the salad between two plates and top each with two salmon cakes.

These salmon cakes can be formed into larger patties and work well as burgers, too.

Ginger-Crab Fried Daikon Rice

Dairy-Free
Low-Cal

TIME TO PREP 15 minutes
TIME TO COOK 15 minutes
SERVES 4

NUTRITIONAL INFORMATION
Calories: 147
Fat: 9 g
Sodium: 1025 mg
Carbohydrate: 6 g
Fiber: 2 g
Sugar: 3 g
Protein: 12 g

ALSO WORKS WELL WITH
Kohlrabi, Turnip

Whenever a New York City chef opens up a sister restaurant in your city, you know you're in the right spot. As a lover of eclectic foods, I was excited to have a chef like Dale Talde enter the scene. Now a go-to of ours, Talde is a popular, casual Asian-American spot known for its outstanding food and lively atmosphere. Every time we're there, we order the Blue Crab Fried Rice, which Lu and I devour together. This spiralized version mimics many of its diverse flavors, so I can enjoy the dish at home in my sweatpants.

1 tablespoon coconut oil

1 garlic clove, minced

1 (1-inch) piece fresh ginger, peeled and minced

¼ teaspoon red pepper flakes (or more if you like more spice)

2 medium daikon radishes, peeled, spiralized with **BLADE D**, then riced and drained

2 large eggs, beaten

1 tablespoon soy sauce

2 to 3 tablespoons fish sauce (I like Red Boat)

1 cup jumbo lump crabmeat

¼ cup roughly chopped cashews

2 scallions, green parts only, diced

¼ cup fresh cilantro

Hot sauce or chile oil, for garnish

1 Heat the coconut oil in a large skillet over medium heat. When the oil has melted, add the garlic, ginger, and red pepper flakes and cook for 1 minute or until fragrant. Stir in the daikon rice and cook for 2 minutes or until softened.

2 Push the rice to the edges of the pan, creating a cavity in the center. Add the eggs to the center and stir continuously to scramble until cooked. Stir the rice back in, combining all the ingredients. Stir in the soy sauce and fish sauce. Fold in the crab and cook for 2 minutes to heat through.

3 Remove the pot from the heat and stir in the cashews, scallions, and cilantro. Garnish with the hot sauce or chile oil, if desired.

There's a big difference between lump and jumbo lump crabmeat, so be sure to pay attention at the store!

Watermelon Radish Nourish Salad

with Lemon-Ginger Vinaigrette and Vegan Parmesan

Vegan
Vegetarian
Gluten-Free
Paleo
Dairy-Free
No Cook

TIME TO PREP 30 minutes

SERVES 2

NUTRITIONAL INFORMATION
Calories: 390
Fat: 36 g
Sodium: 171 mg
Carbohydrate: 15 g
Fiber: 6 g
Sugar: 6 g
Protein: 6 g

ALSO WORKS WELL WITH
Golden Beet, Kohlrabi, Jícama

Sometimes you crave a big, heaping bowl of greens. Or is that just me? There's something comforting about making your own salad—adding whatever you want to it and tossing everything together. Usually when I make salads, I use up whatever I have in my fridge and it becomes one of those "everything but the kitchen sink" meals that I eat out of a big mixing bowl. But there are also times when I want a simple salad with minimal ingredients. I want to sit down and slowly enjoy a nourishing dish, concentrating on chewing, breathing, and feeling my body rejuvenate. This dish is just that: a truly enjoyable salad with stunning watermelon radish slices that pop against dark, leafy kale. The vegan Parmesan adds a graceful sprinkling of nutty flavor.

For the vegan Parmesan
- ¼ cup pine nuts
- 1 teaspoon roasted unsalted sunflower seeds
- 1½ teaspoons nutritional yeast

For the dressing
- Grated zest of ½ lemon
- 1 tablespoon fresh lemon juice
- 1½ teaspoons grated fresh ginger
- 2½ tablespoons extra-virgin olive oil
- 1 teaspoon honey
- 1 tablespoon minced fresh parsley
- Salt and pepper

For the salad
- 1 large watermelon radish
- 4 cups shredded Swiss chard
- ½ avocado, thinly sliced

1 Make the vegan Parmesan. Place all the ingredients for the vegan Parmesan in a food processor and pulse until ground.

2 Make the dressing. In a large bowl, whisk together all the ingredients for the dressing. Taste and adjust the seasoning to your preferences.

3 Make the salad. Slice the watermelon radish halfway through lengthwise to create a slit, being careful not to pierce any farther than its center. Spiralize with **BLADE A** and trim the noodles. Add the noodles and the chard to the bowl with the dressing and toss to combine. Divide the salad between two places and top each with avocado. Finish with the vegan Parmesan.

This vegan Parmesan cheese can be used on pretty much anything in place of regular Parmesan cheese, so grab a sticky note and bookmark the page!

Grilled Steak
with Mustard Greens and Radish Noodles

I've never really been a steak person. I love a masterfully braised short rib or a sumptuous Bolognese, but a slab of steak doesn't appeal to me. The only way I've ever enjoyed it has been sliced on a salad. There's something about having a green vegetable in every bite that makes the steak more appealing to me. Whatever your reason for liking steak salads, this one is simple and honest, and it has plenty of crunch.

Gluten-Free
Paleo
Dairy-Free

TIME TO PREP 15 minutes
TIME TO COOK 15 minutes
SERVES 4

NUTRITIONAL INFORMATION
Calories: 413
Fat: 30 g
Sodium: 347 mg
Carbohydrate: 8 g
Fiber: 3 g
Sugar: 5 g
Protein: 27 g

ALSO WORKS WELL WITH
Pear, Potato

1 pound New York strip steak or your preferred cut

Salt and pepper

1 tablespoon extra-virgin olive oil

For the dressing

¼ cup extra-virgin olive oil

2 tablespoons balsamic vinegar

1 teaspoon honey

¼ teaspoon garlic powder

1 teaspoon Dijon mustard

Salt and pepper

For the salad

4 cups chopped mustard greens

1 *large radish, peeled, spiralized with* **BLADE D**, *noodles trimmed*

1 cup chopped endives

1 Season the steak generously with salt and pepper on both sides.

2 Heat a grill pan over medium-high heat. When the pan is hot, add the olive oil. When the oil is shimmering, add the steak and cook for about 4 minutes per side for medium-rare or 6 minutes per side for medium-well. Transfer to a carving or cutting board to rest for 3 to 5 minutes. Slice the steak thinly (about ¼-inch-thick slices) against the grain.

3 While the steak cooks, make the salad. Whisk together all the ingredients for the dressing in a large bowl. Add the mustard greens, radish noodles, and endives and toss to combine.

4 Divide the salad among four plates and top with slices of steak. Pour any juices from the cutting board back over the steak.

Watermelon radish, black radish, and daikon all work well in this recipe. If mustard greens aren't your favorite, swap in spinach or another mild green.

Clear Immunity Soup
with Daikon Noodles

In an attempt to bolster our immune systems and avoid falling ill in the winter, many of us drink green juices, have hot water with lemon, fix matcha tea lattes, and sip bone broth. My favorite way to ward off any sickness is to whip up this clear immunity-boosting soup. The simple healing powers of garlic and ginger will leave you feeling nourished, rejuvenated, and ready to conquer the chilly temperatures. It's a great way to protect yourself from the person next to you in line who just sneezed all over your shoulder!

Vegan
Vegetarian
Gluten-Free
Paleo
Dairy-Free
Low-Cal
One Pot

TIME TO PREP 20 minutes
TIME TO COOK 30 minutes
SERVES 4

NUTRITIONAL INFORMATION
Calories: 70
Fat: 3 g
Sodium: 25 mg
Carbohydrate: 8 g
Fiber: 2 g
Sugar: 3 g
Protein: 3 g

ALSO WORKS WELL WITH
Carrot, Zucchini, Turnip

---

1 tablespoon extra-virgin olive oil

1 *small white onion, peeled spiralized with* **BLADE A**, *noodles trimmed*

2 celery stalks, diced

2 scallions, sliced, white and green parts kept separate

3 garlic cloves, thinly sliced

2 teaspoons finely grated fresh ginger

Salt

¼ teaspoon white pepper

8 ounces button mushrooms, trimmed and thinly sliced

1 medium daikon radish, peeled, spiralized with *BLADE C*, noodles trimmed

1 cup pea shoots

1 Heat the oil in a large stockpot over medium heat. When the oil is shimmering, add the onion, celery, white parts of the scallions, garlic, and ginger. Season with salt and cook for 3 minutes or until the onion is softened.

2 Add 8 cups water and the white pepper. Increase the heat to medium-high and bring the soup to a strong simmer. Cook for 10 minutes, then add the mushrooms and daikon noodles and simmer for 5 minutes more or until the daikon is al dente.

3 Ladle the soup into bowls. Top with the pea shoots and scallion greens.

For more flavor, use chicken broth instead of water. Even better if it's homemade!

Rutabaga

Like celery roots, rutabagas are tough cookies—er, veggies. They have a very waxy exterior and take time to properly peel. They tend to be larger in both size and weight for a vegetable. But don't let all that intimidate you—once you've prepped your rutabaga, it spiralizes easily and yields loads of noodles. Rutabagas are perhaps the most resilient of spiralized vegetables, able to withstand all types of cooking methods and hold all kinds of sauces.

Raw rutabaga generally carries a mild and slightly bitter taste, as it's in the same family as the turnip. (In fact, rutabagas are sometimes known as wax turnips and Swedish turnips, or swedes.) But once it's cooked, rutabaga steals the show, with a golden color and a slight sweetness, making them popular mashed, roasted, and stirred into stews. They're less starchy and therefore less carbohydrate-heavy than regular potatoes, so they may be a better option for you, depending on your goals.

When picking out a rutabaga at the store, look for one that's not too heavy or large (under 6 inches in diameter, preferably). Properly ripened rutabagas should have a purple-tinged skin without any major blemishes or a shriveled appearance.

NUTRITIONAL BENEFITS: A solid source of zinc, rutabagas help support the immune system and metabolism. They are also high in vitamin C and dietary fiber.

PREPARATION AND STORAGE: Peel the rutabaga entirely and slice the ends off to leave flat, even surfaces. If the rutabaga is large, to get better leverage, slice each side off to leave flat, even surfaces until you have a thinner, more rectangular vegetable that's no more than 6 to 7 inches wide. Store in an airtight container in the refrigerator for up to 6 days. Rutabaga noodles can be frozen for up to 8 months for future use.

BEST BLADES TO USE
- Blade A
- Blade B
- Blade C
- Blade D

BEST COOKING METHODS
- Boil for 5 to 10 minutes
- Sauté over medium-high heat for 10 to 15 minutes
- Roast at 425 degrees for 20 to 30 minutes, depending on which blade was used

Thai Almond and Pork Curry
with Rutabaga Noodles

〰 Gluten-Free
〰 Paleo
〰 Dairy-Free

TIME TO PREP 15 minutes
TIME TO COOK 30 minutes
SERVES 4

NUTRITIONAL INFORMATION
Calories: 330
Fat: 14 g
Sodium: 992 mg
Carbohydrate: 22 g
Fiber: 3 g
Sugar: 15 g
Protein: 29 g

ALSO WORKS WELL WITH
Zucchini, Sweet Potato,
Turnip, Kohlrabi, Carrot

Where do you stand in the almond butter versus peanut butter battle? Nine times out of ten I'm on team almond, simply based on flavor alone. Whichever way you sway, trust me: almond butter is the way to go in this recipe. The rutabaga makes a hearty noodle, similar in texture to chewy soba. The light pork doesn't overpower the curry, and absorbs the Thai flavors well.

2 small rutabagas, peeled, spiralized with **BLADE C**, noodles trimmed

Salt and pepper

1 (14-ounce) can lite coconut milk

3 tablespoons fish sauce (I like Red Boat)

3 tablespoons honey

¼ cup smooth almond butter

1 tablespoon coconut oil

1½ pounds pork tenderloin, sliced into ½-inch-thick strips

1 garlic clove, sliced

2 scallions, diced, white and green parts separated

3 tablespoons red curry paste

1 teaspoon chile paste

2 tablespoons chopped fresh cilantro, for garnish

2 tablespoons roughly crushed and chopped almonds, for garnish

Feel free to replace the pork tenderloin with chicken, tofu, or your preferred protein source. It won't affect the overall flavors too much.

1 Preheat the oven to 425 degrees. Line a baking sheet with parchment paper. Lay out the rutabaga noodles on the baking sheet, spacing them apart, and season with salt and pepper. Bake for 15 to 20 minutes or until al dente.

2 Meanwhile, in a medium bowl, whisk together the coconut milk, fish sauce, honey, and almond butter until smooth.

3 Heat the coconut oil in a large skillet over medium heat. When the oil has melted, add the pork and cook for 5 to 7 minutes, turning occasionally to brown on all sides. Transfer the pork to a plate.

4 Immediately add the garlic, white parts of the scallions, curry paste, and chile paste to the same pan and stir continuously until combined, about 30 seconds. Add the coconut milk mixture and cooked pork and stir to combine. Reduce the heat to medium-low and simmer for 10 minutes or until the sauce has thickened.

5 Divide the cooked rutabaga noodles among four plates and spoon the pork curry over each. Garnish with the cilantro, scallion greens, and almonds.

Rutabaga Gratin
with Leeks

Casseroles are the best way to feed a crowd, ideal to bring to dinner parties or serve at your own gatherings. And of the casseroles, gratins are king. They tend to lean on the heavier side, often incorporating ingredients like cream and flour, but this recipe is loaded with clean eating–friendly ingredients like cashews, garlic, leeks, and, of course, rutabaga. With simple components and big flavor, this shareable vegan dish is sure to become your go-to potluck recipe.

Vegan
Vegetarian
Gluten-Free
Paleo
Dairy-Free

TIME TO PREP 20 minutes plus 2 hours to soak cashews

TIME TO COOK 50 minutes

SERVES 4 to 6

NUTRITIONAL INFORMATION
(for 1 of 6 servings)
Calories: 317
Fat: 22 g
Sodium: 269 mg
Carbohydrate: 24 g
Fiber: 4 g
Sugar: 7 g
Protein: 10 g

ALSO WORKS WELL WITH
Sweet Potato, Butternut Squash, Potato, Parsnip

Cooking spray

For the sauce

2 cups low-sodium vegetable broth

2 cups raw cashews, soaked overnight (or for at least 2 hours) and drained

1 tablespoon nutritional yeast

2 teaspoons fresh lemon juice

2 large garlic cloves, roughly chopped

Salt and pepper

For the gratin

1 tablespoon extra-virgin olive oil

1 small yellow onion, diced

2 cups thinly sliced leeks

2 garlic cloves, minced

1½ tablespoons fresh thyme

Salt and pepper

1 *medium rutabaga, peeled, spiralized with* **BLADE A**, *noodles trimmed*

1 Preheat the oven to 400 degrees. Coat a medium casserole dish with cooking spray.

2 Make the sauce. Place all the ingredients for the sauce in a high-speed blender or food processor and pulse until creamy. Add salt and pepper to taste.

3 Make the gratin. Heat the olive oil in a large skillet over medium-high heat. When the oil is shimmering, add the onion and leeks and cook for 5 minutes or until softened. Add the garlic and cook until fragrant, about 30 seconds. Add the sauce and the thyme. Season with salt and pepper. Stir to combine thoroughly, then remove the skillet from the heat.

4 Spread about ¼ cup of the leek mixture over the bottom of the prepared casserole dish. Add a layer of the rutabaga noodles on top. Continue these layers with the remaining ingredients, finishing with the remaining leeks. Season with pepper.

5 Cover with foil and bake for 30 minutes or until the rutabaga is fork-tender. Turn the oven to broil, remove the foil, and return the gratin to the oven for 2 minutes or until the top is browned. Cut into portions and serve.

Mussels
over Rutabaga Pasta

≋ | Gluten-Free
≋ | Dairy-Free
| Low-Cal

TIME TO PREP 15 minutes
TIME TO COOK 30 minutes
SERVES 4

NUTRITIONAL INFORMATION
Calories: 228
Fat: 6 g
Sodium: 515 mg
Carbohydrate: 21 g
Fiber: 4 g
Sugar: 8 g
Protein: 16 g

ALSO WORKS WELL WITH
Zucchini, Chayote, Turnip,
Kohlrabi

In the wintertime, sweet potatoes and rutabaga compete for my attention. Luckily, there's plenty of veggie love to go around, but if I *had* to pick, it would be rutabaga. This news may be surprising, since sweet potatoes, touted as a superfood, usually steal the spotlight. But these mild, buttery noodles coated in a simple light tomato and white wine sauce with garlic and fresh parsley shine underneath fresh mussels. They look so much like spaghetti that you'll have guests searching your recycling bin for an empty box! If you're looking for a dish to warm up your winter blues, this is the one.

2 small rutabagas, peeled, spiralized with
   BLADE D, noodles trimmed

1 teaspoon garlic powder

   Salt and pepper

4 garlic cloves, minced

1 shallot, minced

½ cup dry white wine

2 pounds mussels, rinsed, scrubbed, and
   debearded

1 (14.5-ounce) can diced tomatoes

1 tablespoon extra-virgin olive oil

¼ teaspoon red pepper flakes

¼ teaspoon dried oregano

¼ teaspoon dried basil

¼ cup chopped fresh curly parsley

1 tablespoon finely grated lemon zest

1 Preheat the oven to 425 degrees. Line a baking sheet with parchment paper. Lay out the rutabaga noodles on the baking sheet, spacing them apart, and season with the garlic powder, salt, and black pepper. Bake for 15 to 20 minutes or until al dente.

2 Meanwhile, place a Dutch oven or large, wide skillet with a lid over high heat. When water flicked onto the pan sizzles, add three-quarters of the garlic, the shallot, and the wine. Bring to a boil, then add the mussels. Cover and cook, shaking the pan occasionally, for about 3 minutes, but no more than 5 minutes, until the mussels open up. Transfer to a large bowl, discarding any unopened mussels.

3 While the mussels cook, place the tomatoes in a food processor and pulse a few times until coarsely ground—not completely smooth, but with no large chunks remaining.

4 When the mussels are cool enough to handle, remove half of them from their shells. Taste-test one; if it's sandy, rinse them all in a colander.

5 Wipe clean the Dutch oven or skillet in which you cooked the mussels and heat the olive oil over medium heat. When the oil is shimmering, add the

remaining garlic and red pepper flakes and cook until fragrant, about 30 seconds. Add the pureed tomatoes, oregano, and basil. Increase the heat to medium-high, and bring to a strong simmer. Cook, stirring often, for 5 to 10 minutes or until the tomatoes have reduced slightly. Add all the cooked mussels to the pan, cover, reduce the heat to low, and cook for 5 minutes more to let the flavors develop.

6 Transfer the rutabaga to a large serving bowl or platter. Uncover the pan with the mussels and fold in the parsley. Garnish with the lemon zest and pour the mussels over the rutabaga. Serve family-style.

Chicken Cacciatore
over Rutabaga Noodles

Gluten-Free
Dairy-Free
Saves Well

TIME TO PREP 20 minutes
TIME TO COOK 40 minutes
SERVES 4

NUTRITIONAL INFORMATION
Calories: 493
Fat: 22 g
Sodium: 485 mg
Carbohydrate: 38 g
Fiber: 11 g
Sugar: 18 g
Protein: 38 g

ALSO WORKS WELL WITH
Zucchini, Turnip, Celeriac

If you're searching for a hearty dish to impress a crowd, look no further. Rutabaga noodles' resilience makes them ideal for serving with this classic chicken Italian dish—they won't break up on your guests' plates! The veggie's soft, buttery texture soaks up the flavors of the stewed tomatoes, herbs, garlic, and onions, ensuring this dish a spot in your weekly dinner rotation, too.

3 small rutabagas, peeled, spiralized with BLADE D, noodles trimmed

Cooking spray

1 teaspoon garlic powder

Salt and pepper

½ cup almond flour

1¼ pounds skin-on, bone-in chicken thighs

2 carrots, diced

1 large red bell pepper, diced

1 medium yellow onion, peeled, spiralized with BLADE A, noodles trimmed

2 large garlic cloves, minced

¼ teaspoon red pepper flakes

½ teaspoon dried rosemary

½ cup dry white wine (I like sauvignon blanc)

1 (28-ounce) can no-salt-added diced tomatoes

1 cup low-sodium chicken broth

1½ teaspoons dried oregano

¼ cup roughly chopped fresh basil

If you prefer chicken breasts over thighs, you can substitute them. Just let them cook a bit longer—25 to 30 minutes—and use only four.

1 Preheat the oven to 425 degrees. Line a baking sheet with parchment paper. Lay out the rutabaga noodles on the baking sheet, spacing them apart. Spray them with cooking spray and season with the garlic powder, salt, and black pepper. Bake for 20 to 30 minutes or until al dente.

2 On a large plate, season the almond flour with salt and black pepper. Season the chicken all over with salt and black pepper, then dredge it in the flour, pressing to adhere.

3 Place a large skillet over medium-high heat and coat with cooking spray. When water flicked onto the skillet sizzles, add the chicken in a single layer, working in batches if necessary. Cook until browned on the outside, about 5 minutes per side. Transfer to a plate and set aside.

4 Add the carrots, bell pepper, onion, fresh garlic, red pepper flakes, and rosemary to the skillet. Season with salt and black pepper. Cook for 5 minutes or until the vegetables are softened. Add the wine and simmer until reduced by half, about 5 minutes. Add the tomatoes and their juices, broth, and oregano.

5 Return the chicken to the skillet, nestling it into the vegetables. Spoon some sauce over each piece of chicken, then reduce the heat to medium-low and simmer for about 20 minutes or until the chicken is cooked through.

6 Using tongs, transfer the chicken to a large plate. Add the cooked rutabaga noodles to the skillet and toss to coat. Cook for 2 minutes or until the flavors are melded.

7 Using tongs, divide the rutabaga pasta among four plates and top each with chicken. Garnish with the basil and serve.

Rutabaga Baked Ziti
with Mushrooms and Kale

≋ Vegetarian
≋ Gluten-Free
Saves Well

TIME TO PREP 25 minutes
TIME TO COOK 35 minutes
SERVES 4 to 6

NUTRITIONAL INFORMATION
Calories: 320
Fat: 18 g
Sodium: 794 mg
Carbohydrate: 20 g
Fiber: 5 g
Sugar: 8 g
Protein: 22 g

ALSO WORKS WELL WITH
Sweet Potato, Potato

You'd be hard-pressed to find an Italian person—or maybe any person—who doesn't love baked ziti and lasagna. But what you might find are people who don't regularly eat these dishes because of their high calorie, fat, and carbohydrate counts. This Inspiralized version calls for rutabaga noodles instead of rigatoni or penne pasta. I promise you won't miss it—the rutabaga holds its own against the melted cheeses. The mushrooms and kale squeeze in extra vegetables and nutrients, and add an earthy flavor to this comforting ziti.

Cooking spray

1 tablespoon extra-virgin olive oil

2 garlic cloves, minced

1 small onion, diced

5 cups curly kale, chopped

4 cups sliced baby portobello mushrooms

Salt and pepper

1 *medium rutabaga, peeled, spiralized with* **BLADE C**, *noodles trimmed*

1 (14.5-ounce) can crushed tomatoes

2 teaspoons dried rosemary

2 teaspoons dried oregano

½ teaspoon red pepper flakes

1 cup ricotta cheese

1 cup grated Parmesan cheese

1½ cups shredded mozzarella cheese

Meat lovers can add crumbled sausage or ground turkey to this dish for extra flavor and protein.

1 Preheat the oven to 400 degrees. Coat a medium baking dish with cooking spray.

2 Heat the olive oil in a large saucepan or Dutch oven over medium-high heat. When the oil is shimmering, add the garlic and onion and cook for 3 to 5 minutes or until the onion is translucent. Add the kale and mushrooms, season with salt and black pepper, and cook for 5 minutes or until the kale is wilted. Transfer the mixture to a medium bowl.

3 Add the rutabaga to the same pan and cook for 5 minutes or until it begins to soften. Return the kale mixture to the pan and toss thoroughly to combine. Stir in the tomatoes, rosemary, oregano, and red pepper flakes. Increase the heat to medium-high and bring to a simmer, then remove the pan from the heat.

4 Meanwhile, in a medium bowl, stir together the ricotta, Parmesan, and 1 cup of the mozzarella. Add the mixed cheeses to the pot with the rutabaga and toss to combine.

5 Transfer the mixture to the prepared baking dish and top with the remaining mozzarella. Cover with foil and bake for 20 minutes. Remove the foil and bake for 10 minutes more or until the rutabaga is al dente and the cheese is golden brown. Serve immediately.

Sweet Potato

When you're grocery shopping for sweet potatoes to spiralize, you'll see signs for "sweet potatoes" and "yams." What's the difference? Both are tuberous root vegetables, but they actually *aren't* related, and depending on which area of the world you live in, they may be entirely different.

Yams are most commonly identified by their blackish or brown, rough, thick skin and white, purple, or reddish flesh. They're a bit starchier than sweet potatoes and drier—not as ideal for the spiralizer. The two major types of sweet potatoes you'll find in supermarkets are firm and soft. Firm potatoes have golden skin and paler flesh, and can be a little bit waxy and more difficult to spiralize. The soft ones have a copper skin and orange flesh. (You may find this variety labeled as a yam, although technically it is not.) When you are selecting a sweet potato for spiralizing, look for the latter type. If you're unsure which it is, scratch the skin to reveal the color of the flesh. I prefer to use these in my recipes, as they become creamy, fluffy, and moist when cooked. The potato should be medium to large in size and as tubular as possible. One more thing: Don't ever boil sweet potatoes—they'll turn into mush on your plate and break apart!

NUTRITIONAL BENEFITS: Sweet potatoes are an excellent source of vitamins A, B_6, and C. They also contain iron, which is a necessary mineral to maintain adequate energy levels, and magnesium, essential for healthy arteries and nerve function. Sweet potatoes have a lower glycemic index and are more nutritionally dense than traditional white potatoes, making them a better option for maintaining a healthy diet.

PREPARATION AND STORAGE: Peel the sweet potato, if you prefer. Slice off the ends to leave flat, even surfaces. Store in an airtight container in the refrigerator for up to 5 days. Sweet potato noodles can be frozen for up to 8 months for future use.

BEST BLADES TO USE
- Blade A
- Blade C
- Blade D

BEST COOKING METHODS
- Sauté over medium-high heat for 5 to 7 minutes
- Roast at 425 degrees for 10 to 15 minutes

Tandoori Chicken
over Sweet Potato Rice

∞ Gluten-Free
∞ Paleo
∞ Dairy-Free
    Saves Well

TIME TO PREP 35 minutes
TIME TO COOK 35 minutes
SERVES 4

NUTRITIONAL INFORMATION
Calories: 329
Fat: 21 g
Sodium: 111 mg
Carbohydrate: 20 g
Fiber: 4 g
Sugar: 5 g
Protein: 16 g

ALSO WORKS WELL WITH
Butternut Squash, Turnip,
Kohlrabi

If you're ever in the mood for a super-well-seasoned, somewhat spicy piece of chicken, make it tandoori. Of Indian origin, tandoori chicken is traditionally prepared with yogurt. In this version, we use coconut cream to keep it dairy-free and to add a lightly sweet flavor in a subtle sauce that coats the sweet potato rice. While the classic is marinated and cooked on a skewer for hours, this quick version requires only an oven and a skillet, and is done in about an hour.

½ cup coconut cream (see page 19)

½ teaspoon onion powder

1 teaspoon garlic powder

1 teaspoon ground turmeric

1 teaspoon cayenne pepper

1 teaspoon paprika

½ teaspoon ground cumin

½ teaspoon ground coriander

Juice of ½ lemon

Salt and pepper

4 skin-on, bone-in chicken breasts or legs and thighs

1 tablespoon extra-virgin olive oil

2 garlic cloves, minced

2 medium sweet potatoes, peeled, spiralized with BLADE D, then riced (see page 16)

½ cup low-sodium chicken broth

2 tablespoons chopped fresh cilantro

¼ cup sliced blanched almonds

1 Preheat the oven to 450 degrees. Line a baking sheet with parchment paper.

2 In a medium bowl, stir together the coconut cream, onion powder, garlic powder, turmeric, cayenne, paprika, cumin, coriander, and lemon juice. Season with salt and black pepper. Transfer to a large resealable plastic bag or container. Add the chicken and turn to coat. Set aside to marinate for 20 minutes at room temperature or up to 2 hours in the refrigerator.

3 Remove the chicken from the marinade, allowing the excess to drip off. Transfer to the prepared baking sheet and bake for 25 minutes or until charring on the outside and cooked through.

4 Heat the olive oil in a large skillet over medium-high heat. When the oil is shimmering, add the garlic and cook for 30 seconds or until fragrant. Add the sweet potato rice and broth, cover, and cook for 7 minutes or until softened. Stir in the cilantro and almonds.

5 Divide the rice among four plates and top each with a piece of chicken.

Sweet Potato Pizza Skillet

If you'd like to re-create pizza with your spiralizer, you have options. You can make a mini pizza with a spiralized bun, or regular pizza by creating a larger version of the bun. But if you're craving pizza and need it now, this simple skillet version is all you need. With cooked spiralized sweet potatoes covered in plentiful seasonings, toppings, and cheese, there's not much more to it. You may be tempted to eat the whole thing yourself, so grab a friend to share it!

Vegetarian
Gluten-Free
One Pot
Saves Well

TIME TO PREP 25 minutes
TIME TO COOK 35 minutes
SERVES 4

NUTRITIONAL INFORMATION
Calories: 315
Fat: 15 g
Sodium: 812 mg
Carbohydrate: 35 g
Fiber: 5 g
Sugar: 15 g
Protein: 13 g

ALSO WORKS WELL WITH
Rutabaga, Potatoes

- 1 tablespoon extra-virgin olive oil
- 3 medium sweet potatoes, peeled, spiralized with BLADE C, noodles trimmed
- 1 teaspoon garlic powder
- Salt and pepper
- 1½ cups marinara sauce (I like Victoria Fine Foods)
- ½ teaspoon dried oregano
- 1¼ cups shredded mozzarella cheese
- ¼ cup sliced black olives
- ½ small red onion, thinly sliced
- 1 small green bell pepper, thinly sliced
- 2 tablespoons chopped fresh basil, for garnish
- 1 tablespoon grated Parmesan cheese, for garnish

1 Preheat the oven to 425 degrees.

2 Heat the olive oil in a 10-inch skillet over medium-high heat. When the oil is shimmering, add the sweet potato noodles and season with the garlic powder, salt, and black pepper. Cook for about 5 minutes or until beginning to soften.

3 Pour the marinara sauce over the noodles, sprinkle with the oregano, and layer the mozzarella on top. Top with the olives, onion, and bell pepper.

4 Bake for 20 to 25 minutes or until the cheese is melted and golden.

5 Garnish with the basil and Parmesan before serving.

If there's excess sauce in the skillet once the pizza's out of the oven, pour some out before serving or sop it up with some crusty whole-grain bread.

Chorizo-Sweet Potato Buns
with Tomato and Pepper Jack

Gluten-Free

TIME TO PREP 25 minutes
TIME TO COOK 15 minutes
SERVES 4

NUTRITIONAL INFORMATION
Calories: 403
Fat: 30 g
Sodium: 462 mg
Carbohydrate: 18 g
Fiber: 5 g
Sugar: 3 g
Protein: 15 g

ALSO WORKS WELL WITH
Rutabaga, Potato

Essentially, this dish is an open-faced grilled cheese for adults. The chorizo releases its fats into the pan, which the sweet potato noodles soak up as they cook, setting up this yummy bun. The spiciness and sweetness are tied together by the soft, warm tomato, while the gooey melted cheese finishes everything off under the broiler. The pepper jack brings notes of jalapeños, garlic, rosemary, and sweet peppers, creating a seriously good spiralized sandwich.

2 chorizo links, casings removed

1 *large sweet potato, peeled, spiralized with* BLADE D, *noodles trimmed*

½ teaspoon garlic powder

½ teaspoon paprika

Salt and pepper

2 large eggs, beaten

2 tablespoons olive oil

4 slices of beefsteak tomato

4 slices of pepper jack cheese

1 avocado, sliced

Chopped fresh cilantro, for garnish

Be sure the chorizo is really crumbled. If there are large chunks remaining, it will be difficult to keep the bun bound.

1 Heat a large nonstick skillet over medium heat. When water flicked onto the skillet sizzles, add the chorizo and cook, crumbling the meat with a wooden spoon, for 5 to 7 minutes or until browned. Using a slotted spoon, transfer the chorizo to a medium bowl, reserving any fat in the pan.

2 Immediately add the sweet potato noodles to the skillet and season with the garlic powder, paprika, salt, and pepper. Cook for 5 to 7 minutes or until the noodles are softened and lightly browned. Transfer to the bowl with the chorizo and let cool for 1 to 2 minutes. Stir in the eggs, tossing to coat.

3 Fill four 6-ounce ramekins halfway with the noodles. Cover each with a piece of foil or wax paper, pressing it down firmly onto the noodles to compress them. Refrigerate for at least 15 minutes to set.

4 Heat 1 tablespoon of the olive oil in a large nonstick skillet over medium heat. When the oil is shimmering, add the buns, two at a time, flipping each out of its ramekin into the skillet and patting the bottom until the bun falls out. Cook for 3 minutes or until set, being sure to push in any stray noodles. Carefully

flip and cook for 2 to 3 minutes more, or until the buns are completely set and browned on both sides, flattening with the back of the spatula. Repeat with the remaining olive oil and buns.

5 While buns cook, preheat the broiler. Line a baking sheet with parchment paper.

6 Transfer the buns to the prepared baking sheet. Top each with a tomato slice, then a cheese slice. Broil for 2 minutes or until the cheese has melted.

7 Remove from the oven, top with avocado, and garnish with cilantro.

Vegetarian Full English Breakfast

Vegetarian
Gluten-Free
Dairy-Free

TIME TO PREP 10 minutes
TIME TO COOK 15 minutes
SERVES 4

NUTRITIONAL INFORMATION
Calories: 328
Fat: 9 g
Sodium: 588 mg
Carbohydrate: 58 g
Fiber: 11 g
Sugar: 17 g
Protein: 16 g

ALSO WORKS WELL WITH
Potato

When I studied abroad in London, I made an effort to try all the classic British meals. From toad-in-a-hole to Eton mess, I tasted everything. One of the meals that most surprised me was the full English breakfast—I couldn't believe how much food it was! But now I am a believer in the expression "Eat like a king for breakfast, a prince for lunch, and a pauper for dinner." Eating a big, hearty breakfast revs your metabolism first thing in the morning and fuels your body for whatever the day may bring, helping reduce your chances of overeating later because of hunger pangs. This spiralized vegetarian re-creation of the classic substitutes sweet potato noodles for toast or hash browns, making it more fun to eat *and* cleaner.

- 1 tablespoon extra-virgin olive oil
- 2 medium sweet potatoes, peeled, spiralized with *BLADE D*, noodles trimmed
- ½ teaspoon garlic powder
- Salt and pepper
- 1 (15-ounce) can vegetarian baked beans (I like Amy's Organic)

- 16 ounces button mushrooms, quartered
- 2 garlic cloves, finely minced
- ¼ cup low-sodium vegetable broth
- 2 vine tomatoes, cut into four ½-inch-thick slices
- ¼ teaspoon dried thyme
- Cooking spray
- 4 whole large eggs

1 Heat the olive oil in a large skillet over medium heat. When the oil is shimmering, add the sweet potato noodles and season with the garlic powder, salt, and pepper. Cook for 7 minutes or until al dente. Divide among four plates.

2 Meanwhile, put the baked beans in a small pot and bring to a simmer over medium heat, then reduce the heat to low to keep warm until ready to serve.

3 Place a medium skillet over medium-high heat. When water flicked onto the skillet sizzles, add the mushrooms and garlic, season with salt and pepper, and cook for 2 minutes or until the mushrooms begin to release moisture. Add the broth, cover, and cook for 5 to 7 minutes or until the mushrooms are wilted.

Transfer to the plates with the sweet potato noodles, dividing the mushrooms evenly.

4 Add the tomato slices to the skillet in which you cooked the sweet potato noodles and season with the thyme, salt, and pepper. Cook for 2 minutes per side, flattening with a spatula, until seared and heated through. Add to the plates.

5 Spray the same pan with cooking spray and crack in the eggs, keeping the yolks intact. Cook until the whites are set on the bottom, 3 to 5 minutes. Place one egg on each plate.

6 Finally, divide the simmering baked beans among the plates and serve.

Mexican Eggs
in Pepper Cups

Gluten-Free
Vegetarian
Dairy-Free (opt.)
Low-Cal

TIME TO PREP 10 minutes
TIME TO COOK 25 minutes
SERVES 4

NUTRITIONAL INFORMATION
Calories: 228
Fat: 12 g
Sodium: 287 mg
Carbohydrate: 18 g
Fiber: 4 g
Sugar: 6 g
Protein: 11 g

ALSO WORKS WELL WITH
Potato, Parsnip

Thanks to Pinterest, eggs in pepper cups had their fifteen minutes of fame. Most feature a thin bell pepper slice with a fried egg neatly baked inside, resembling a flower. I've tried these myself and while adorable, they're not exactly satisfying. Instead, this recipe utilizes the *entire* pepper and includes sweet potato noodles, which will both surprise your brunch guests and leave them feeling satisfied! The Mexican flavors add life to this modest breakfast dish, and the gorgeous presentation is still totally Pin-able.

Cooking spray

4 medium bell peppers

1 tablespoon extra-virgin olive oil

1 *large sweet potato, peeled, spiralized with* **BLADE D,** *noodles trimmed*

½ teaspoon garlic powder

½ teaspoon chili powder

½ teaspoon dried oregano

Salt and pepper

½ cup crumbled cotija or feta cheese

4 whole large eggs

2 tablespoons chopped fresh cilantro, for garnish

The egg might not look like much after it's cracked into the bell pepper cup, but it will fluff up. If you're using large peppers, you can cut a little more off the top, or you can use two eggs. You can also slice off the tops after baking if you want a perfectly filled pepper.

1 Preheat the oven to 400 degrees. Coat a medium baking dish with cooking spray.

2 Slice the tops off of the bell peppers and discard. Carefully remove the white flesh and seeds from the pepper using a paring knife. If your peppers are uneven on the bottom, slice off a thin piece so they sit flat, keeping them intact. Stand the bell peppers up in the baking dish and bake for 10 minutes.

3 Meanwhile, heat the olive oil in a large skillet over medium-high heat. When the oil is shimmering, add the sweet potato noodles and season with the garlic powder, chili powder, oregano, salt, and black pepper. Cook for 7 to 10 minutes or until al dente.

4 Stuff the sweet potato noodles into the peppers along with half the cotija cheese, dividing them evenly. Crack one egg into each pepper, keeping the yolks intact, and return to the oven for 12 to 15 minutes or until the egg whites just set.

5 Remove the peppers from the oven and immediately garnish with the remaining cheese, cilantro, and cracked black pepper.

Creamy Chipotle Sweet Potato Pasta
with Chicken and Seasoned Corn

Gluten-Free
Dairy-Free

TIME TO PREP 25 minutes
TIME TO COOK 20 minutes
SERVES 4

NUTRITIONAL INFORMATION
Calories: 464
Fat: 23 g
Sodium: 1950 mg
Carbohydrate: 39 g
Fiber: 6 g
Sugar: 9 g
Protein: 32 g

ALSO WORKS WELL WITH
Butternut Squash, Rutabaga

One of the cardinal rules of healthy eating out is to avoid any recipes with "creamy" in the title. Traditionally, food that is creamy has some amount of butter, sugar, cream, or flour. But it's not hard to re-create those sorts of dishes using alternatives, such as cashew cream. Thanks to that trick, this chicken dish is undeniably decadent . . . without the decadence!

For the corn
- 1 large ear of corn
- Salt
- ½ teaspoon chili powder
- 1 tablespoon fresh lime juice

For the chicken and pasta
- 1 tablespoon extra-virgin olive oil
- 4 skinless, boneless chicken breasts, pounded
- ¼ teaspoon garlic powder
- Salt and pepper
- *1 large sweet potato, peeled, spiralized with* **BLADE C**, *noodles trimmed*

For the sauce
- ¼ cup raw cashews, soaked in water for at least 2 hours (preferably overnight) and drained
- 1 tablespoon coconut oil, melted
- 3 to 4 tablespoons hot sauce (I like Frank's or Tessemae's)
- 1 teaspoon garlic powder
- 1 teaspoon paprika
- 1 tablespoon fresh lemon juice
- 1 tablespoon apple cider vinegar
- Salt

- 1 tablespoon minced fresh cilantro, for garnish

1 Place the corn in a medium pot and add water to cover and a pinch of salt. Bring to a boil, then reduce the heat to medium-low and simmer for 5 minutes or until the kernels are easily pierced with a fork. Drain. When the corn is cool enough to handle, slice the kernels off the cob into a medium bowl. Add the chili powder and lime juice. Toss to combine.

2 Heat 1 tablespoon olive oil in a large skillet over medium-high heat. Season the chicken with the garlic powder, salt, and pepper. When the oil is shimmering, add the chicken and cook for 3 to 5 minutes per side or until golden and cooked through. Transfer to a plate and cut into slices.

3 Immediately add the sweet potato noodles to the skillet. Season with salt and pepper, and cook, tossing frequently, for 10 minutes or until al dente.

4 Puree the cashews in a high-speed blender or food processor until creamy. Add the remaining ingredients for the sauce and pulse until combined. If necessary, add water, 1 tablespoon at a time, until the sauce reaches the desired consistency. Transfer to a small pot and keep warm over low heat.

5 Divide the sweet potato noodles among plates and pour the sauce over the top. Add chicken and seasoned corn and garnish with cilantro.

Braised Short Ribs
over Sweet Potato Pasta

Gluten-Free
Dairy-Free
One Pot
Saves Well

TIME TO PREP 15 minutes
TIME TO COOK 3 hours
SERVES 4

NUTRITIONAL INFORMATION
Calories: 496
Fat: 20 g
Sodium: 432 mg
Carbohydrate: 26 g
Fiber: 5 g
Sugar: 9 g
Protein: 38 g

ALSO WORKS WELL WITH
Zucchini, Butternut Squash,
Rutabaga, Turnip

I never truly appreciated short ribs until I had them in a pasta special at one of my favorite Italian restaurants in Brooklyn, Frankies 457. The tender meat practically melted on my tongue, with the pasta carrying the hearty sauce. I remember every bite of that meal and truly consider it an unforgettable food experience. In this spiralized version, the sweet potato pasta may be even more delicious than its original, thanks to its inherent sweetness. You'll want to make this dish for a special occasion or a loved one—it's exquisite.

3 tablespoons extra-virgin olive oil

4 to 6 beef short ribs (about 2 pounds)

Salt and pepper

4 garlic cloves, sliced

1 small onion, diced

2 carrots, diced

2 celery stalks, diced

3 tablespoons tomato paste

1½ cups red wine (I like Cabernet Sauvignon)

Leaves from 2 sprigs of rosemary

Leaves from 1 sprig of thyme

2 bay leaves

1½ cups low-sodium beef broth, plus more as needed

2 medium sweet potatoes peeled, spiralized with BLADE C or D, noodles trimmed

½ teaspoon garlic powder

1 tablespoon chopped fresh parsley

Top the finished plates off with shaved Parmesan cheese, if you eat dairy, or make the vegan Parmesan on page 192.

1 Preheat the oven to 375 degrees.

2 Heat the olive oil in a Dutch oven or large ovenproof saucepan over medium-high heat. Season the short ribs on both sides with salt and pepper. When the oil is shimmering, add the ribs and cook until golden brown on the outside and beginning to crisp, about 3 minutes per side. Remove and set aside.

3 Immediately add the garlic, onion, carrots, and celery to the pot and season with salt and pepper. Sauté, stirring often, until the vegetables soften, about 5 minutes. Add the tomato paste and stir to coat, about 1 minute. Add the wine and simmer until it has reduced by one-quarter, about 1 minute. Add the rosemary, thyme, bay leaves, and broth.

4 Increase the heat to high and bring the broth to a boil. Return the short ribs to the pot, submerging them halfway. Cover and transfer to the oven. Braise for about 2½ hours or until the meat is fork-tender and falling off the bones. Every 45 minutes, check to make sure the ribs are still about halfway submerged, adding more broth as needed. Remove and discard the bay leaves from the short ribs before serving.

5 Before serving, place the sweet potato noodles in a large skillet and season with the garlic powder, salt, and pepper. Cook over medium-high heat, working in batches if necessary, for 7 minutes or until al dente.

6 Divide the noodles among four plates, add the short ribs, and spoon the sauce over the top. Garnish with the parsley.

Creamy Spinach and Artichoke Sweet Potato Pasta

Vegan
Vegetarian
Gluten-Free
Paleo
Dairy-Free
Low-Cal

TIME TO PREP 25 minutes
TIME TO COOK 25 minutes
SERVES 4

NUTRITIONAL INFORMATION
Calories: 246
Fat: 13 g
Sodium: 756 mg
Carbohydrate: 26 g
Fiber: 10 g
Sugar: 8 g
Protein: 8 g

ALSO WORKS WELL WITH
Rutabaga, Turnip, Carrot, Celeriac

Spinach and artichoke is a popular combination—on pizza, as a dip, in sauces, and in casseroles. Whatever the presentation, it's usually chock-full of cream, cheese, and butter. Spinach is an excellent source of vitamin K and protein, and artichoke hearts are high in antioxidants and dietary fiber—why muck up these nutritional benefits with those processed ingredients? With this spiralized pasta, we highlight the health benefits and keep them top of mind, adding even more with sweet potatoes and cauliflower. This dish is ideal for cozying up with on cold winter nights when you need something warm, comforting, and satisfying.

1 medium head cauliflower, chopped into florets

½ teaspoon garlic powder

2 tablespoons nutritional yeast

½ cup low-sodium vegetable broth

½ teaspoon dried oregano

Salt and pepper

1 tablespoon extra-virgin olive oil

2 medium sweet potatoes, peeled, spiralized with BLADE C, noodles trimmed

1 (13.75-ounce) can halved artichoke hearts, drained and patted dry

1 garlic clove, sliced

4 cups spinach

1 teaspoon red pepper flakes

For a deeper flavor, roast the artichoke halves for 20 minutes at 425 degrees with a tablespoon of extra-virgin olive oil, salt, and pepper. Add them to the pasta after cooking the spinach.

1 Bring a large pot of water to a boil over high heat. Add the cauliflower and cook until easily pierced with a fork, about 10 minutes. Drain and transfer to a food processor. Add the garlic powder, nutritional yeast, broth, and oregano. Season with salt and black pepper and pulse until creamy. Taste and adjust the seasoning to your preference.

2 Meanwhile, heat the olive oil in a large skillet over medium-high heat. When the oil is shimmering, add the sweet potato noodles and season with salt and black pepper. Cook for about 7 minutes or until al dente. Remove from the pan and set aside.

3 Immediately add the artichokes to the skillet and season with salt and black pepper. Cook for 3 minutes or until warmed through. Add the garlic and spinach and cook for 3 minutes or until fragrant and just wilted. Return the sweet potato noodles to the skillet and pour over the cauliflower sauce. Toss to combine thoroughly.

4 Divide among four plates and garnish with the red pepper flakes.

Turnip

Turnips have a bit of a bad reputation, but I'm here to change all that. I'll admit that when served raw or plain, they do have a bitter taste. But with the right seasonings, sauces, and accompaniments, you won't even recognize them—in a good way!

Turnips are a healthy, low-calorie vegetable that should be built into your healthy diet, because they're easy to find, spiralize, and adapt into any pasta or noodle dishes! The noodles have a soft, velvety texture when heated and are durable enough for dressings and sauces to cling to well.

When picking out your turnips at the market, feel for ones with smooth skin. The turnip should be firm with a purple-tinged top. The smaller the turnip, the more palatable the flavor, so aim for one that's 2 inches in diameter—it'll spiralize well and be super tasty. Avoid any shriveled turnips or those with major blemishes.

NUTRITIONAL BENEFITS: A medium turnip provides 54 percent of your recommended daily amount of vitamin C, an immunity-boosting nutrient! Turnips are also high in fiber, which is helpful for weight loss and maintenance. Store in an airtight container in the refrigerator for up to 7 days.

PREPARATION AND STORAGE: Peel the turnip entirely and slice off the ends to leave flat, even surfaces.

BEST BLADES TO USE
- Blade C
- Blade D

BEST COOKING METHODS
- Boil for 2 to 3 minutes
- Sauté over medium-high heat for 5 to 7 minutes
- Roast at 425 degrees for 10 to 12 minutes

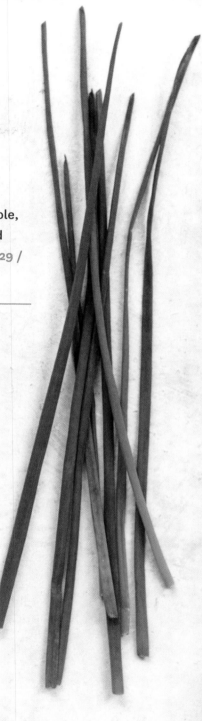

Turnip alla Vodka

Vegan
Vegetarian
Gluten-Free
Dairy-Free
Low-Cal

TIME TO PREP 15 minutes plus
4 hours to soak the cashews
TIME TO COOK 20 minutes
SERVES 4

NUTRITIONAL INFORMATION
Calories: 248
Fat: 14 g
Sodium: 766 mg
Carbohydrate: 20 g
Fiber: 4 g
Sugar: 9 g
Protein: 6 g

ALSO WORKS WELL WITH
Rutabaga, Zucchini

At restaurants, I've always steered clear of the creamier pasta dishes, even before I was Inspiralized. I much prefer a dusting of Parmesan or a dollop of ricotta to a cup of cream. With too much cream, you lose the taste of the noodle! So I've always had a love-hate relationship with vodka sauces . . . until now. This lightened-up version offers that iconic, luxurious texture and taste, without the processed ingredients and sugar roller coaster. Instead, you get *healthy* fat and a little bit of protein from the cashew cream. The sauce lets these turnip noodles shine. Grab some bread—something tells me you'll want to soak up every last drop!

¼ cup raw cashews, soaked for at least 4 to 5 hours, drained

Low-sodium vegetable broth, as needed

1 tablespoon extra-virgin olive oil

1 large garlic clove, minced

¼ teaspoon red pepper flakes

½ red onion, diced

1 (14-ounce) can crushed tomatoes

½ teaspoon dried oregano

½ teaspoon dried basil

¼ cup vodka (I like Tito's)

2 turnips, peeled, spiralized with BLADE D, noodles trimmed

Salt and pepper

¼ cup vegan Parmesan cheese (see page 192)

2 tablespoons chopped fresh curly parsley

1 Place the cashews in a high-speed blender or food processor and pulse until creamy. Add the broth 1 tablespoon at a time as needed until the sauce reaches a smooth consistency, similar to a vodka sauce or alfredo.

2 Heat the olive oil in a large skillet over medium-high heat. When the oil is shimmering, add the garlic, red pepper flakes, and onion and cook for 3 minutes or until the onion is soft and translucent. Add the tomatoes, oregano, basil, vodka, and turnip noodles and season with salt and black pepper. Reduce the heat to low and simmer for about 5 minutes or until the alcohol cooks off.

3 Stir in the cashew sauce and Parmesan and cook for 1 minute more or until the turnip noodles are al dente.

4 Divide the pasta among four plates and garnish with the parsley.

Cauliflower Steak
over Roasted Garlic Tomato Turnip Noodles

≋ Vegan
≋ Vegetarian
≋ Gluten-Free
Paleo
Dairy-Free
Low-Cal
Saves Well

TIME TO PREP 25 minutes
TIME TO COOK 50 minutes
SERVES 4

NUTRITIONAL INFORMATION
Calories: 279
Fat: 12 g
Sodium: 1333 mg
Carbohydrate: 40 g
Fiber: 9 g
Sugar: 18 g
Protein: 9 g

ALSO WORKS WELL WITH
Butternut Squash, Parsnip,
Sweet Potato

Cauliflower steak is the vegetarians' best-kept secret, but ever so slowly it's starting to make its way onto restaurant menus and into home kitchens everywhere. They can be seasoned lightly or dramatically, depending on what kind of dish you're trying to create. With the proper accompaniments, you can enjoy a steak dinner without the steak! Here the warm, thick, and hearty star of this dish sits atop a bed of roasted garlic tomato turnip pasta, adding Italian flair and completing a robust meal that's fully vegetarian.

- 1 head of garlic, outer skin peeled
- 1 tablespoon plus 1 teaspoon extra-virgin olive oil
- 1 large head cauliflower
- Salt and pepper

For the sauce and pasta

- 1 tablespoon extra-virgin olive oil
- 1 small red onion, finely diced
- 1 tablespoon tomato paste
- ¼ teaspoon red pepper flakes
- ½ teaspoon Italian seasoning
- 1 (28-ounce) can crushed tomatoes
- Salt and pepper
- 2 tablespoons roughly chopped fresh basil
- 2 large or 3 medium turnips, peeled, spiralized with BLADE D, noodles trimmed
- 2 tablespoons vegan Parmesan cheese (see page 192), for garnish (optional)

1 Preheat the oven to 400 degrees and set a rack in the center.

2 Slice off about ¼ inch from the top of the head of garlic so that you can just see the tops of the cloves. Drizzle the exposed part with 1 teaspoon of the olive oil. Wrap the garlic in foil and set on a baking sheet. Roast for 40 to 50 minutes or until lightly caramelized and very soft when pierced with a knife or fork. Remove from the oven, remove the foil, and set aside to cool, then peel all the cloves.

3 While the garlic is roasting, line a baking sheet with parchment paper. Remove the leaves from the head of cauliflower and, using a sturdy, large knife, slice the cauliflower from top to base into four ¾-inch-thick "steaks." Season each with salt and pepper.

recipe continues

4 Heat the remaining 1 tablespoon olive oil in a large skillet over medium-high heat. When the oil is shimmering, add the cauliflower steaks in a single layer, working in batches if necessary. Sear for about 1 minute per side or until golden, then transfer to the prepared baking sheet. Roast for 15 to 20 minutes or until tender and cooked through.

5 Meanwhile, make the sauce and pasta. In the same skillet you used to cook the cauliflower, heat the olive oil over medium-high heat. When the oil is shimmering, add the onion and cook for 3 to 5 minutes or until soft and translucent. Add the tomato paste, red pepper flakes, and Italian seasoning and cook for 1 minute, stirring to combine. Add the tomatoes and season with salt and pepper. Increase the heat to high and bring to a boil, then reduce the heat to medium-low and simmer for 20 minutes or until reduced by one-quarter.

6 Transfer the sauce to a food processor, along with the roasted garlic cloves. Blend until creamy. Taste and adjust the seasoning to your preferences.

7 Return the skillet to medium heat, pour in the sauce, and fold in the basil. Add the turnip noodles and toss to coat. Cover and cook for 5 to 7 minutes or until warmed through and al dente.

8 Divide the turnip noodles among four plates and top each with a cauliflower steak. Garnish with vegan Parmesan, if desired.

If you'd like to make your own Italian seasoning blend instead of using a premade store-bought one, combine ⅛ teaspoon each of dried rosemary, dried oregano, dried basil, and dried parsley.

White Beans, Escarole, and Turnip Noodles
in Parmesan Broth

Gluten-Free
Low-Cal
Saves Well

TIME TO PREP 15 minutes
TIME TO COOK 15 minutes
SERVES 2

NUTRITIONAL INFORMATION
Calories: 213
Fat: 8 g
Sodium: 300 mg
Carbohydrate: 26 g
Fiber: 10 g
Sugar: 7 g
Protein: 10 g

One of my mother's best dishes was her white beans and escarole in a salty chicken broth. Whenever I came home from college or break, I'd ask her to make it for me. This spiralized version adds turnip noodles to soak up the flavors from the buttery beans, earthy escarole, and Parmesan-infused broth. Not quite a soup, not quite a pasta, this dish is something I like to whip up in a pinch for lunch or a late dinner.

- 1 tablespoon extra-virgin olive oil
- 1 large garlic clove, minced
- Pinch of red pepper flakes
- 1 bunch escarole, rinsed and chopped into 2-inch pieces
- 1 *large turnip, peeled, spiralized with* BLADE C, *noodles trimmed*
- 1 cup low-sodium chicken broth
- Salt and pepper
- ½ cup canned white beans, rinsed and drained
- 2 tablespoons grated Parmesan cheese

1 Heat the olive oil in a large skillet over medium heat. When the oil is shimmering, add the garlic and red pepper flakes and cook for 30 seconds or until fragrant. Add the escarole, turnip noodles, and broth and season with salt and black pepper. Cover and cook for 5 to 7 minutes or until the escarole is wilted and the noodles are al dente. Using tongs, transfer the escarole and noodles to bowls, dividing them evenly and reserving the broth in the pan.

2 Immediately add the beans and Parmesan to the broth and remove from the heat. Stir continuously until the beans are warmed through, about 2 minutes.

3 Spoon the beans and Parmesan broth over the noodles and serve immediately.

Pan-Seared Pork Chops
with Mushroom Gravy and Turnip Noodles

Gluten-Free
Paleo
Dairy-Free
Low-Cal
Saves Well

TIME TO PREP 20 minutes
TIME TO COOK 35 minutes
SERVES 4

NUTRITIONAL INFORMATION
Calories: 229
Fat: 10 g
Sodium: 158 mg
Carbohydrate: 12 g
Fiber: 2 g
Sugar: 5 g
Protein: 21 g

ALSO WORKS WELL WITH
Celeriac, Zucchini, Rutabaga

The difference between bone-in and boneless pork chops is astounding—with the former, the flavors intensify as the meat soaks in the juices released from the bone. If you're not a meat-eater, I apologize for that descriptive sentence, but if you are—this dish has it all. The turnip noodles' earthy taste complements the mushrooms and holds up to the gravy, just like real pasta. If you don't eat meat, omit the pork chop and make this sauce with vegetable broth—it will taste like a marsala!

1 tablespoon extra-virgin olive oil

2 bone-in pork chops, about ½ inch thick, fat trimmed

¼ teaspoon paprika

Salt and pepper

1 *small onion, peeled, spiralized with* **BLADE A**, *noodles trimmed*

2 garlic cloves, minced

8 ounces sliced cremini mushrooms

½ cup low-sodium chicken broth

1 cup lite coconut milk

1 teaspoon dried thyme

2 *medium turnips, peeled, spiralized with* **BLADE C**, *noodles trimmed*

2 tablespoons minced fresh parsley, for garnish

1 Heat the oil in a large skillet over medium heat. Season the pork chops with paprika, salt, and pepper. When the oil is shimmering, add the pork chops in a single layer, working in batches if necessary, and cook for 3 to 4 minutes per side or until browned. Transfer to a plate and tent with foil to keep warm.

2 Add the onion noodles, garlic, and mushrooms to the pan and season with salt and pepper. Cook until the onions are caramelized, about 10 minutes. Add the broth and scrape up any browned bits from the bottom of the pan. Stir until the liquid has evaporated, about 5 minutes. Add the coconut milk, thyme, salt, and pepper. Cook for 7 to 10 minutes, until thickened. Transfer to a bowl and set aside.

3 Immediately add the turnip noodles to the pan, season with salt and pepper, cover, and cook for 5 to 7 minutes or until noodles wilt and are al dente, uncovering occasionally to toss. Add the mushroom gravy and toss for 1 to 2 minutes or until turnips are coated and everything is warmed through.

4 Plate the pork chops and stir any collected juices into the noodles. Pour the noodles and sauce over the pork chops and garnish with parsley.

Turnip Risotto
with Crispy Pancetta and Chives

Gluten-Free
Dairy-Free (opt.)
Low-Cal
Saves Well

TIME TO PREP 10 minutes
TIME TO COOK 15 minutes
SERVES 4

NUTRITIONAL INFORMATION
Calories: 186
Fat: 12 g
Sodium: 755 mg
Carbohydrate: 9 g
Fiber: 2 g
Sugar: 5 g
Protein: 9 g

ALSO WORKS WELL WITH
Kohlrabi, Butternut Squash,
Sweet Potato

When I first discovered how to make rice out of spiralized vegetables, I experimented with about a dozen types of dishes, from stuffed peppers to burrito bowls. I can tell you with confidence that the dish most similar in consistency to the real thing is risotto. The spiralized "rice" fluffs up when cooked with broth, collecting flavor. It's much faster than traditional risotto—and much simpler! Adding pancetta here infuses flavor into every bite of turnip. Everyone will think you slaved over the stove for hours!

- 1 cup diced pancetta
- 2 garlic cloves, minced
- 2 tablespoons minced shallot
- ½ teaspoon red pepper flakes
- *2 large turnips, peeled, spiralized with* **BLADE D**, *then riced (see page 16)*
- Salt and pepper
- 1 cup low-sodium vegetable broth
- ¼ cup finely chopped fresh chives
- ½ cup grated Parmesan cheese (see Tip)

1 Cook the pancetta in a large skillet over medium heat for 7 minutes or until browned, flipping. Transfer to a paper towel–lined plate to drain. Reserve 1 tablespoon of the rendered fat in the pan and discard the remainder.

2 Add the garlic, shallot, and red pepper flakes to the skillet with the pancetta fat and cook for 30 seconds or until fragrant. Add the turnip rice, season with salt and black pepper, and cook for 2 minutes or until the rice is beginning to soften.
Add the broth and cook for 5 minutes more or until the rice is al dente.

3 Fold in the half the pancetta, half the chives, and the cheese. Remove the skillet from the heat and stir continuously to melt the cheese completely.

4 Divide the risotto among four bowls and top with the remaining pancetta and chives.

If you eat don't eat dairy, stir in ½ cup coconut cream (see page 19) instead of the Parmesan.

White Potato

We all know that potatoes are buttery, creamy, and rich. Their starchy goodness is undeniably addictive and universally complementary to all types of meals. If you're trying to convince a stubborn friend or family member to try spiralizing but he or she is a "meat and potatoes" kind of person, this chapter is the obvious place to start. There's a whole lot more to potatoes than fries, mash, and chips!

There are many varieties of potatoes, and we use a lot of them in this chapter. Some of my favorites to spiralize are the russet, Yukon Gold, Red Gold, and Idaho. The differences among these are their starch and sweetness levels, but they all spiralize easily and yield plentiful noodles. For example, russet potatoes have an earthier, mild flavor, while red-skinned potatoes are slightly more sweet—but both carry moderate levels of starch.

Keep in mind as you're preparing your recipes that when potatoes are peeled and/or spiralized, they quickly oxidize (a chemical reaction that happens when their flesh is exposed to oxygen, resulting in browning and black spots). To avoid this, you have two options: wait to spiralize the potato until right before it's used in the recipe or, after you spiralize, place the noodles in a bowl of cold water and set it in the refrigerator for up to 24 hours.

NUTRITIONAL BENEFITS: Potatoes are high in vitamin B_6, potassium, and copper, all of which help lower blood pressure and support basic metabolic function.

PREPARATION AND STORAGE: Peel the potato, if desired, and slice off the ends to leave flat, even surfaces. Store in a container filled with water in the refrigerator for up to 24 hours. Potato noodles can be frozen for up to 8 months for future use.

BEST BLADES TO USE
- Blade A
- Blade B
- Blade C
- Blade D

BEST COOKING METHODS
- Sauté over medium-high heat for 5 to 7 minutes
- Roast at 425 degrees for 10 to 15 minutes

Potato-Wrapped Roasted Carrots

with Moroccan Black Lentils and Feta

Vegetarian
Gluten-Free
Dairy-Free (opt.)
Saves Well

TIME TO PREP 15 minutes

TIME TO COOK 50 minutes

SERVES 4

NUTRITIONAL INFORMATION
Calories: 389
Fat: 21 g
Sodium: 324 mg
Carbohydrate: 45 g
Fiber: 9 g
Sugar: 9 g
Protein: 14 g

ALSO WORKS WELL WITH
Sweet Potato, Rutabaga

If you're a reader of the *Inspiralized* blog, you might have seen that for Halloween, I created potato-wrapped carrots that resembled mummies. I knew I wanted to turn them into a full meal. This dish squeezes in complex carbohydrates (the good kind!), and has a comforting taste enhanced by Moroccan spiced black lentils and salty feta. Wrapping the carrots is an impressive presentation and also adds nutrients. If you want to try this recipe but don't want to deal with that intricacy, cook the potato noodles separately and stir them into the lentils.

---

1 cup uncooked black Beluga lentils, rinsed

2 cups low-sodium vegetable broth, plus more as needed

Leaves from 1 sprig of thyme

1 pound heirloom carrots, scrubbed clean (unpeeled) and patted dry

2 *large red potatoes, or 1 medium Yukon Gold potato, spiralized with BLADE D, untrimmed*

1½ tablespoons extra-virgin olive oil

½ teaspoon ground cumin

Salt and pepper

For the dressing

1 tablespoon fresh lemon juice

1 teaspoon honey

3 tablespoons extra-virgin olive oil

½ teaspoon ground cumin

¼ teaspoon ground cinnamon

¼ teaspoon ground ginger

¼ teaspoon smoked paprika

¼ teaspoon ground coriander

⅛ teaspoon cayenne pepper

¼ cup chopped fresh cilantro, for garnish

½ cup crumbled feta cheese

1 Preheat the oven to 425 degrees. Line a baking sheet with parchment paper.

2 Place the lentils, broth, and thyme in a medium saucepan. Bring to a boil over medium-high heat, cover, then reduce the heat to low and simmer for 20 to 30 minutes or until the lentils are tender but not mushy. If the liquid evaporates before the lentils are cooked, add more broth, ¼ cup at a time.

3 Lay out the carrots on the prepared baking sheet, spacing them apart. Roast for 15 minutes or until slightly tender. Remove and set aside until cool enough to handle. Then, working from end to end, twirl the potato noodles around the carrots.

4 In a small bowl, whisk together the oil and cumin. Brush the mixture over the carrots and season with salt and pepper. Return the carrots to the oven to roast for 30 to 40 minutes more or until fork-tender.

5 Meanwhile, make the dressing. Whisk together all the ingredients for the dressing in a small bowl. Taste and adjust the seasoning to your preferences.

6 Serve the carrots over the lentils. Drizzle with the dressing and garnish with the cilantro and feta.

Choose the longest spiralized potato noodles possible, discarding any extra noodles that are too short to wrap around the carrot or saving them for another use.

Asparagus, Egg, and Potato Noodles
with Kale

 Vegetarian
Gluten-Free
Paleo
Dairy-Free

TIME TO PREP 10 minutes
TIME TO COOK 15 minutes
SERVES 2

NUTRITIONAL INFORMATION
Calories: 365
Fat: 26 g
Sodium: 86 mg
Carbohydrate: 25 g
Fiber: 5 g
Sugar: 3 g
Protein: 11 g

ALSO WORKS WELL WITH
Sweet Potato

On those nights when you get home late from a long day at school, tiring meetings at work, or an exhausting fitness class, this dish is for you. There's no point in making a big meal before you go to bed—your body doesn't need that much fuel to sleep. Instead, this quick recipe offers all you need to nourish yourself and turn in feeling light: leafy greens, protein-packed eggs, complex carbohydrates, and fiber-filled asparagus.

3 tablespoons extra-virgin olive oil

8 large asparagus spears, ends trimmed

Salt and pepper

1 *medium russet potato, spiralized with BLADE D, noodles trimmed*

¼ teaspoon garlic powder

⅛ teaspoon paprika

3 cups roughly chopped kale leaves

Cooking spray

2 whole large eggs

To turn this dish into a more filling meal, add avocado and/or some bacon.

1 Heat 1½ tablespoons of the olive oil in a large skillet over medium heat. When the oil is shimmering, add the asparagus and season with salt and pepper. Cook for 5 minutes or until the asparagus is bright green and fork-tender. Divide between two plates.

2 Heat the remaining olive oil in the same skillet. When the oil is shimmering, add the potato noodles and season with the garlic powder, paprika, salt, and pepper. Cover and cook for about 5 minutes or until mostly wilted. Stir in the kale, cover, and cook for 5 minutes more or until the noodles are al dente. Divide the mixture between the plates with the asparagus.

3 Immediately coat the skillet with cooking spray and set it over medium-high heat. Crack in the eggs and cook until the whites are just set but the yolks are still runny, about 3 minutes.

4 Transfer an egg to each plate and serve immediately.

Half and Half Pasta

Vegetarian
Gluten-Free
Saves Well

TIME TO PREP 10 minutes
TIME TO COOK 15 minutes
SERVES 2

NUTRITIONAL INFORMATION
Calories: 382
Fat: 20 g
Sodium: 367 mg
Carbohydrate: 39 g
Fiber: 6 g
Sugar: 5 g
Protein: 14 g

If you know someone who is resisting becoming Inspiralized, beg for one more chance—and then make this recipe. This pasta is exactly what it sounds like: half zucchini, half potato noodles! The latter offers a familiar starchiness that your regular pasta-loving pal will welcome. When the Parmesan cheese melts and coats both noodles together, he or she will only know that dinner tastes delicious. Oh, and here's a pro tip: peel the zucchini before spiralizing—without the green, it will look more like the real thing!

2 tablespoons extra-virgin olive oil

2 garlic cloves, finely minced

¼ teaspoon red pepper flakes

1 medium russet potato, peeled, spiralized with BLADE D, noodles trimmed

Salt and pepper

1 large zucchini, spiralized with BLADE D, noodles trimmed

½ cup grated Parmesan cheese

Minced fresh parsley, for garnish

1 Heat 1 tablespoon of the olive oil in a large skillet over medium heat. When the oil is shimmering, add the garlic and red pepper flakes and cook for 30 seconds or until fragrant. Add the potato noodles, season with salt and black pepper, and toss to combine. Cover and cook, tossing occasionally, for 7 minutes or until al dente. Remove from the pan and set aside.

2 Immediately add the zucchini noodles to the skillet and cook, tossing occasionally, for 3 to 5 minutes or until al dente.

3 Return the potato noodles to the skillet. Drizzle over the remaining 1 tablespoon oil and toss to combine thoroughly. Turn off the heat, fold in the Parmesan, and toss until the cheese has melted.

4 Garnish with parsley and serve immediately.

For the *most* stubborn of nonbelievers, you can replace the potato noodles with regular pasta. Baby steps!

Pan con Tomate
with Serrano Ham

Gluten-Free
Dairy-Free
Low-Cal

TIME TO PREP 10 minutes
TIME TO COOK 30 minutes
SERVES 2

NUTRITIONAL INFORMATION
Calories: 272
Fat: 15 g
Sodium: 52 mg
Carbohydrate: 26 g
Fiber: 3 g
Sugar: 2 g
Protein: 6 g

My childhood friend Sarah and I have birthdays within three days of each other, and for years, we've celebrated together. We both studied in Europe during our junior year of college, and that year we met up in Barcelona, the land of tapas. We discovered that one of the most ubiquitous and inexpensive tapas is *pan con tomate* ("bread with tomato"). We ate so much that by the end of our visit, we were in a carb coma. This spiralized version replaces the bread with a potato noodle bun and adds a little something extra with the ham. Bring on the cava!

4 teaspoons extra-virgin olive oil

1 russet potato, peeled, spiralized with **BLADE D**, *noodles trimmed*

¼ teaspoon smoked paprika

Salt and pepper

1 large egg, beaten

1 large ripe tomato

1 garlic clove, smashed and chopped

2 thin slices of Serrano ham

To make this dish vegetarian, omit the ham and sprinkle a little bit of smoked sea salt on top.

1 Heat 2 teaspoons of the olive oil in a large nonstick skillet over medium heat. When the oil is shimmering, add the potato noodles and season with the paprika, salt, and pepper. Cook for 5 to 7 minutes or until the noodles are softened and lightly browned.

2 Transfer the noodles to a medium bowl and let cool for 2 minutes. Stir in the egg and toss to coat.

3 Fill two ramekins halfway with the noodles. Cover each with a piece of foil or wax paper, pressing it down firmly onto the noodles to compress them. Refrigerate for at least 15 minutes to set.

4 Heat the remaining 2 teaspoons oil in the same skillet over medium heat. When the oil is shimmering, add the buns two at a time, flipping each out of its ramekin into the skillet and patting the bottom until the bun falls out. Cook for 3 minutes or until set on the bottom, being sure to push in any stray noodles. Carefully flip and cook for 2 to 3 minutes more or until the buns are completely set and browned on both sides, flattening with the back of the spatula.

5 While the potato buns cook, using the largest holes on a box grater, grate the tomato. Smear each potato bun with the garlic, then spoon on the grated tomato. Top each bun with a slice of ham and serve.

Loaded Potatoes
with BBQ Sauce

Twice-baked loaded potatoes are essential for the Sunday football party spread. With melted cheese and bacon, something about them is just perfect for fun and celebrating. This spiralized version is a healthy spin that omits the traditional butter and sour cream. The potato noodles are shareable and almost resemble nachos! Does that make them even more perfect for sport-watching? Maybe.

〰〰 | Gluten-Free
〰〰 | Low-Cal

TIME TO PREP 15 minutes
TIME TO COOK 20 minutes
SERVES 4

NUTRITIONAL INFORMATION
Calories: 261
Fat: 16 g
Sodium: 359 mg
Carbohydrate: 28 g
Fiber: 4 g
Sugar: 2 g
Protein: 11 g

ALSO WORKS WELL WITH
Sweet Potato, Rutabaga

---

4 bacon slices

4 red potatoes, peeled, spiralized with **BLADE D**, noodles trimmed

½ teaspoon garlic powder

¼ teaspoon chili powder

Salt and pepper

1 large avocado

1 tablespoon fresh lime juice

¼ teaspoon paprika

¼ cup shredded cheddar cheese

¼ cup shredded Monterey Jack cheese

2 scallions, green parts only, sliced

2 tablespoons bottled barbecue sauce (I like Tessemae's Matty's BBQ Sauce)

1 Preheat the broiler.

2 Cook the bacon in a large skillet over medium-high heat, flipping occasionally, for about 10 minutes or until browned and beginning to crisp. Transfer to a paper towel–lined plate to drain. Reserve 1 tablespoon of the rendered fat in the pan; discard the remainder.

3 Add the potato noodles to the skillet with the bacon fat and season with the garlic powder, chili powder, salt, and pepper. Toss to combine and cook for about 7 minutes or until al dente. Transfer the potato noodles to a medium baking dish.

4 Meanwhile, use the back of a fork to mash together the avocado and lime juice in a medium bowl until no large chunks remain. Season with the paprika, salt, and pepper.

5 Mound together the potato noodles in the center of the baking dish. Crumble half the bacon over the noodles and sprinkle with the cheeses. Broil for 2 minutes or until the cheese is melted and bubbling.

6 Remove from the oven and immediately top with the scallions. Crumble the remaining bacon over the top. Drizzle with barbecue sauce and finish with dollops of the avocado mash.

Zucchini & Summer Squash

Last but not least: zucchini. Like a first love, it will always have a special place in my heart—and on my plate. Whenever I introduce people to spiralizing, I always encourage them to start with this vegetable, like I did.

Zucchini is the most popular vegetable to spiralize: it requires barely any prep, moves through the gadget effortlessly, and has a consistency similar to that of real pasta. The noodles are also resilient, so they won't break up in the pan.

When you cook zucchini, it releases quite a bit of moisture. To minimize this effect, there are a few steps you can take:

- Pat the noodles dry to blot out excess moisture as soon as they're spiralized.
- Cook the noodles in their own pan and drain them in a colander before topping them with any sauces or dressings.
- If you're cooking the noodles directly in a sauce, transfer the finished dish to the serving plate using pasta tongs, allowing the excess moisture to drip off into the pan rather than collect on the plate.
- Keep your noodle-to-sauce ratio heavier on the noodles, as their liquid will add to (and thin out) the sauce.

When picking out your zucchini, make sure it's firm, bright in color, at least 1½ inches in diameter, and no longer than 8 inches (any longer and their taste becomes bitter).

NUTRITIONAL BENEFITS: Zucchini is very low-caloric and contains moderate amounts of folates, which help with cell function. It is also a good source of potassium and vitamin C. Since it is composed of so much water, it also has detoxifying and hydrating benefits. Peeling is not necessary, so keep the skin on, as it carries many nutrients, including dietary fiber.

PREPARATION AND STORAGE: Slice off the ends to leave flat, even surfaces. Seal in an airtight container lined with paper towels in the refrigerator for up to 5 days.

BEST BLADES TO USE
- Blades A, B, C, and D

BEST COOKING METHODS
- Raw
- Simmer in soups
- Sauté over medium-high heat for 2 to 5 minutes

Thai Steak Salad

~~~
~~~     Dairy-Free
~~~     Saves Well
~~~

TIME TO PREP 20 minutes
TIME TO COOK 20 minutes
SERVES 4

NUTRITIONAL INFORMATION
Calories: 408
Fat: 27 g
Sodium: 484 mg
Carbohydrate: 15 g
Fiber: 4 g
Sugar: 9 g
Protein: 29 g

ALSO WORKS WELL WITH
Kohlrabi

If I'm going to eat steak, the rest of the plate must be filled with heart-healthy vegetables. Here, the spiralized vegetables expertly complement the heartiness of the meat and add beautiful color. The slightly sweet, nutty sauce brings life to the raw zucchini noodles, and the longer they sit, the more they soften. No matter how you like your steak cooked, it shines in this Thai-inspired dish.

1 tablespoon extra-virgin olive oil

1 pound NY strip or flank steak

Salt and pepper

For the dressing

¼ cup almond butter

1½ tablespoons fresh lime juice

1 tablespoon rice vinegar

1 tablespoon soy sauce

1½ teaspoons sesame oil

1½ teaspoons honey

1 teaspoon grated fresh ginger

1 teaspoon hot sauce

2 *medium zucchini, peeled, spiralized with* **BLADE C,** *noodles trimmed*

1 *large carrot, peeled spiralized with* **BLADE D,** *noodles trimmed*

1 *large red bell pepper, spiralized with* **BLADE A,** *noodles trimmed*

½ cup sliced scallions

2 tablespoons slivered raw almonds

¼ cup packed fresh cilantro

1 Heat the olive oil in a grill pan or large skillet over medium-high heat. Season the steak generously with salt and pepper. When the oil is shimmering, add the steak and sear for 4 minutes per side until medium-rare. Transfer to a cutting board to rest for about 10 minutes. Slice it thinly against the grain, then cut each slice into thirds.

2 While the steak rests, make the dressing. Place all the ingredients for the dressing in a food processor and pulse until creamy. Add water, 1 tablespoon at a time, as needed to reach the desired consistency. Taste and adjust the seasoning to your preferences.

3 In a large bowl, combine the zucchini, carrot, and bell pepper noodles and add the scallions, almonds, and cilantro. Pour the dressing over the salad and toss thoroughly to combine. If desired, marinate the salad in the refrigerator for 15 minutes or until the zucchini softens.

4 Divide the noodle salad among four plates and top evenly with the sliced steak.

~~~~~~~~~~

I prefer to serve the steak chilled in this dish, so if you have the time, let it sit in the refrigerator after it rests for about 30 minutes. Hello, cold steak salad leftovers!

~~~~~~~~~~

Hoisin Salmon
with Zucchini Slaw

Many people ask me if I ever eat the same thing twice. Everyone figures I'm always testing new recipes, experimenting, and cooking different styles of meals. While that's certainly true, I definitely have my lazy meals—the ones I default to when I'm not feeling inspired. One of those is hoisin salmon, and it may quickly become *your* lazy meal, too! Hoisin sauce is a thick, barbecue sauce–like condiment used in Chinese cooking to flavor dishes—it's both sweet and spicy. The zucchini slaw absorbs all the flavors from the hoisin sauce and adds a nice crunch. Consider this lazy meal upgraded!

Dairy-Free

TIME TO PREP 25 minutes
TIME TO COOK 25 minutes
SERVES 2

NUTRITIONAL INFORMATION
Calories: 424
Fat: 10 g
Sodium: 2300 mg
Carbohydrate: 45 g
Fiber: 8 g
Sugar: 24 g
Protein: 42 g

ALSO WORKS WELL WITH
Sweet Potato, Butternut Squash, Turnip, Chayote

For the glaze
   Juice of 2 limes
¼ teaspoon red pepper flakes
⅓ cup low-sodium soy sauce
⅓ cup hoisin sauce
1 (1½-inch) piece fresh ginger, peeled and chopped
2 garlic cloves, pressed

2 (4-ounce) salmon fillets
2 medium zucchini, spiralized with **BLADE D**, noodles trimmed
3 scallions, thinly sliced
2 carrots, peeled, spiralized with **BLADE D**, noodles trimmed
1 red bell pepper, spiralized with **BLADE A**, noodles trimmed
2 tablespoons chopped fresh cilantro
1 teaspoon white sesame seeds, for garnish

The hoisin sauce is very sticky, so you might want to clean as you cook.

1 Preheat the oven to 400 degrees. Line a baking sheet with parchment paper.

2 Make the glaze. Place all the ingredients for the glaze in a food processor and pulse until smooth.

3 Place a medium skillet over medium-high heat. When water flicked onto the skillet sizzles, add the prepared glaze, reserving ¼ cup in a small bowl. Simmer until it has reduced and thickened into a syrup, about 15 minutes. Remove the pan from heat.

4 Set the salmon fillets on the prepared baking sheet and brush with a thin layer of the reserved glaze.

5 Bake the salmon for 9 to 12 minutes or until it is opaque and flakes easily.

6 Meanwhile, heat a large skillet over medium-high heat. When water flicked onto the skillet sizzles, add the zucchini, scallions, carrots, and bell pepper and cook until al dente, about 3 minutes. Drain the vegetables in a colander, then return them to the skillet over medium-high heat and immediately pour over the reserved glaze. Toss to coat with the glaze for about 1 minute, then stir in the cilantro.

7 Divide the slaw between two plates and top each with a salmon fillet. Garnish with sesame seeds.

Green Goddess Zucchini Pasta

Vegan
Vegetarian
Gluten-Free
Dairy-Free (opt.)
No Cook
Saves Well

TIME TO PREP 35 minutes
TIME TO COOK 5 minutes
SERVES 2

NUTRITIONAL INFORMATION
Calories: 413
Fat: 32 g
Sodium: 65 mg
Carbohydrate: 31 g
Fiber: 8 g
Sugar: 6 g
Protein: 10 g

This recipe is for my fellow green goddesses out there—those of us who proudly embrace a healthy lifestyle full of wholesome, nourishing foods, including, of course, lots of greens. You'll feel and shine like your goddess self after eating this bowl of, well, green noodles. With anti-inflammatory avocado, immune-boosting ginger, and detoxifying lemon, this dish will truly make you feel like you're glowing from the inside out. Whether it was the second slice of birthday cake at lunch or an emotionally draining week that led to a junk food bender, we've all been there—and this meal will get you back to feeling like the goddess you are!

¼ cup quinoa

For the dressing
  1 small garlic clove
  ½ medium avocado
  ¼ cup minced fresh basil
  2 tablespoons minced fresh parsley
  2 tablespoons minced fresh chives
  3 tablespoons extra-virgin olive oil
  ¼ cup sliced scallions (green parts only)
  ½ teaspoon lemon zest
    Juice of 1 small lemon
  1 tablespoon red wine vinegar
    Salt and pepper

2 medium zucchini, spiralized with BLADE A, noodles trimmed
  2 tablespoons slivered almonds
  1 cup packed watercress
  2 tablespoons crumbled goat cheese, optional

As you spiralize the zucchini, apply very soft pressure and crank the handle slowly, yielding thinner-than-usual ribbons. If you're not sure on how to do this, just spiralize with blade D instead.

1 Place the quinoa and ⅔ cup water in a small saucepan. Cover and bring to a boil over high heat, then uncover, reduce the heat to medium-low, and simmer for 15 minutes or until the quinoa fluffs up. Transfer the quinoa to a small bowl and refrigerate for 30 minutes.

2 Meanwhile, make the dressing. Place all the ingredients for the dressing plus 1 tablespoon water in a food processor and pulse until smooth. It should be thick, but add more water, 1 tablespoon at a time, as needed until the desired consistency is reached. Taste and adjust the seasoning to your preference.

3 Put the zucchini noodles in a large bowl. Pour the dressing over the noodles and toss to combine. Set aside to soften for 5 minutes.

4 Place a small skillet over medium-high heat. Toast the almonds in the skillet, tossing to avoid burning, for about 5 minutes or until fragrant and golden brown. Immediately remove them from the pan.

5 Add the watercress and quinoa to the bowl with the zucchini and toss to combine. Divide the zucchini pasta between two plates and top with the toasted almonds and, if desired, goat cheese.

Dairy-Free Clam Chowder
with Zucchini Noodles

Gluten-Free
Dairy-Free
Low-Cal

TIME TO PREP 15 minutes
TIME TO COOK 30 minutes
SERVES 4

NUTRITIONAL INFORMATION
Calories: 200
Fat: 4 g
Sodium: 476 mg
Carbohydrate: 35 g
Fiber: 9 g
Sugar: 13 g
Protein: 9 g

ALSO WORKS WELL WITH
Kohlrabi

Clam chowder is a New England summer classic. Traditionally made with milk and flour, it's not the lightest, but is so universally desirable that I had to create an Inspiralized version. A seasoned cauliflower mash gives this chowder its chunky, thick consistency, just like the original. The moment after you sip your last spoonful of this soup, you'll look down at the bowl and say, "Was that really dairy-free?!" The addition of zucchini noodles lends substance and a slight crunch. If there's a little bit of broth left over, sop it up with some toasted multigrain bread and imagine yourself on the Cape.

- 1 large head of cauliflower, chopped into florets
- 1 tablespoon extra-virgin olive oil
- 1 small onion, diced
- 2 garlic cloves, minced
- 1 carrot, diced
- 1 celery stalk, diced
- 2 bay leaves
- 1½ cups low-sodium chicken broth
- 2 (6.5-ounce) cans chopped clams in juice
- ½ teaspoon garlic powder
- 2 tablespoons nutritional yeast, plus more if needed
- 1 teaspoon fresh thyme leaves
- Salt and pepper
- 1 teaspoon chili powder
- 2 small zucchini, peeled, spiralized with *BLADE D*, noodles trimmed
- 1 cup frozen organic corn, thawed

If you'd like to make a thinner soup, use only half the cauliflower florets and add another ½ cup chicken broth.

1 Bring a large pot of water to a boil over high heat. Add the cauliflower and cook until fork-tender, about 10 minutes. Drain and transfer to a food processor.

2 Wipe the pot clean and heat the olive oil over medium-high heat. When the oil is shimmering, add the onion, garlic, carrots, and celery and sauté for 5 minutes or until the vegetables are softened. Add the bay leaves, 1 cup of the broth, and the clams along with their juice. Reduce the heat to medium and simmer.

3 Add the garlic powder, nutritional yeast, thyme, and remaining ½ cup broth to the cauliflower and season with salt. Blend until smooth. Taste and adjust the seasoning to your preference with more nutritional yeast, salt, or pepper.

4 Add the cauliflower mixture and chili powder to the simmering clam broth and stir to combine thoroughly. Season with pepper, then season generously with salt. Simmer for 10 minutes to allow the flavors to develop.

5 Add the zucchini noodles and corn to the chowder and cook for 5 minutes, until the noodles are al dente. Taste and adjust the seasoning, if needed. Before serving, remove the bay leaves.

Italian-Style Chicken Sliders

Gluten-Free
Paleo
Dairy-Free
Low-Cal
Saves Well

TIME TO PREP 20 minutes
TIME TO COOK 15 minutes
SERVES 4 (2 sliders per serving)

NUTRITIONAL INFORMATION
Calories: 120
Fat: 9 g
Sodium: 52 mg
Carbohydrate: 4 g
Fiber: 1 g
Sugar: 2 g
Protein: 12 g

This probably won't shock you, but my theory is that everything is better with zucchini noodles. So why not stir them into your burgers? It's a fun, quick, and super-easy way to sneak more vegetables into your meals. This recipe uses ground chicken, keeping the fat content low while incorporating the same great juicy flavors as a traditional burger. Those green swirls are sure to be a conversation starter at a dinner party.

- *1 small zucchini, spiralized with* **BLADE D**, *noodles roughly chopped*
- **1 pound lean ground chicken**
- **1 large garlic clove, minced**
- **2 teaspoons dried parsley**
- **1 teaspoon dried oregano**
- **1 teaspoon dried basil**
- **½ teaspoon onion powder**
- **¼ teaspoon red pepper flakes**
- **Salt and pepper**
- **2 tablespoons extra-virgin olive oil**
- *½ small red onion, peeled, spiralized with* **BLADE A**, *noodles trimmed*
- **8 leaves Boston lettuce**
- **8 Roma (plum) tomato slices (from about 2 tomatoes)**
- **2 cups microgreens**
- **Ketchup, for serving (optional)**

1 In a large bowl, combine the zucchini noodles, chicken, garlic, parsley, oregano, basil, onion powder, and red pepper flakes and season with salt and black pepper. Using your hands, form the mixture into eight small patties (or four large). Refrigerate for about 10 minutes to set.

2 Heat the olive oil in a grill pan or large skillet over medium-high heat. When the oil is shimmering, add the onions to one half of the pan and the patties to the other, working in batches if necessary. Season the onions with salt and pepper and sear, tossing occasionally, until mostly caramelized. Sear the patties for 5 minutes per side or until browned and cooked through.

3 On a serving platter, lay out the lettuce leaves and place a burger on each (if you made sliders). Top each with a tomato slice, caramelized onion, and microgreens. (Top with another piece of lettuce if you made larger burgers.) Serve with ketchup, if desired.

I love packing in even more vegetables by putting burgers on thick roasted slices of sweet potato as the "bun." You can also make spiralized buns (see page 16). Give it a try!

Chocolate Chip Zucchini Noodle Bread
with Coconut Cream Frosting

~ Gluten-Free
~ Paleo
~ Dairy-Free
Saves Well

TIME TO PREP 20 minutes
TIME TO COOK 50 minutes
SERVES 6 to 8

NUTRITIONAL INFORMATION
(for 1 of 6 servings)
Calories: 481
Fat: 31 g
Sodium: 238 mg
Carbohydrate: 43 g
Fiber: 7 g
Sugar: 24 g
Protein: 10 g

In gluten-free baking, there are many healthy types of flours to use, like coconut, tapioca, and almond. These flours come from vegetables, nuts, and fruits, making treats baked with them more nutritiously valuable than if wheat flour were used—plus, they're gluten-free! Spiralizing the zucchini here makes this recipe a million times easier than the grating called for in your standard zucchini bread recipe; plus, it adds a cool texture and visual appeal. The coconut cream in the sweet, fluffy frosting complements the coconut notes of the flour.

For the zucchini bread
- 1 medium zucchini
- ¼ cup tapioca flour
- ½ cup coconut flour
- ¾ teaspoon baking soda
- ¾ teaspoon baking powder
- ½ teaspoon salt
- 2 teaspoons ground cinnamon
- ½ teaspoon ground nutmeg
- 3 large eggs, beaten
- 3 tablespoons maple syrup
- 2 teaspoons vanilla extract
- ¼ cup plain unsweetened almond milk
- 1 tablespoon coconut oil, melted and cooled to room temperature
- 1 ripe banana, mashed until no large chunks remain
- ½ cup chopped walnuts
- ½ cup dairy-free chocolate chips (I like Enjoy Life)

For the frosting
- 1½ heaping cups coconut cream (see page 19)
- 1½ teaspoons vanilla extract
- 1 tablespoon honey

1 Make the zucchini bread. Preheat the oven to 350 degrees. Line a 9 x 5-inch loaf pan with parchment paper, leaving the paper overhanging on two sides.

2 Slice off the ends of the zucchini and then slice it halfway through lengthwise to create a slit, being careful not to pierce any farther than its center. Spiralize with **BLADE D**. Trim the noodles and pat them dry.

3 In a medium bowl, combine the tapioca flour, coconut flour, baking soda, baking powder, salt, cinnamon, and nutmeg.

4 In a large bowl, stir together the eggs, maple syrup, vanilla, almond milk, coconut oil, and banana.

5 Add the dry ingredients to the wet ingredients and stir to combine. Add the zucchini noodles and stir until the batter is mostly smooth. Fold in the walnuts and chocolate chips.

recipe continues

6 Pour the batter into the prepared pan and bake for 40 to 50 minutes or until a toothpick inserted into the center of the bread comes out clean and the bread is browned on top. Lift the bread out of the pan using the parchment paper. Discard the paper and set the bread on a wire rack to cool for at least 10 minutes.

7 Meanwhile, make the frosting. Using a hand mixer, beat together the coconut cream, vanilla, and honey in a medium bowl for 5 minutes or until whipped. Alternatively, use a stand mixer fitted with the whisk attachment and beat on high, or get in a good bicep workout with a whisk.

8 When the bread has cooled, cut it into thick slices or squares and top each with a generous dollop of the coconut cream.

It's important to let this bread cool completely to let it firm up—and so the frosting doesn't melt on top of it. Don't skip that step!

Greek-Style Shrimp Scampi

~~~

Gluten-Free
Dairy-Free (opt.)
Low-Cal

TIME TO PREP 15 minutes
TIME TO COOK 10 minutes
SERVES 4

NUTRITIONAL INFORMATION
Calories: 266
Fat: 10 g
Sodium: 670 mg
Carbohydrate: 13 g
Fiber: 4 g
Sugar: 7 g
Protein: 29 g

ALSO WORKS WELL WITH
Kohlrabi, Chayote

If you're searching for an easy weeknight dinner, look no further—nothing beats shrimp scampi. Fast-cooked in garlic, olive oil, and wine with herbs and traditionally served over pasta, this classic Italian-American dish gets a makeover here, with the addition of tomato and salty feta for a slightly Greek flair. On top of zucchini noodles, this zesty dish is suitable for any night. It also *looks* fancy!

- 2 tablespoons extra-virgin olive oil
- 1 tablespoon minced garlic
- ¼ teaspoon red pepper flakes
- 1 pound large shrimp, defrosted, peeled, and deveined
- Salt and pepper
- 1 cup diced seeded tomato
- ¼ cup dry white wine
- ½ teaspoon lemon zest
- 2 tablespoons fresh lemon juice
- 3 medium zucchini, spiralized with BLADE D, noodles trimmed
- 2 tablespoons chopped fresh parsley
- ¼ cup crumbled feta, for garnish

1 Heat the olive oil in a large skillet over medium heat. When the oil is shimmering, add the garlic and red pepper flakes and cook for 30 seconds or until fragrant. Add the shrimp, season with salt and black pepper, and cook for about 2 minutes per side or until pink, opaque, and cooked through. Using tongs or a slotted spoon, remove the shrimp and set aside.

2 Immediately add the tomato, wine, lemon zest, and lemon juice to the pan and scrape up any browned bits from the bottom of the pan with a wooden spoon. Cook for 2 minutes or until reduced slightly. Add the zucchini noodles and season generously with pepper. Cook for 2 to 3 minutes or until al dente.

3 Return the shrimp to the pan. Stir in the parsley and divide the pasta among four plates. Sprinkle the feta over the top before serving.

Use chopped lobster tail meat instead of shrimp for an amped-up scampi.

Minestrone
with Zucchini Noodles

Vegan
Vegetarian
Gluten-Free
Dairy-Free
One Pot
Saves Well

TIME TO PREP 15 minutes
TIME TO COOK 30 minutes
SERVES 4

NUTRITIONAL INFORMATION
Calories: 373
Fat: 8 g
Sodium: 720 mg
Carbohydrate: 60 g
Fiber: 15 g
Sugar: 16 g
Protein: 18 g

When I was vegan and went to my grandparents' house for Sunday dinner, aside from a few wisecracks here and there, my family was totally supportive of my diet. My grandmother would always prepare a *pasta e fagioli* or a minestrone soup especially for me. Minestrone is an Italian soup made with diced vegetables, beans, and pasta. If I had known about spiralizing back then, I definitely would have had her make this version! Even though I'm no longer vegan, whenever I'm in the mood for something comforting and hearty, I always opt for this version with zucchini noodles—it does the trick.

2 tablespoons extra-virgin olive oil

2 garlic cloves, minced

½ teaspoon red pepper flakes

1 cup diced red onion

1 cup diced carrots

1 cup diced celery

2 bay leaves

1 (28-ounce) can crushed tomatoes

6 cups low-sodium vegetable broth

1 teaspoon dried oregano

½ teaspoon dried rosemary

1 teaspoon dried thyme

½ teaspoon dried basil

Salt and pepper

2 *medium zucchini*

2 (15-ounce) cans cannellini beans, rinsed and drained

The longer the zucchini sits in this soup, the more it releases its water and dilutes the flavor of the soup. It's best to serve it right away.

1 Heat the olive oil in a medium pot over medium heat. When the oil is shimmering, add the garlic and red pepper flakes. Cook for 30 seconds or until fragrant. Add the onion, carrots, and celery. Sauté until softened, about 7 minutes.

2 Add the bay leaves and stir in the tomatoes, broth, oregano, rosemary, thyme, and basil and season with salt and pepper. Increase the heat to high and bring the soup to a boil, then reduce the heat to medium-low, cover, and simmer for 20 minutes to allow the flavors to develop.

3 While soup simmers, slice the zucchini halfway through lengthwise to create a slit, being careful not to pierce any farther than their centers. Spiralize with **BLADE D**.

4 Uncover the saucepan and add the beans and zucchini noodles. Cook for about 3 minutes or until the zucchini noodles soften. Remove the bay leaves and serve immediately.

Gluten-Free Chicken Parmesan
over Zucchini Noodles

≋ | Gluten-Free
≋
≋

TIME TO PREP 20 minutes
TIME TO COOK 30 minutes
SERVES 4

NUTRITIONAL INFORMATION
Calories: 461
Fat: 23 g
Sodium: 805 mg
Carbohydrate: 24 g
Fiber: 8 g
Sugar: 13 g
Protein: 44 g

ALSO WORKS WELL WITH
Sweet Potato, Butternut
Squash, Rutabaga

I've always loved chicken parm, but I rarely order it in restaurants because it's breaded, fried, covered with melted cheese, and usually served with a bowl of pasta alongside. This gluten-free version uses a nutrient-dense almond meal blend to coat the chicken, which gets baked in the oven and is then served with a mound of tomato-basil zucchini noodles. The ultimate Italian-American meal, without the heavy calorie or carb count, it's my go-to Friday night dinner—and you're about to find out why.

For the bread crumbs
- ¾ cup almond meal
- ½ teaspoon garlic powder
- Salt and pepper
- ½ teaspoon dried parsley
- ½ teaspoon dried oregano
- ¼ teaspoon onion powder
- 3 tablespoons grated Parmesan cheese

- 1 large egg
- 4 (¼-inch-thick) skinless, boneless chicken breasts
- 1 tablespoon extra-virgin olive oil
- ½ cup diced onion
- 2 garlic cloves, minced
- ½ teaspoon red pepper flakes
- 1 (28-ounce) canned diced tomatoes
- 1 teaspoon dried oregano
- Salt and pepper
- ¼ cup chopped fresh basil
- 4 (¼-inch-thick) slices mozzarella cheese
- 4 zucchini, spiralized with BLADE D, noodles trimmed

1 Preheat the oven to 400 degrees. Line a baking sheet with parchment paper.

2 Set up your dredging station. On a large plate, combine all the ingredients for the bread crumbs and stir to combine. Beat the egg in a shallow medium bowl. Set the dishes side by side. Working one piece at a time, dip the chicken first in the egg and allow the excess to drip back into the bowl. Then dip it in the bread crumbs, turning to coat and pressing to adhere. Place on the prepared baking sheet and bake for 15 to 20 minutes or until cooked through and no longer pink.

3 While the chicken bakes, heat the oil in a large skillet over medium heat. When the oil is shimmering, add the onion, garlic, and red pepper flakes and cook for 2 minutes or until the onion begins to soften. Add the tomatoes with their juices and the oregano, and season with salt and pepper. Crush the tomatoes with the back of a wooden spoon. Reduce the heat to low and simmer for 10 minutes or until the sauce thickens. Stir in the basil. Transfer half the sauce to a medium bowl and set aside, reserving the remainder in the skillet over low heat.

4 Remove the baking sheet from the oven and pour the sauce from the bowl over the chicken. Top each piece with a mozzarella slice and return to the oven to bake for 5 to 10 minutes more or until the cheese has melted.

5 Return the skillet with the remaining sauce to medium-high heat. Add the zucchini noodles and cook for about 5 minutes or until al dente. Divide the noodles among four plates. Top with the chicken.

Seared Scallops
over Zucchini Noodles
with Roasted Bell Pepper Sauce

Gluten-Free
Paleo
Dairy-Free
Low-Cal

TIME TO PREP 15 minutes
TIME TO COOK 40 minutes
SERVES 2

NUTRITIONAL INFORMATION
Calories: 239
Fat: 13 g
Sodium: 387 mg
Carbohydrate: 19 g
Fiber: 5 g
Sugar: 10 g
Protein: 14 g

ALSO WORKS WELL WITH
Butternut Squash

Some jarred dressings and pasta sauces are so good that if you're crunched for time, there's no need to make your own. But it can be difficult to find a healthy version of some types. In my opinion, red bell pepper sauce is always better made from scratch, free of any dairy, preservatives, or added sugars—like this one! The sauce is light but with a deep, roasted flavor, and coats the zucchini noodles beautifully. This dish feels like a gourmet meal!

Cooking spray

2 red bell peppers

1 tablespoon plus 2 teaspoons olive oil

2 garlic cloves, minced

¼ teaspoon red pepper flakes

¼ cup diced white onion

1 teaspoon dried oregano

⅓ cup low-sodium chicken broth

2 medium zucchini, spiralized with BLADE C, noodles trimmed

6 large scallops, patted dry

Salt and pepper

1 tablespoon chopped fresh parsley, for garnish

Blade B also works well in this recipe. Try it for a change in texture!

---

1 Preheat the oven to 400 degrees. Lightly coat a baking sheet with cooking spray.

2 Slice off the tops and bottoms of the peppers, then halve them lengthwise. Keeping the peppers intact, remove and discard the seeds. Place them cut-side up on the prepared baking sheet. Roast for 25 minutes, then transfer the roasted peppers to a food processor and pulse until mostly smooth.

3 Heat 1 tablespoon of the olive oil in a large skillet over medium heat. When the oil is shimmering, add the garlic, red pepper flakes, and onion and sauté until the onion is soft, about 5 minutes. Stir in the roasted bell pepper puree and the oregano, then add the broth. Cook for 5 to 7 minutes or until the mixture thickens. Reduce the heat to low and bring to a simmer to allow the flavors to develop.

4 Heat a separate large skillet over medium-high heat. When water flicked onto the pan sizzles, add the zucchini noodles and cook for 3 to 5 minutes or until al dente. Drain and set aside in a large bowl.

5 Add the remaining 2 teaspoons olive oil to the skillet you used for the zucchini and heat over medium-high heat. Season the scallops generously with salt and pepper. When the oil is shimmering, add the scallops and cook for 2 to 3 minutes per side or until opaque and cooked through.

6 Pour the bell pepper sauce over the zucchini noodles in the bowl and toss to coat. Divide the noodles between two plates, top each with three scallops, and garnish with parsley.

Zucchini Ravioli
with Tomato Basil and Cashew Cheese

If you aren't already sold on the spiralizer being the most incredible kitchen gadget on the planet, these spiralized raviolis should seal the deal. This version uses cashew cheese, which raw vegans have been making ravioli with for ages. But to me, there's just something about this dish that needs to be warm and velvety smooth. So I've combined the best of both worlds: the zucchini slices are warmed up in a pan before the vegan cheese is added, then the dish is topped off with a cozy and aromatic tomato-basil sauce.

Vegan
Vegetarian
Gluten-Free
Paleo
Dairy-Free
Low-Cal

TIME TO PREP 30 minutes plus 2 hours for the cashews

TIME TO COOK 15 minutes

SERVES 4 (3 ravioli per serving)

NUTRITIONAL INFORMATION
Calories: 59
Fat: 4 g
Sodium: 100 mg
Carbohydrate: 5 g
Fiber: 1 g
Sugar: 2 g
Protein: 2 g

For the cashew cheese
- ¾ cup raw, unsalted cashews, soaked in water for at least 2 hours (preferably overnight) and drained
- 1 tablespoon nutritional yeast
- ¼ teaspoon dried oregano
- ¼ teaspoon dried basil
- ¼ teaspoon dried parsley
- ¼ teaspoon garlic powder
- 1½ tablespoons fresh lemon juice
- Salt and pepper

For the ravioli
- 1 medium zucchini
- 1 cup tomato-basil sauce (I like Victoria's Tomato Herb)
- ¼ cup chopped fresh basil, for garnish

The size of your ravioli will depend on the width of your zucchini. Opt for a medium zucchini (about 1½ inches in diameter) for optimal results.

1 In a food processor or high-speed blender, combine the cashews, yeast, herbs, garlic powder, and lemon juice. Season with salt and pepper. Pulse a few times to break down the cashews until they have a coarse texture. Add 2 tablespoons water, 1 tablespoon at a time, and pulse until the cashew cheese has the consistency of thick hummus.

2 Make the ravioli. Slice the zucchini lengthwise to create a slit, taking care not to pierce any farther than its center. Spiralize with **BLADE A**. Select 24 zucchini slices, saving any additional for future use.

3 Heat the tomato sauce in a small pot over medium-high heat. Bring to a simmer, then reduce the heat to low to keep the sauce warm until ready to serve.

4 Heat a large skillet over medium heat. When water flicked onto the skillet sizzles, add the zucchini in a single layer, working in batches if necessary. Cook for 2 minutes or until heated through, then transfer to foil or parchment paper, keeping them separated.

5 Lay out one zucchini round on each of four plates. Spoon 1 tablespoon of cashew cheese on top, then add another round, pressing firmly to form a ravioli. Repeat until each plate has three ravioli. Pour ¼ cup of sauce over each plate and garnish with basil.

Avocado BLT Zucchini Pasta

Gluten-Free
Paleo
Dairy-Free

TIME TO PREP 10 minutes
TIME TO COOK 20 minutes
SERVES 2

NUTRITIONAL INFORMATION
Calories: 330
Fat: 21 g
Sodium: 432 mg
Carbohydrate: 28 g
Fiber: 12 g
Sugar: 9 g
Protein: 20 g

ALSO WORKS WELL WITH
Butternut Squash, Parsnip, Chayote, Broccoli, Sweet Potato

When Lu and I go back to restaurants we've visited before, we always try to order something new—especially at our neighborhood staples. There's one restaurant, however, where Lu refuses to order any other thing on the menu, despite having ordered it dozens of times. That's the BLAT: a bacon, lettuce, avocado, and tomato sandwich. He loads it up with a fried egg, chicken, and a heaping pile of sweet potato fries alongside. He just can't resist it! This zucchini pasta is a healthier, lighter version of Lu's favorite sandwich. It comes together quickly and works well for brunch or dinner.

- 1 cup cherry tomatoes
- 1 tablespoon extra-virgin olive oil
- ½ teaspoon garlic powder
-   Salt and pepper
- 4 bacon slices
-   Cooking spray
- 1 garlic clove, minced
- ¼ teaspoon red pepper flakes
- 2 medium zucchini, spiralized with **BLADE C**, noodles trimmed
- 3 to 4 cups chopped kale leaves
- ½ ripe avocado, cubed

Make this dish vegetarian by using the coconut or shiitake bacon on pages 93 and 156, respectively.

1 Preheat the oven to 400 degrees. Line a baking sheet with parchment paper.

2 In a medium bowl, toss the tomatoes and olive oil to coat. Add the garlic powder, season generously with salt and black pepper, and toss again. Spread the tomatoes on the prepared baking sheet, spacing them apart. Roast for 25 minutes or until the tomatoes collapse and their skins are charred. Remove from the oven, lift the parchment paper, and pour the tomatoes and their juices from the paper into a medium bowl.

3 Meanwhile, place the bacon in a large skillet. Cook over medium-high heat, flipping occasionally, for 8 to 10 minutes or until crispy. Transfer to a paper towel-lined plate to drain.

4 Discard most of the rendered bacon fat and let the pan cool for a few minutes. Return the pan to medium heat and add the fresh garlic and red pepper flakes. Cook until fragrant, about 30 seconds. Add the zucchini noodles, kale, and avocado. Cook, tossing frequently, for 2 to 3 minutes or until the noodles are al dente. Add the tomatoes and their juices and crumble the bacon over the top, tossing to combine. Serve immediately.

Lemon Halibut
with Summer Squash Gratin and Tomato Coulis

Gluten-Free
Paleo
Dairy-Free

TIME TO PREP 30 minutes
TIME TO COOK 15 minutes
SERVES 4

NUTRITIONAL INFORMATION
Calories: 338
Fat: 18 g
Sodium: 168 mg
Carbohydrate: 22 g
Fiber: 4 g
Sugar: 9 g
Protein: 27 g

ALSO WORKS WELL WITH
Potato, Sweet Potato,
Rutabaga, Butternut
Squash, Golden Beet

Because they're typically heavy, gratins are usually reserved for cold winter nights. I happen to love gratins, so I wanted to create a warm-weather version with a light, dairy-free sauce. This recipe not only uses zucchini, but also yellow squash, making it a true celebration of summer produce. The halibut sits delicately in a tomato coulis and matches the freshness of the gratin.

For the tomato coulis
- 1½ pounds ripe Roma (plum) tomatoes, seeded and chopped
- 1 garlic clove, pressed
- 2 fresh basil leaves
- Salt and pepper

For the cashew cream
- 1 cup raw unsalted cashews, soaked in water for at least 2 hours, rinsed and drained
- 1 cup low-sodium vegetable broth
- 1 tablespoon fresh lemon juice
- 1 tablespoon nutritional yeast
- Salt and pepper

For the gratin
- 1 *green zucchini*
- 1 *yellow summer squash*
- Cooking spray
- 2 teaspoons extra-virgin olive oil
- 2 garlic cloves, minced
- 1 tablespoon minced shallot
- 2 tablespoons chopped fresh basil

For the halibut
- 4 (3- to 4-ounce) skinless halibut fillets
- 1 lemon, cut into 4 slices
- Salt and pepper
- 2 teaspoons extra-virgin olive oil, plus more as needed

1 Preheat the oven to 450 degrees.

2 Make the tomato coulis. Place all the ingredients for the coulis in a food processor and pulse until smooth. Season with salt and pepper, transfer to a medium bowl, and set aside. Clean the food processor bowl and blade.

3 Make the cashew cream. Place all the ingredients for the cashew cream in the food processor and pulse until creamy. Taste and adjust the seasoning to your preferences.

4 Make the gratin. Slice the zucchini and yellow squash halfway through lengthwise to create a slit in each, being careful not to pierce any farther than their centers. Spiralize with **BLADE A** and trim the noodles so that the pieces lay flat, rather than in spirals.

5 Coat a medium baking dish with cooking spray and create a layer of alternating zucchini and squash slices over the bottom.

6 Heat the olive oil in a large skillet over medium-high heat. When the oil is shimmering, add the garlic and shallot and cook for 30 seconds or until fragrant. Add the cashew cream and basil and stir to combine.

7 Pour ¼ cup of the cashew cream mixture into the baking dish, then top with another layer of alternating zucchini and squash slices. Repeat twice more, ending with the cashew cream. Season the top with salt and pepper. Bake for 15 to 20 minutes or until easily pierced with a fork.

8 Meanwhile, make the halibut. Coat a separate medium baking dish with cooking spray. Spread the tomato coulis evenly over the bottom. Place the halibut on top and layer the lemon slices over the fish. Season the halibut with salt and pepper and drizzle each fillet with ½ teaspoon of the olive oil. Transfer to the oven to bake alongside the gratin for 10 to 12 minutes or until the fish is opaque and cooked through.

9 Remove both dishes from the oven. Spoon the coulis back over the top of the halibut fillets. Serve each fillet with a portion of the gratin.

To enhance the flavor of the gratin, drizzle some of the tomato coulis over the squash slices before topping them with the sauce.

Cauliflower Pizza
with Zucchini, Ricotta, Corn, and Pesto

≋ Vegetarian
≋ Gluten-Free
≋ Low-Cal

TIME TO PREP 20 minutes
TIME TO COOK 35 minutes
SERVES 4

NUTRITIONAL INFORMATION
Calories: 270
Fat: 16 g
Sodium: 173 mg
Carbohydrate: 20 g
Fiber: 6 g
Sugar: 7 g
Protein: 16 g

A couple of years back, I read an article that proclaimed, "Cauliflower is the new kale!" Well, I've seen it everywhere—as a stand-in for chicken (see page 143), as rice, and, like here, as a pizza crust. I guess whoever wrote that article was right! While this cauli-crust doesn't have the same texture as a regular wheat crust (it's not quite as thick or resilient), it dutifully serves its purpose—to hold delicious toppings! After all, without the toppings, a pizza would just be a giant piece of baked dough, right? The ricotta, pesto, and corn showcase delicious summer flavors on top of a fluffy, soft mound of zucchini noodles.

1 head cauliflower, cut into florets

1 teaspoon dried oregano

½ teaspoon dried basil

½ teaspoon garlic powder

2 large eggs, beaten

2 tablespoons grated Parmesan cheese

¼ cup almond flour

Salt and pepper

Cooking spray

1 ear of corn, kernels sliced off

For the pesto

2 cups packed fresh basil leaves

1 large garlic clove, minced

2 teaspoons pine nuts

1 tablespoon extra-virgin olive oil, plus more as needed

1 tablespoon grated Parmesan cheese

Salt and pepper

½ cup ricotta cheese

1 medium zucchini, spiralized with BLADE D, noodles trimmed

1½ teaspoons red pepper flakes (optional)

recipe continues

1 Preheat the oven to 425 degrees. Line a baking sheet or 10-inch pizza pan with parchment paper.

2 Place the cauliflower florets in a food processor and pulse until ricelike. Transfer to a piece of cheesecloth or a very thin kitchen towel and wring out all the excess moisture. Transfer to a large bowl and add the oregano, basil, garlic powder, eggs, Parmesan, and almond flour. Season with salt and black pepper and mix thoroughly with a fork until doughlike.

3 Spread the dough over the prepared pan, packing it in until it's about ½ inch thick all around. Bake for 10 to 15 minutes or until the crust is firm and lightly golden brown on the edges. Remove from the oven and transfer the crust on the parchment paper to a wire rack.

4 While the crust bakes, place a medium skillet over medium-high heat and coat with cooking spray. When water flicked onto the pan sizzles, add the corn and sauté for 5 minutes or until fork-tender.

5 Meanwhile, make the pesto. Place all the ingredients for the pesto in a food processor and pulse until creamy. Taste and adjust the seasoning to your preference.

6 Assemble the pizza. Spread the pesto evenly around the crust, leaving a ¾-inch-wide border. Dollop the ricotta on top, spreading it out evenly with the back of a spoon. Season with salt and black pepper. Lay out the zucchini noodles and scatter the corn over the crust.

7 Return the pizza, still on the parchment paper, to the baking sheet or pizza pan. Bake for 10 minutes more or until the zucchini noodles wilt and the crust is browned on the bottom. Remove and sprinkle the red pepper flakes, if desired, over the pizza. Let rest for 5 minutes, until the crust solidifies. Using a pizza wheel or a sharp knife, cut the pizza into slices and serve.

Be sure your crust is at least ½ inch thick; otherwise, it will crumble too easily. If you're worried, add an extra 2 tablespoons almond flour to help it bind a bit more. Depending on the size of your pan, your crust may not fill its whole surface.

Vegetable Ribbon and Barley Salad

with Basil-Feta Vinaigrette

Vegetarian
Gluten-Free
Low-Cal
Saves Well

TIME TO PREP 15 minutes
TIME TO COOK 60 minutes
SERVES 4

NUTRITIONAL INFORMATION
Calories: 172
Fat: 11 g
Sodium: 263 mg
Carbohydrate: 13 g
Fiber: 3 g
Sugar: 5 g
Protein: 5 g

Before there were vegetable noodles, there were vegetable ribbons. Ribbons can be made simply using a vegetable peeler, shaving the vegetables into thin strips—or they can be made using light pressure on your spiralizer with Blade A (see page 000). This salad combines my favorite vegetables with a healthy whole grain and a salty, fresh basil–feta vinaigrette. It's ideal for a summer get-together—it feeds a crowd well and looks beautiful, with those plush, colorful strands of vegetables. Note that you'll still have to rely on the peeler for the asparagus.

½ cup pearl barley

1 tablespoon olive oil

1 *medium zucchini, spiralized into ribbons with* **BLADE A**, *noodles trimmed*

1 *large carrot, peeled, spiralized into ribbons with* **BLADE A**, *noodles trimmed*

12 large asparagus spears, shaved into ribbons with a peeler

Salt and pepper

For the vinaigrette

3 tablespoons sliced fresh basil

½ cup crumbled feta

1 shallot, minced

1 tablespoon fresh lemon juice

Salt and pepper

2 tablespoons olive oil

2 tablespoons red wine vinegar

1 Put the barley and 1½ cups water in a large pot with a lid and bring to a boil over high heat. Reduce the heat to medium-low, cover, and simmer until tender, about 45 minutes.

2 Make the vinaigrette. Place all the ingredients for the vinaigrette in a food processor and pulse until blended and creamy.

3 Heat the olive oil in a large skillet over medium-high heat. When the oil is shimmering, add the zucchini, carrots, and asparagus. Season with salt and pepper and cook for 3 to 5 minutes or until the vegetables are lightly softened. Transfer to a large bowl.

4 Add the barley to the vegetables and pour the vinaigrette over the top. Toss thoroughly to combine.

If you're maintaining a grain-free diet, use a cup of cauliflower rice in place of the barley.

Sausage and Peppers
with Zucchini Noodles

Gluten-Free
Paleo
Dairy-Free
Saves Well

TIME TO PREP 15 minutes
TIME TO COOK 30 minutes
SERVES 4 to 6

NUTRITIONAL INFORMATION
Calories: 399
Fat: 32 g
Sodium: 488 mg
Carbohydrate: 16 g
Fiber: 3 g
Sugar: 10 g
Protein: 15 g

I daresay that, with a loaf of oven-toasted semolina bread alongside for dipping, sausage and peppers is my absolute favorite Italian dish to indulge in during the summertime. From June to September, almost every time I stopped by my grandparents' house, there were sausage and peppers. In an attempt to fill up on fiber-filled vegetables and resist the bread, I've tossed in raw zucchini noodles here. They add an al dente pasta–like crunch and bulk up this dish, making it a fully satisfying meal. And yes, there's a lot of olive oil here, because it wouldn't be the same without it. It's all about balance, right?

5 tablespoons extra-virgin olive oil

2 sweet fennel Italian sausage links

2 spicy Italian sausage links

2 *medium yellow onions, peeled, spiralized with* BLADE A, *noodles trimmed*

1 *red bell pepper, spiralized with* BLADE A, *noodles trimmed*

1 *orange bell pepper, spiralized with* BLADE A, *noodles trimmed*

1½ tablespoons tomato paste

¼ teaspoon red pepper flakes

4 garlic cloves, minced

½ teaspoon dried oregano

1 cup low-sodium chicken broth

Salt and pepper

2 tablespoons finely chopped fresh curly parsley

2 *medium zucchini, spiralized with* BLADE D, *noodles trimmed*

If you're serving this dish in the summer, try fresh basil instead of parsley to garnish.

1 Heat 2 tablespoons of the olive oil in a large skillet with a lid over medium-high heat. When the oil is shimmering, add the sausages and cover the pan. Cook for about 7 minutes or until just browned on the bottom. Uncover and cook for 5 minutes more, turning, until browned on the outside but not yet cooked through. Using tongs, transfer the sausage to a cutting board and slice into 1-inch pieces. Set aside.

2 Immediately add the remaining 3 tablespoons olive oil, the onion noodles, and the bell pepper noodles to the same skillet. Cook for about 5 minutes or until the vegetables soften. Add the tomato paste, and stir to cook the vegetables. Add the red pepper flakes and garlic and cook for 30 seconds or until fragrant. Return the sausage to the pan and add the oregano and broth. Season with salt and black pepper. Cover the skillet and simmer until the sausage is cooked through, about 10 minutes. Uncover and simmer until the sauce has reduced by a quarter, about 5 minutes more. Stir in the parsley.

3 Transfer to a large serving platter or bowl and add the zucchini noodles. Toss thoroughly until the noodles begin to wilt and are fully incorporated. Serve immediately.

Recipes by Category

Recipe Title	Gluten-Free	Paleo	Vegetarian	Vegan	One Pot	Saves Well	Dairy-Free/ optional	Low Calorie	No Cook
Crabless Crab Cakes with Green Apple Guacamole	X		X				X		
Creamy Roasted Butternut Squash Soup with Apple Noodles	X	X	X	X			X		
Apple-Walnut Muffins	X	X	X			X		X	
Curried Apple Egg Salad Wrap	X		X					X	X
Ginger Pear and Apple Sangria			X				X		X
Spiced Lamb Skewers with Beet Noodles	X								
Tahini Beet Noodle Bowl with Falafel	X		X				X	X	
Chicken Tagine with Apricot Golden Beet Rice	X								
Green Curry Golden Beet Noodle Bowl	X	X	X	X					
Oven-Fried Goat Cheese with Figs, Bitter Greens, and Beet Noodles	X		X						
Spiralized Shakshuka	X	X	X		X		X		
Turkey Picadillo with Green Bell Pepper Noodles	X	X				X	X		
Quick Steak and Bell Pepper Stir-Fry						X	X	X	
Bell Pepper Taco Skillet	X					X	X		
Roasted Bell Pepper Chicory Salad with Anchovy–White Bean Dressing and Soft-Baked Eggs	X						X		
Summer Ratatouille	X	X	X	X	X	X	X	X	
Foil Pouch Sea Bass	X	X					X	X	
Grams's Tuna and Macaroni Salad	X						X	X	
Sun-Dried Tomato, Chicken, and Broccoli Pasta	X					X	X	X	
Shrimp Tom Kha with Broccoli Noodles	X				X		X		
Butternut Squash Rice and Beans	X		X	X		X	X	X	

Recipe Title	Gluten-Free	Paleo	Vegetarian	Vegan	One Pot	Saves Well	Dairy-Free/optional	Low Calorie	No Cook
Pumpkin-Rosemary Alfredo with Crispy Prosciutto	X	X				X	X		
Butternut Squash Ravioli with Sage and Toasted Pine Nuts	X		X					X	
Butternut Squash Noodles with Almond Ricotta and Coconut Bacon	X	X	X	X			X		
Pear, Pomegranate, and Roast Turkey Salad with Butternut Squash and Maple-Sesame Vinaigrette						X	X		
Winter Lasagna with Brussels Sprouts and Chicken Sausage	X					X			
Teriyaki Mini Meatballs over Roasted Scallions and Butternut Squash Noodles						X	X		
Oven-Fried Avocado Tacos with Chipotle Cream	X	X	X				X	X	
Butternut Squash Noodles with Butter Beans and Sun-Dried Tomato Cream Sauce	X		X	X			X	X	
Crunchy Bok Choy and Cabbage Salad	X	X	X			X	X	X	X
Spanish Cabbage Stew with Cod and Saffron	X	X					X	X	
Spicy Cabbage and Carrot Detox Soup	X	X			X	X	X	X	
Cabbage Buddha Bowl with Chickpea-Avocado Mash and BBQ Tahini	X		X	X			X		X
Roasted Carrot Noodles with Smoked Salmon, Avocado, and Creamy Herb Dressing	X	X					X		
Garlic-Miso Soup with Carrot Noodles, Seaweed, and Tofu	X		X	X			X	X	
Mom's Matzo Ball Soup with Carrot Noodles			X				X	X	
Za'atar Chickpeas over Radicchio and Carrot	X		X				X	X	
Slow-Cooker Spiced Lentils and Cauliflower over Carrot Rice	X	X	X			X	X	X	
Stuffed Cabbage Rolls with Celeriac Rice and Adzuki Beans	X		X	X		X	X		

Recipe Title	Gluten-Free	Paleo	Vegetarian	Vegan	One Pot	Saves Well	Dairy-Free/optional	Low Calorie	No Cook
Chicken and Celeriac Rice Soup	X	X				X	X	X	
Celeriac Spaghetti and Vegetarian Meatballs			X			X	X		
Buffalo Wings with Celeriac Slaw	X								
Slow-Cooker Carnitas Soup with Chayote Noodles	X	X				X	X		
Chayote Tex-Mex Bowls with Tomatillo Sauce	X		X	X			X		
Blackened Tilapia over Chayote-Mango Pasta Salad	X	X					X	X	
Turkey, Spinach, and Hummus Cucumber Noodle Roll-Ups	X						X	X	X
California Roll Sushi Bowl with Ginger-Carrot Dressing							X	X	
Lamb-Feta Burgers with Greek Cucumber Noodle Salad	X								
Chicago-Style Carrot Dogs with Spiralized Pickles			X	X		X	X	X	
Poached Salmon over Jícama Noodle Salad with Cilantro-Lime Yogurt Dressing	X							X	
No-Lettuce Jícama Cobb Salad	X						X		
Vietnamese Cold Jícama Noodle Salad	X	X				X	X	X	X
Carne Asada with Manchego Chimichurri and Jícama Noodles	X								
Kohlrabi Spaghettini Aglio e Olio	X		X			X	X	X	
General Tso's Cauliflower with Kohlrabi Rice			X				X	X	
Spicy Kohlrabi Tortilla Soup with Shrimp	X				X	X	X		
Fried Green Tomatoes with Avocado Ranch Kohlrabi	X	X	X				X		
Chicken Mole with Kohlrabi Rice	X	X				X	X		
Kale and Quinoa Salad with Pickled Onions and Caesar Dressing	X		X				X	X	X

Recipe Title	Gluten-Free	Paleo	Vegetarian	Vegan	One Pot	Saves Well	Dairy-Free/ optional	Low Calorie	No Cook
Wedge Salad with Caramelized Onions, Mushroom Bacon, and Greek Yogurt–Balsamic Dressing	X		X						
Rosemary, Olive, and Onion Frittata with Arugula Salad and Parmesan Vinaigrette	X		X				X	X	
Almond-Crusted Lemon Sole with Tomato, Sweet Onion, and Caper-Parsley Salad	X	X					X		
No-Cheese French Onion and Lentil Soup	X				X	X	X		
Parsnip-Chive Waffles and Gluten-Free Oven-Fried Chicken	X	X					X		
Hearty Beef Stew with Parsnip and Carrot Noodles	X					X	X	X	
Avocado "Toast" with Cherry Tomato Jam	X	X					X		
Parsnip Pasta with Caramelized Leeks and Ham	X					X	X	X	
Broccoli Rabe and Sausage Parsnip Pasta	X					X	X	X	
Grilled Halloumi, Lentils, and Arugula with Roasted Fennel and Pear Noodles	X		X						
Chai-Spiced Pear Oatmeal	X		X	X			X	X	
Pear Noodle Bowl with Maple-Roasted Acorn Squash and Pomegranate Dressing	X		X	X			X	X	
Cinnamon and Pecan Pear Noodle Pancakes	X	X	X				X	X	
Easy Pork Chops with Shredded Brussels Sprout, Kale, and Pear Noodle Salad	X	X				X	X		
Hot-and-Sour Soup with Daikon Noodles			X		X	X	X	X	
Black Radish and Orange Salad with Radicchio and Salmon Cakes	X								
Ginger-Crab Fried Daikon Rice							X	X	

Recipe Title	Gluten-Free	Paleo	Vegetarian	Vegan	One Pot	Saves Well	Dairy-Free/optional	Low Calorie	No Cook
Watermelon Radish Nourish Salad with Lemon-Ginger Vinaigrette and Vegan Parmesan	X	X	X	X			X		X
Grilled Steak with Mustard Greens and Radish Noodles	X	X					X		
Clear Immunity Soup with Daikon	X	X	X	X	X		X	X	
Thai Almond and Pork Curry with Rutabaga Noodles	X	X					X		
Rutabaga Gratin with Leeks	X	X	X	X			X		
Mussels over Rutabaga Pasta	X						X	X	
Chicken Cacciatore over Rutabaga Noodles	X					X	X		
Rutabaga Baked Ziti with Mushrooms and Kale	X		X			X			
Tandoori Chicken over Sweet Potato Rice	X	X				X	X		
Sweet Potato Pizza Skillet	X		X		X	X			
Chorizo–Sweet Potato Buns with Tomato and Pepper Jack	X								
Vegetarian Full English Breakfast	X		X				X		
Mexican Eggs in Pepper Cups	X		X				X	X	
Creamy Chipotle Sweet Potato Pasta with Chicken and Seasoned Corn	X						X		
Braised Short Ribs over Sweet Potato Pasta	X				X	X	X		
Creamy Spinach and Artichoke Sweet Potato Pasta	X	X	X	X			X	X	
Turnip alla Vodka	X		X	X			X	X	
Cauliflower Steak over Roasted Garlic Tomato Turnip Noodles	X	X	X	X		X	X	X	
White Beans, Escarole, and Turnip Noodles in Parmesan Broth	X					X		X	
Pan-Seared Pork Chops with Mushroom Gravy and Turnip Noodles	X	X				X	X	X	
Turnip Risotto with Crispy Pancetta and Chives	X					X	X	X	

Recipe Title	Gluten-Free	Paleo	Vegetarian	Vegan	One Pot	Saves Well	Dairy-Free/ optional	Low Calorie	No Cook
Potato-Wrapped Roasted Carrots with Moroccan Black Lentils and Feta	X		X			X	X		
Asparagus, Egg, and Potato Noodles with Kale	X	X	X				X		
Half and Half Pasta	X		X			X			
Pan Con Tomate with Serrano Ham	X						X	X	
Loaded Potatoes with BBQ Sauce	X							X	
Thai Steak Salad						X	X		
Hoisin Salmon with Zucchini Slaw							X		
Green Goddess Zucchini Pasta	X		X	X		X	X		X
Dairy-Free Clam Chowder with Zucchini Noodles	X						X	X	
Italian-Style Chicken Sliders	X	X				X	X	X	
Chocolate Chip Zucchini Noodle Bread with Coconut Cream Frosting	X	X				X	X		
Greek-Style Shrimp Scampi	X						X	X	
Minestrone with Zucchini Noodles	X		X	X	X	X	X		
Gluten-Free Chicken Parmesan over Zucchini Noodles	X								
Zucchini Ravioli with Tomato Basil and Cashew Cheese	X	X	X	X			X	X	
Avocado BLT Zucchini Pasta	X	X					X		
Seared Scallops over Zucchini Noodles with Roasted Bell Pepper Sauce	X	X					X	X	
Lemon Halibut with Summer Squash Gratin and Tomato Coulis	X	X					X		
Cauliflower Pizza with Zucchini, Ricotta, Corn, and Pesto	X		X					X	
Vegetable Ribbon and Barley Salad with Basil-Feta Vinaigrette	X		X			X		X	
Sausage and Peppers with Zucchini Noodles	X	X				X	X		

Acknowledgments

You know when you take a photo to capture a gorgeous sunset on the beach or a bright skyline in a big city like New York, and then you go home and share those pictures with a friend or loved one? As you look at the photos with that person, you start to realize that the pictures don't adequately capture what you saw and felt in that moment. Scrolling through the photos, you exclaim, "The photos don't do it justice!" Well, that's how I feel when someone asks me about Inspiralized. Words like "blessed" and "grateful" immediately come to mind, but they don't do this feeling justice!

Every day, I get to help thousands of people find their healthy stride through spiralizing. Ironically, over these past three years, the Inspiralized community has helped *me* attain the healthiest, happiest, and most inspired version of *myself*. Their daily encouragement means more to me than they'll ever know. So first, to all of my loyal, kind readers and followers—*grazie*!

Aside from my #inspiralizedsquad, there are a few others who have supported me along this path and helped me grow Inspiralized bigger than I ever thought I could, and for that, I'll always be thankful.

To the Clarkson Potter team, thank you for ensuring this cookbook has a special place in the kitchens of so many home cooks. Doris, thank you for taking a chance on this Inspiralized dream of mine. Kate, Carly, and Erica, thank you for showing the world what this cookbook can do. To everyone behind the scenes (Stephanie, La Tricia, Amy, Mark, Alex, and Heather), this book is as much yours as it is mine, and I hope you feel as proud as I do—what a labor of love!

And of course, thank you to my editor, Amanda Englander, for getting me and letting me be me! You took my haphazard spiralized recipe list and birthed it into this stunning must-have cookbook. You held my hand when I needed it and pushed me out there alone when I was ready. Thank you for being in my corner and teaching me to embrace "shimmering oil" and the Oxford comma. Cheers to many more champagne lunches with great news!

Alyssa Reuben (Sedrish!), thank you for being my sounding board and standing up for me and this crazy vision of mine. The unbelievable opportunities that keep coming my way since my first cookbook would not have happened if it weren't for your trust in me. I can't wait to see what *Inspiralize Everything* brings. Next stop: world domination.

They say it "takes a village," and it couldn't be truer! Thank you to the photography crew that brought life to my printed words. Even though I spiralize every single day, they'll never look as good as you've made them look in this book! Evan Sung, thank you for managing the show with absolute Zen-like composure. You're a true star, a pro, and now a life-long friend. Your ability to make my home-cooked healthy meals look like something you'd find on a plate in a Michelin-star restaurant is uncanny, and I cherish these photos almost as much as our laughs on set! Undoubtedly, this wouldn't have happened without the support of the rest of the team—prop stylist Carla Gonzalez-Hart, you scrunch up napkins and lay down spoons with such artistic precision, it amazes me, and food stylist extraordinaire Suzanne Lenzer, I'm happy to have worked with such a talented woman, but most important, one who shares in my belief that a little olive oil, salt, and pepper is all you need.

Laura Arnold, thanks for testing all of the recipes in this cookbook, especially so quickly, and I hope you've been #inspiralized and dig the final product.

Meaghan, Meaghan, Meaghan. Meaghan Prenda, I love you like family! Amongst other things in my life (like my wedding, the Inspiralizer, and overall work-life balance), this cookbook truly would not have been possible without you. Your commitment to Inspiralized and me is humbling, and I am so grateful to have you on my team every single day to laugh and eye-roll with, vent to, bounce ideas off of, and to answer "those" emails with a smile. I'm so excited for what's to come with this little brand we're building together, and I'll forever be thankful for your kindness and hustle.

Felicia, you'll always be my little sister, and I'll always want to make you proud. I'm so happy you moved in next door in Jersey City so we can spend more time together, procrastinating on our workouts and drinking Karen Specials. Thank you for Inspiralizing all of your friends, because we all know you're more popular than I am. I love you so much, Feesh. And a special shout-out to Ben, who should be on the payroll, he promotes Inspiralized so much! You guys are a great team, and I can't wait to see what life brings us all. Wink, wink.

Dad, since my first book, you've become my business partner and the father-in-law to the love of my life. I'm blessed to have you along in this Inspiralized journey. As I grow older, I realize more and more how alike we are, and I'm proud to be like you! I'm so happy I followed your footsteps into entrepreneurship. This life is so much better! And as this book publishes, we'll be celebrating your sixtieth birthday. Happy birthday, Dad!

Mom. WO-man. You're my best friend, and Inspiralized would never have happened without you. Literally, you discovered spiralizing and brought it to me, but aside from that, you have been there for me every single step of the way, supporting and encouraging me. I know you believe in me and I carry that confidence with me in every aspect of my life. Thank you for welcoming Lu into the family last year and making me feel loved and cared for every day of my life. I can only dream of being as good of a mother as you are one day!

Grams and Pops. Your love and faith is beautifully infectious, and we need more of it in the world. Grams, thank you for being there for Poppy during this past beyond-tough year. I know you pray for everyone in our family, and it's those prayers that keep us together. You're the sweetest woman in the world, and I find inspiration in my everyday from the lessons you've taught me. Pops: Although devastatingly scary, your struggle with cancer has only proved that you're the strongest man in the world. You've been through too much and continue to live life to its fullest with a optimistic perspective and a love for family and the good things in my life (like food!). I love you so much, and I have you in my heart everywhere I go.

Lu. I could fill this cookbook with how much thanks I'd like to give to you. Instead, I figured I'd immortalize a portion of the vows I wrote and made to you on our wedding day, by printing it in this cookbook—because after all, this cookbook is filled with anecdotes and inspiration from our lives together!

For those of you who don't know, Lu comes home almost every day to me still working at my desk on Inspiralized, another dream of mine he made happen. In our apartment, there's a little hallway where I can't see Lu until he turns the corner and enters the living room, where my desk is. In the three seconds it takes for you to open the door and get into the apartment, my heart skips a beat the moment I hear your keys open the lock, and I get butterflies in my stomach because, even though it's only been eight hours since I saw you last, I get so excited to see you, kiss you, and have you back in my arms. I want to feel that same way every single day of my life, forever.

Thank you for completing me, baby. I love you.

Index

Note: Page numbers in *italics* indicate recipe photos.